The Elizabethan conquest of Ireland sparked off two linguistic events of enduring importance: it initiated the language shift from Irish to English, which constitutes the great drama of Irish cultural history, and it marks the beginnings of English linguistic expansion. The Elizabethan colonisers in Ireland included some of the leading poets and translators of the day. In *Language and Conquest in Early Modern Ireland*, Patricia Palmer uses their writings, as well as material from the State Papers, to explore the part which language played in shaping colonial ideology and English national identity. Palmer shows how manoeuvres of linguistic expansion rehearsed in Ireland shaped Englishmen's encounters with the languages of the New World, and frames that analysis within a comparison between English linguistic colonisation and Spanish practice in the New World. This is an ambitious comparative study which will interest literary and political historians.

PATRICIA PALMER is a lecturer in the Renaissance School in the Department of English and Related Literature at the University of York. She has published and broadcast on language issues. This is her first book.

LANGUAGE AND CONQUEST IN EARLY MODERN IRELAND

English Renaissance literature and Elizabethan imperial expansion

PATRICIA PALMER

CAMBRIDGE UNIVERSITY PRESS

PUBLISHED BY THE PRESS SYNDICATE OF THE UNIVERSITY OF CAMBRIDGE
The Pitt Building, Trumpington Street, Cambridge, United Kingdom

CAMBRIDGE UNIVERSITY PRESS
The Edinburgh Building, Cambridge CB2 2RU, UK
40 West 20th Street, New York NY 10011–4211, USA
10 Stamford Road, Oakleigh, VIC 3166, Australia
Ruiz de Alarcón 13, 28014 Madrid, Spain
Dock House, The Waterfront, Cape Town 8001, South Africa

http://www.cambridge.org

First published 2001

Printed in the United Kingdom at the University of Cambridge

Typeface 11/12.5pt Baskerville   *System* 3b2   CE

A catalogue record for this book is available from the British Library

Library of Congress Cataloguing in Publication data
Palmer, Patricia Ann, 1957–
Language and conquest in early modern Ireland: English Renaissance literature and
Elizabethan imperial expansion / Patricia Ann Palmer.
p.   cm.
Includes bibliographical references (p.) and index.
ISBN 0 521 79318 1
1. English literature – Early modern, 1500–1700 – History and criticism. 2.
Ireland – Foreign public opinion, English – History – 16th century. 3. English
language – Political aspects – Ireland. 4. Ireland – History – 1558–1603 – Historiography. 5.
Ireland – History – To 1603 – Historiography. 6. British – Ireland – History – 16th century. 7.
Irish language – Political aspects. 8. Language policy – Ireland. 9. Imperialism in
literature. 10. Ireland – In literature. 11. Renaissance – England. 12. Ireland – Languages.
I. Title.

PR129.I7 P35 2001
820.9′9417′09031–dc21   2001025394

ISBN 0 521 79318 1 hardback

To my parents, William and Catherine Palmer, *le grá*.

Contents

Acknowledgements

Conversation of one kind or another is central to this work. A book which explores the origins of the troubled conversation between Irish and English – both speakers and languages – is itself the outcome of conversations of far less troubled kinds that have criss-crossed these islands. This work grows out of an Oxford doctoral thesis, 'The Grafted Tongue: Linguistic Colonisation and the Native Response in Sixteenth-Century Ireland', and I am eternally grateful to my supervisor, Bernard O'Donoghue, for his enthusiasm, kindness and wisdom and for supervisions that flowed with laughter and good talk. Professors David Norbrook and Clare Carroll, my examiners, have given generously of their time and encouragement over the years. I am also behoven to Richard MacCabe for giving me the benefit of his insightful reading of the work at a vital stage. I've been fortunate to have Deana Rankin as a reader and critic, friend and neighbour. We talked early modern Ireland until it seemed almost as real as *fin-de-siècle* Oxford. I owe a particular debt to Wes Williams for his exceptionally perceptive reading of this work at different stages and for the energy and stimulation of the discussions that followed. I am grateful to Gillian Wright for her careful reading of part of the final draft.

My debt to Patricia Coughlan goes back to my undergraduate days in University College, Cork and I have drawn from her sharp intellect, good humour and generosity ever since. I am indebted to Kenneth Nicholls of the History Department UCC for sharing with me some of his unparalleled knowledge of sixteenth-century Ireland. Hiram Morgan, also of the History Department, has very kindly read sections of this work and tried to save me from error. Mícheál Mac Craith, Professor of Modern Irish at the National University of Ireland, Galway, has been singularly unselfish in responding to my work and in sharing his scholarship with me. I owe a huge debt to

Professor Donal Dineen of the University of Limerick for his generous encouragement and for facilitating the study leave during which much of this was written. Catherine La Farge furnished not only fine, lively talk but perfect spaces for writing, in both Oxford and Galway. I can hardly thank enough those whose stalwart friendship and bountiful conversation has sustained me: Lionel Pilkington, Fionnuala Murphy, Miriam Deane – and Sylvia Berney who taught me something about talking to the English.

Abbreviations

ALC   *Annals of Loch Cé: A Chronicle of Irish Affairs, 1014–1590,* ed. and trans. William M. Hennessy, vol. 2, Dublin: Irish Manuscripts Commission, 1939

ARÉ   *Annála Ríoghachta Éireann / Annals of the Kingdom of Ireland by the Four Masters from the Earliest Period to the Year 1616,* ed. and trans. John O'Donovan., 3 vols. Dublin: Hodges and Smith, 1848.

CBC   *The Compossicion Booke of Conought,* trans. Alexander M. Freeman, Dublin: Irish Manuscripts Commission, 1936

CCCHA   'Colin Clouts Come Home Again'

CCM   *Calendar of the Carew Manuscripts,* vols. 1–5, ed. J. S. Brewer and William Bullen, London: Longmans, Green, 1867–71

CPR   *Calendar of the Patent and Close Rolls of Chancery of Ireland,* vol. 1, ed. James Morrin, Dublin: Thom, 1861–2

CSPDom.   *Calendar of State Papers preserved in the Public Records Office, Domestic Series, 1581–90,* ed. Robert Lemon, London: Longmans, Green, 1865
         1598–1601, ed. M. A. Everett Green, London, 1869

CSPI   *Calendar of State Papers, Ireland,1509–1573,* 13 vols., London: His Majesty's Stationary Office, 1860–1912

DIL   *Dictionary of the Irish Language, based mainly on Old and Middle Irish materials,* ed. E. G. Quin *et al.,* Dublin: Royal Irish Academy, 1913–76

Egmont   *Report on the Manuscripts of the Earl of Egmont,* vol. 1, pt. 1, London: Historical Manuscripts Commission, 1905

FQ   Edmund Spenser, *The Faerie Queene,* ed. Thomas P. Roche, Penguin, 1978

JRHAAI   *Journal of the Royal Historical and Archaeological Association of Ireland,* 4th series. vol. 1

PRO SP   Irish State Papers, Public Record Office, Kew
Salis   *Calendar of the Manuscripts of the Marquis of Salisbury*, vols.
            I–XIII, London: Historical Manuscripts Commission,
            1883–1915
SPH8   *State Papers, King Henry VIII*, vols II & III, London, 1834
Stats   *The Statutes at Large from the First Year of King Edward the*
            Fourth to the end of the Reign of Queen Elizabeth, ed. Danby
            Pickering, London, 1763
Stats. Irl.   *The Statutes at Large Passed in the Parliaments held in Ireland*,
            vol. I, Dublin, 1786
UJA   *Ulster Journal of Archaeology*, vols. 2–6, 1854–8

Introduction

> We traffic with time in the arts of language, and with history and its events.
>
> Robert Welch, *Changing States*, p. 4

The Elizabethan conquest of Ireland is that point in history where the fortunes of two languages briefly intersect, then spectacularly diverge. For one, the conquest marks the inaugural episode of its imperialist expansion. For the other, it is the originary moment of a language shift that constitutes the great drama of Irish cultural history. The present book, written from the perspective of an Irish anglophone awkwardly aware that those troubled origins continue to shadow Irish speech, explores how far that moment of encounter throws light on an enduring paradox: that Irish literature in English – a literature rooted in the silencing of Irish and animated by that rupture – itself participates in that most Elizabethan of concepts, 'the triumph of English'.

A sense of discontinuity, self-estrangement, of living beyond the faultline of a fractured tradition haunts Irish writing. Anglophone Ireland, cut off from its Irish-speaking antecedents, is 'adrift among the accidents of translation' (Thomas Davis, quoted in Lloyd, 'Translator as Refractor', p. 145). The 'semantics of remembrance' are impaired; cultural amnesia is inescapable: 'there no longer exists any inherited reservoir of meaning' (Steiner, *After Babel*, p. 494; Kearney, *Transitions*, p. 13). The past is available only in translation and not everything – not much – can jump the gap. In a context where 'mother tongue' and 'native language' do not necessarily seem synonymous, language is made strange. Declan Kiberd's *Idir Dhá Chultúr* captures in its title – 'Between Two Cultures' – the displacement of modern Irish literature which, he argues, sprouts in the cracks between the two languages. When an Irish writer like Samuel

Beckett takes up his pen, argues David Wheatley, 'titeann scáth teanga trasna a shaothair' (the shadow of language falls across his work[1]) ('Beckett', p. 17). A sense of being exiled from 'another tradition, encoded in the lost language of a nation' complicates Irish writers' relationship with their medium (Boland, *Object Lessons*, pp. 80–1).

The most complete expression of the predicament comes in the final chapter of James Joyce's *A Portrait of the Artist as a Young Man*, a chapter threaded through with fragmentary allusions to 'the age of Dowland and Byrd and Nash' (p. 210). When the English Dean queries his use of 'tundish', Stephen feels 'with a smart of dejection that the man to whom he was speaking was a countryman of Ben Jonson'. His sense of holding imperfect title to the language he speaks, of never being fully at home in it, is the simultaneously uncomfortable and enabling perspective of Irish writing in English:

> The language in which we are speaking is his before it is mine . . . His language, so familiar and so foreign, will always be for me an acquired speech. I have not made or accepted its words. My voice holds them at bay. My soul frets in the shadow of his language. (p. 172)

Dowland, Byrd, Nash, Jonson . . . Tell-tale flashes of historical consciousness return us time and again to the Elizabethan source of the quandary. Seamus Heaney, 'a wood-kerne / Escaped from the massacre' ('Exposure'), seeks to 're-enter memory' ('Bone Dreams') but hears only the 'Soft voices of the dead': 'I cock my ear / at an absence' ('Gifts of Rain'). His laconically ambivalent formula, 'We are to be proud / Of our Elizabethan English', marks out the distance separating 'us' from the Elizabethans who 'tell of us' – and it explains his recoil from the 'whinging' MacMorris, 'gallivanting / round the Globe' ('Traditions'). In 'Ocean's love to Ireland', he reconfigures the sixteenth-century conquest as a linguistic rape: Ralegh 'Speaking broad Devonshire . . . drives inland'; 'The ruined maid complains in Irish'. After her spoliation, 'Iambic drums / Of English beat the woods.'

John Montague's *The Rough Field*, too, meditates on the legacy of a colonialism that was, to a striking degree, linguistic. Montague feels keenly the 'harsh . . . humiliation' of growing 'a second tongue' (p. 39); 'A Severed Head', interleaved with woodcuts of conquest from John Derricke's *The Image of Irelande*, provides an oblique and halting commentary on the long legacy of the Elizabethan campaign:

Dumb
bloodied, the severed
head now chokes to
speak another tongue.   (p. 39)

These fleeting apparitions of the Elizabethan moment are doubly
revealing. Historical intuition draws writers to this pivotal episode in
the encounter between Irish and English; scholars' commensurate
inattention to the linguistic face of the conquest, however, reduces
their access to a fuller engagement with it. The problem is illustrated
by Frank McGuinness's *Mutabilitie*, set in Kilcolman during the Nine
Years War. Theatrically, the stage is shared among the English
characters, 'Edmund' the poet and 'William' the playwright, and an
Irish woman poet, 'File', a dispossessed chieftain, Sweney, and his
queen, Maeve. Linguistically, however, no alterity is recognised; the
play reproduces the colonial texts' effacement of Irish. In the world
of *Mutabilitie*, the triumph of English is already accomplished.
McGuinness's elision of Irish goes beyond the conventions necessary
for mediating a diglossic world to an English-speaking audience.[2]
His alterations to his source text, *A View of the Present State of Ireland*,
erase Spenser's acknowledgement of the potency of Irish. Whereas
Spenser writes 'the speech being Irish, the heart must needs be so,
for out of the abundance of the heart, the tongue speaketh',
'Edmund' says 'Out of the abundance of the heart, the tongue
speaks, and here it speaks of Rome' (*View*, p. 68; *Mutabilitie*, p. 48). By
substituting 'Rome' for 'Irish', McGuinness is anachronistically
privileging religious over linguistic nationalism. Hugh, the chieftain's
son, refuses William's request to 'speak to me in your own language'
with the retort 'You are hearing my own language' (p. 68). The effect
of representing sixteenth-century Munster as uncomplicatedly anglophone is deeply problematic. Edmund speaks commanding Spen-
serian prose;[3] William descants Shakespearean sonnets (p. 23); the
natives, culturally unhoused neophytes astray in a richly textured
world of English, have access only to howls, hobbling rhymes (p. 43)
and inarticulate violence: 'Revenge, beautiful word. Say it' (p. 28).
Almost inevitably, given the natives' linguistic disadvantage, *Mutabilitie*, with its pastiche *hommage* to *King Lear* and *A Midsummer Night's
Dream*, links their empowerment to English. This leads McGuinness
into ascribing anachronistic sentiments of cultural dependency – 'I
require your eloquence' (p. 23) – to a sixteenth-century *file* who is
made to prophesyse improbably that an English poet 'shall give us

the gift of tongues' (p. 2).[4] McGuinness's engagement with the seminal moment of linguistic encounter is circumscribed precisely because its perspective is that of most literary critics on 'Elizabethan Ireland', that give-away term. Like such critics, it is positioned on the far side of the break, deep inside an anglophone universe of discourse. It is in dialogue only with the canonical English texts and so it replicates their elision of Irish and of its worldview.

Such exiguous attention as the language encounter has so far attracted has focused on the nineteenth century, the century of 'silence', and on the subsequent demographics of decline (Kinsella, 'Divided Mind', p. 209; cf. Welch, *Changing States*; Hindley, *Death of the Irish Language*); the originary moment of the encounter, the sixteenth century, is ignored almost completely. This is to write history as autopsy. To focus on the silence as it settles rather than on the intensity and engagement of its sixteenth-century prelude is intellec- tually confining: we lose the chance to understand how power intersects with language and to study the patterns of resistance and accommodation as they are set down. But it is also impoverishing at a simpler, human level: to concentrate only on the silent prevents us from listening in to the urgent volubility of their sixteenth-century antecedents. 'Elizabethan' Ireland is the last moment when a confident Irish-speaking world confronts its English nemesis and, as its moment slips away, records its loss and makes its adjustments. The Elizabethan tracts of conquest defused Irish-speakers' insistent contestation by suppressing their expression textually; not to attempt now to reconstruct the polyphony and incipient hybridity of the encounter is to repeat that effacement. It is to truncate our under- standing of the past by tuning in to one set of voices only and to elide our perspective with those with whom we share – or have come to share – a common language. 'The Elizabethan mind', Foster tells us, 'found the native Irish . . . incomprehensible' (*Modern Ireland*, p. 9). That incomprehension was, at its simplest level, linguistic; it is all too easy to replay that lack of understanding and to collapse our horizon of interpretation with that of the Elizabethan texts – as Foster himself does by remarking that 'the English colonial presence in Ireland remained superimposed upon an ancient identity, *alien and bizarre*' (p. 3; my emphasis).

'Maireann lorg an phinn, ach ní mhaireann an béal a chan' (The trace of the pen lives on, but not the mouth that sang). The proverb captures an imbalance, pronounced in colonial contexts, which this work is concerned with addressing – an imbalance which critical practice has often been more successful in replicating than in challenging. New Historicism with its 'reciprocal concern with the historicity of texts and the textuality of history' (Montrose, 'Professing the Renaissance', p. 20) is useful in sanctioning my own recourse to non-literary texts of conquest – State Papers, account books, campaign journals, statutes, depositions, trial reports – in seeking to reconstruct the linguistic corollary of the conquest. But less enabling is its paradoxical mesmerism with the colonial canon: Christopher Highley, for instance, spectacularly consigns Irish-language writers of the period to a footnote: they 'remain outside the discourse of Ireland as I define it' (*Crisis*, p. 164, fn. 2). Nor does mainstream postcolonial practice greatly advance matters. As well as being strangely ill-adapted to the early modern period (Adorno, 'Colonial Discourse'), its inclination to think in polarities such as European/ Other tends to 'make Ireland invisible' (Miller, *Invested with Meaning*, p. 18). When writing about early modern Ireland, postcolonialists' fixation on English literary texts – once more unto the breach with *Henry V* – quite unintentionally ends up representing colonial discourse as triumphantly omnipotent. Said salutes writers like Friel who 'can truly read the great colonial masterpieces' and write back (*Culture and Imperialism*, p. 35). But it is not enough just to read the 'colonial masterpieces': the 'minorpieces' of the colonised also must be read. The 'trace of the pen' left by sixteenth-century Irish is faint: fewer than a hundred manuscripts from the period survive (Ó Cuív, 'Irish Language', p. 513); fewer still – bardic poems and annals – have a place in our story; as the endpieces of a broken tradition, they have not travelled as well in time as the 'colonial masterpieces'. Yet, they represent an essential counterpoint to the voluminous colonial record. Equally, one must read with an eye for what did not get written. Though the colonial texts systematically exclude 'the mouth that sings' in Irish, critical approaches such as feminism help us to recover the voices of the silenced or, failing that, alert us to the strategies that silenced them.

To escape the temporal and theoretical impediments that block our engagement with the sixteenth-century encounter, I have found it necessary to escape a spatial one as well. Seán Ó Tuama muses that the Tudors' 'subjugation of Ireland may well have been unique in the attention they paid to cultural as well as territorial conquest' ('Gaelic Culture', p. 28). That conviction, which holds up poorly against comparisons with French and Spanish colonial practice, results in the kind of insular and, at times, rancorous victimhood that marks De Fréine's *The Great Silence* and which is never far from the surface in Kinsella's *The Dual Tradition*. But the Irish case, though often portrayed as a unique misfortune (Lee, *Ireland*, p. 663), and while unusual in a European context, is by no means singular. The Tudor (re)conquest of Ireland is part of a much larger pattern of sixteenth-century colonial expansion. It comes sandwiched between the massive Spanish *empresa* in the New World and England's first colonial ventures in the Americas. To view linguistic colonisation in Ireland from that broader spatial perspective, in a manner prepared for by historians like Nicholas Canny, but never followed up by those studying language, allows us to situate events in Ireland in their wider historical context. The great advantage of the broader spatial perspective is that it expands our theoretical framework as well. It opens up the possibility of transferring to the study of linguistic colonisation in Ireland the methodologies and discursive practices which have uncovered the philosophical underpinnings and practical procedures of Spanish linguistic colonisation.

This book seeks to understand the nature of the encounter between Irish and English under the press of the Elizabethan conquest and to reinsert Irish interlocutors into the discussion in a way that avoids replacing a colonial imbalance with a postcolonial one – one that turns the colonists into the critic's 'Other'. In doing so I am indebted, imaginatively and procedurally, to the 'New World' scholarship. I draw on writers like Francis Affergan, whose analysis of colonial and anthropological strategies of silencing also explores how the voice of the other can be brought back into dialogue; or like Le Clézio, who finds a way to let 'le silence . . . immense, terrifiant' that followed the *conquista* resonate (*Rêve mexicain*, p. 231).

This work analyses the engagement between Irish and English from, roughly, Elizabeth I's accession in 1558 to the flight of the earls in 1607. Chapter 1 draws on the 'Spanish-American' model to establish a methodological framework for exploring how language and power move into alignment in the context of conquest. Chapters 2, 3 and 4 uncover the pattern of Elizabethan linguistic colonisation in its paired guises of denigrating Irish and promoting English. Chapters 2 and 3 examine how the Elizabethans' textual elision of Irish and their negative evaluations of it prepared for their strategy of silencing. Chapter 4 explores how far the Elizabethans' adventure in Ireland consolidated English linguistic nationalism. Chapter 5 offers an oblique commentary on both processes by exploring how colonists who graduated from Ireland to the New World engaged with native languages there. Chapter 6 focuses on Irish reaction to linguistic colonisation and traces the origins of the vigorous conflictual dialogue that opened up *between* Irish and English and, as the language shift got under way, *within* an English made polyvalent by the experience. By bringing both sets of voices into dialogue, I hope to open up 'a space of translation', as Homi Bhabha enjoins the critic to do (*Location*, p. 25), which can make possible an art that 'does not merely recall the past as social cause or aesthetic precedent; [but] renews the past, refiguring it as a contingent "in-between" space, that innovates and interrupts the performance of the present' (7).[5]

To examine the language shift from the temporal, spatial and theoretical perspective which I am proposing not only helps us to 'live back' more fully but to live in the present more alertly. It points us towards the enduring questions raised by linguistic colonisation for contemporary cross-cultural communications: how is comprehension achieved in a way that respects the opacity and singularity of the other without reducing him to either sameness or exoticism? How are power relations disentangled from the often economically unequal weight of languages in contact? And, at the beginning of a century in which an unprecedented number of languages are threatened with extinction,[6] we need to understand how languages are silenced and through such understanding hear, perhaps, in the responses of a future literature, a singing out of silence.

CHAPTER I

Conquest, colonial ideologies and the consequences for language

Les discours sont, eux aussi, des événements.

Tzvetan Todorov, *Nous et les Autres*, p. 14

The sixteenth century in Ireland was action-packed and dynamic. The transformations that occurred were so sweeping that the century, which opened with Gerald FitzGerald, the future ninth earl of Kildare and Lord Deputy, travelling to Court to marry Elizabeth Zouche, seems to close, on the eve of Kinsale, on a different world. In that time, Ireland had moved from being an almost forgotten 'distant border province' (Ellis, *Tudor Ireland*, p. 86), left to its own devices and those of its Old English and Gaelic magnates, to a colony in revolt at the centre of Elizabethan attention. In the interim, the country was the stage for a bewildering variety of policy changes; the cast was swelled by an influx of bureaucrats, aristocrats, adventurers, soldiers, settlers and proselytisers; and the nature of the military engagement shifted from marcher skirmishes to full-scale war with an international dimension. Caught up in all of this was language: as medium of negotiation, as subject of interdictions, as badge of identity, as index of civility, as symbol of otherness, as bearer of ideology, as words in the mouth of a preacher, as battlecry, as lines tumbling off the newly established printing presses, as – when O'Donnell, on a hosting in Sligo, slaughtered all males unable to speak Irish (O'Sullivan, *Ireland under Elizabeth*, p. 82) – death-warrant. The history of the period is, in part, the history of a shift in the balance of power between the island's two languages. When the Englishwoman Elizabeth Zouche married into the greatest of the Old English dynasties, in 1503, she immediately set about learning Irish: using the direct method which Baron Delvin later adapted to produce an Irish primer for Queen Elizabeth, 'in shorte tyme she learned to reade, write, and perfectlye speake the tongue' (Gilbert,

8

Facsimiles, IV.1, p. xxxv). A hundred years later, when Hugh O'Neill, Earl of Tyrone and overlord of the Nine Years War (1595–1603), submitted after Kinsale, he did so in English.

My purpose is to explore how the century's vertiginous political changes mapped on to the engagement between Irish and English. Historians of early modern Ireland bring us part of the way. They chart the political and military developments that transformed the island's polity and the relations between its two communities – 'mere' Irish, Old English – and the Crown; and they reconstruct the ideologies that underpinned England's growing colonial entanglement in Ireland. But they leave the question of language hanging. Yet ideologies of conquest had implications for language – as the Spanish *empresa* in the New World demonstrated. This chapter, therefore, moves from reconstructing the political and ideological context of sixteenth-century Ireland to opening up a comparison between English linguistic colonisation in Ireland and its Spanish equivalent in the New World. Because language was so central to Spanish discourses of colonisation and because academic research into the *conquista* correspondingly highlights language issues, the Spanish-American model provides a template for exploring the connection between colonial ideologies and language policy and helps to point up the particularity of English linguistic colonisation.

THE HISTORICAL BACKGROUND

Sixteenth-century Irish historiography is a domain almost as contested as the territory it surveys. Yet while individual historians may disagree – hotly – about when the drift towards conquest and colonisation set in, and clash over which ideologies shaped those policies, the agreed *grandes lignes* of sixteenth-century history are not in dispute. Though officially an English colony since the Norman invasion in 1169, Ireland had gradually slipped from English attention and settled into a de facto partition between the Gaelic lordships and the Pale. English rule, as far as it ran, was delegated to the principal Old English families, the FitzGeralds of Kildare and the Butlers of Ormond. In the early 1530s, however, Old English reformers persuaded the Crown to involve itself in regenerating the residual colony. The ambitions of the reformers soon extended to the whole island, ushering in a phase of 'unitary sovereignty'. This phase ran from 1540, with the arrival of Lord Deputy St Leger, until conciliation and reform were abandoned and the drift towards conquest and colonisation began.

Offering such a neatly delineated chronology is not without its dangers. While the schema is useful, we should not be seduced into accepting its periodisation as absolute, much less into taking it over uncritically to force a matching language scheme into the same mould. Brady and Gillespie warn against a simplified view of Ireland as moving from a kingdom, with a constitution similar to England's, to a colony ripe for exploitation. The distinctiveness of sixteenth-century Ireland, they insist, is that it was 'a constitutional anomaly, neither the "kingdom" of England nor a "colony" in North America' (*Natives and Newcomers*, p. 17). England's Irish policy was never monolithic or clear-cut but characterised by 'periodic oscillations and simultaneous inconsistencies' (Brady, 'Court', p. 23).

Our focus is the interaction between Irish and English under the press of increased English engagement in Ireland after 1541. The period immediately preceding the Crown's renewed involvement in Ireland provides a point of reference and comparison. Politically, the fifteenth and early sixteenth centuries were characterised by duality: the incompleteness of the Anglo-Norman conquest meant that, from the Statutes of Kilkenny (1366) until the reign of Henry VIII, London had little option but to accept the status quo and to interfere only minimally (Quinn and Nicholls, 'Ireland in 1534', p. 39). The duality was reflected in the colonists' continuing sense of their Englishness and in their more developed political consciousness which contrasted with the 'particularist and dynastic' mentality of the Gaelic lords (Ellis, *Tudor Ireland*, p. 94). But, while in the political domain 'duality' betokened boundaries and the existence of parallel political and administrative worlds, culturally, it signalled permeability. The Old English moved comfortably between both worlds: there was a 'widespread predilection for the Irish language and Gaelic cultural forms at all levels in the Pale' (Bradshaw, *Constitutional Revolution*, p. 41).

The initial expansion of the English state into Ireland combined limited military action under Lord Leonard Grey with bureaucratic reform. Bradshaw stresses the distinctiveness of this initial reform period, characterised as it was by collaboration between Old English reformers and Tudor administrators. Reform got under way in 1534 with Thomas Cromwell's *Ordinances for Ireland*. Its ambitions, limited to 'particular reform' of the Pale, were at first modest. But, while

necessary, consolidation of the English colony alone, prey as it was to
Gaelic incursions, would not be enough. Moreover, the Old English
reformers' commitment to the humanist ideal of the commonwealth
brought the whole island within their purview, nudging them
towards a 'general reform' which embraced the Gaelic lordships: the
movement towards unitary sovereignty was on. It received an urgent
push in 1539 with the rising of the Geraldine League which
assembled an unusually united aggregation of Gaelic parties. This
threat from outside the newly reformed Pale 'proved the inadequacy
of Cromwell's programme in failing to come to grips with the
constitutional problem of the Irishry' (Bradshaw, *Constitutional Revolution*, pp. 127, 184).

In the early 1540s, therefore, the Crown finally adopted a policy of
general reform. Henry VIII's assumption of the title 'King of
Ireland', proclaimed by the Irish parliament in June 1541, marked a
new stage in relations between the two islands, de jure to begin with,
but increasingly de facto. 'The change of title signified a commitment
to effective and total rule' (Foster, *Modern Ireland*, p. 3). It inaugurated
a policy of 'unification by assimilation' (Brady, 'Court', p. 27).
English law now encompassed the whole island, ending its effective
partition into Gaelic and English jurisdictions (Ellis, *Tudor Ireland*,
p. 140). Significantly, the proposal to extend the king's title to Ireland
came from the Irish reformers, not the Crown; they were also behind
the policy of 'surrender and regrant' adopted by St Leger (Bradshaw,
Constitutional Revolution, p. 91). The policy sought 'to incorporate the
Gaelic lordship by consent into a new fully anglicised kingdom of
Ireland' (Ellis, *Tudor Ireland*, p. 137). But the new constitutional status
remained paradoxical: 'neither a colony nor yet an independent
sovereign entity, Ireland was a curious hybrid, a kingdom whose own
sovereign denied its autonomy' (Brady, 'Court', p. 29). Ironically,
unitary sovereignty sidelined the Irish administration and its Old
English officials. As power became centralised, it became centralised
in London (Bradshaw, *Constitutional Revolution*, p. 141). With this shift,
the influence of the Old English reformers waned. At the same time,
Edward VI's accession in 1547 introduced a far less conciliatory
brand of Protestantism under Protector Somerset.

The period after Henry VIII's death in 1547 saw a breakdown
in the reforming impulse and a slide towards militarisation,
religious polarisation and colonisation. While warning against any
facile pinpointing of the precise moment of 'the radical shift from

conciliation to coercion', Brady and Gillespie have no hesitation in pronouncing Tudor policy in Ireland a failure precisely in terms of that slippage: 'they had aimed to fashion a kingdom and had laid instead the foundations of a colony' (Brady and Gillespie, *Natives and Newcomers*, p. 14; Brady, 'Court', p. 49). 'Three novel elements' were creeping into Irish affairs: cultural conflict, religious cleavage and a palpable hardening of English administrative policy (Bottigheimer, 'Kingdom and Colony', p. 52). Edward VI's short reign (1547–53) marks a turning point: impatient with the pace of reform, Somerset greatly reinforced the army and an increased reliance on the 'military solution' entailed a corresponding scaling-down of the policy of incorporation by consent (Ellis, *Tudor Ireland*, p. 176). Sir Edward Bellingham, appointed Deputy in 1548, approached Ireland as a soldier rather than as an administrator. Almost immediately, he garrisoned and colonised Leix, thereby setting in motion a radical new policy (Bradshaw, *Constitutional Revolution*, p. 261).

While Henry VIII's reforms had been accepted with relative equanimity, the more militantly Protestant Edwardian reforms were not. Religious policy now exacerbated tensions: the Gaels identified it with military conquest and plantation as part of a general anglicising policy; the Old English regarded it as a reform too far. The growing alienation of the bicultural Old English is a key development of the period. The centralisation implicit in unitary sovereignty saw Dublin being increasingly by-passed for London. The Dublin Parliament was called less often and was packed with placemen. As Ireland became a 'significant prize in court faction-fighting', the English administrators – now less dependent on the Old English – enjoyed a new freedom of manœuvre (Ellis, *Tudor Ireland*, p. 245). Moreover, English attention switched from the Pale to Gaelic Ireland. From 1547 onwards, therefore, Tudor policy was increasingly conducted independently of the Old English, leading to what Ellis identifies as 'a breakdown in consensus between crown and community'. As the influence of the Old English waned, so their restraining counsel fell on deaf ears. The way was left open for military conquest and colonisation on a scale otherwise impossible (pp. 179, 177). Moreover, the 'removal of the Old English as a buffer had the effect of exacerbating the clash of cultures' (Bottigheimer, 'Kingdom and Colony', p. 51).

By mid-century, the Tudor state had become increasingly embroiled in Ireland. The claims and ambitions of royal government had been greatly extended; the agenda had broadened to include thoroughgoing religious reform and, ineluctably, military conquest. The Gaelic lords who had been wooed by 'surrender and regrant' were embittered by the abandonment of conciliation. Their alienation and that of the Old English was beginning to coalesce into 'an articulate opposition movement which cut across traditional factional politics'. Administratively and militarily, the colonial state was over-stretched. By the time Elizabeth came to the throne in 1558, coercion and the alienation it provoked made a return to consensus politics almost impossible. Reform on contemporary English lines was no longer an option. Instead, the government found itself resorting to the radical solution of 'Anglicization . . . by force' (Ellis, *Tudor Ireland*, pp. 228, 180). Canny documents the increasing ferocity of the military campaigns and shows that commanders like the first Earl of Essex, campaigning in Ulster in 1575, were establishing the principle that military conquest would be a necessary prelude to establishing a colony (*Elizabethan Conquest*, p. 90): the movement towards colonisation was becoming inexorable.

IDEOLOGIES OF CONQUEST

Bound up in the drift towards colonisation traced by the historians was language; but the historians leave that story untold. They exhibit little curiosity about language and take its transparency largely for granted, cheerfully recording parleys between Englishmen and Gaels without pausing to explore how, precisely, such attempted communications were managed. McCarthy Morrogh, exceptionally, wonders 'whether they could speak the same language' and recognises a blindspot: 'The question is of obvious importance when dealing with relations between different societies, yet nothing specific has been written on this topic' ('English Presence', p. 189). Speech, passing so quickly into silence and leaving no apparent trace, presents a particular challenge to the historical method. Language is rarely the historians' focus. They rarely conceive of it as being directly involved in the process or as being in any way constitutive of it. Conquest proceeds by its own rules; language adjustments may follow in its wake. The linguistic landscape, they imply, can be surveyed after the gunsmoke clears.

There has been no systematic attempt to analyse how the policy shift to 'Anglicization . . . by force' affected the relationship between the Irish and English languages. Commentators shy away from making the connection between colonisation and linguistic anglicisation. Ó Cuív portrays language shift as the half-unexpected fall-out of conquest. He implies that it was self-wrought for utilitarian reasons and locates the turning-point in the early seventeenth century, arguing that it was the plantations and 'the upheaval among the landholders rather than any official measures against the Irish language that gained for English a foothold in the Irish countryside' ('Irish Language', p. 529). Meanwhile, sociolinguists bridle at the notion that the triumph of English owes anything to crude historical processes rather than to intrinsic linguistic virtue. R. W. Bailey contends that it would be a 'mistake' to attribute the advance of English in Ireland to any 'consistent imperial impulse' ('Conquests', p. 16). Wardhaugh tries to remove language from the realm of history to that of forensic medicine, arguing that 'the language was not killed but committed suicide' ('Languages in Competition', p. 91). Durkacz, too, discounts colonial causation. He rejects Hechter's 'internal colonialism' theory – which relies on an implicitly neo-imperialistic annexation of Ireland as an 'internal', albeit 'fringe', region in a British polity – but then, by insisting on seeing Scotland, Wales and Ireland as 'peripheral', goes on to replay it. He argues that 'the persistent trend has been the westward march of English into ever more peripheral areas. Wherever the languages clashed, English invariably predominated – a reflection of the economic vigour and cultural buoyancy of the English-speaking peoples' (*Decline*, p. 214). His formula attempts to abstract language from politics and the operation of power, imagining instead the prodigious marching metonym, 'English', ousting rivals less fitted for survival in a species of linguistic Darwinism. But language does not inhabit so autonomous a realm. In the sixteenth century, English was not so much the 'reflection' of 'economic vigour and cultural buoyancy' as the shadow that fell in the shade of the sword.

Anglicisation was neither incidental to the conduct of conquest nor a mere spin-off from it. Language was intimately bound up with the ideologies that legitimised colonisation and shaped its unfolding. The colonists' estimation of their own language and their attitudes towards that of the enemy are as much constitutive of such ideologies as they are consequences of them. We need to review the ideologies which shaped the Elizabethans' drift from reform to conquest in order to identify the role of language in their construction and operation. While it could, crudely, be argued that the late Tudors could move on the unfinished business of conquest because theirs was the drier gunpowder, such superiority, of itself, cannot launch – or continue to justify – a colonial enterprise. Starting with the Spanish and Portuguese, sixteenth-century colonialism was notably articulate in legitimating its operations. The Irish adventure marks the moment when England joins that discourse.

Some historians have competed to reconstruct a single ideology to explain all. Most partisan have been Nicholas Canny and Brendan Bradshaw, the former promoting 'Renaissance anthropology' (the discourse that pitted colonial civility against native barbarism), the latter advancing Protestant Reformation pessimism. Brady and Gillespie, sceptically reviewing their colleagues' penchant for emphasising 'ideological factors as determinants of the course of early modern Irish history' deplore their 'highly schematised approaches', insisting rather that sixteenth-century Ireland escapes rigid categorisation: policy was 'so problematic and its results so multifarious and uncertain' that it 'no longer seems possible to regard any single factor as dominant in shaping English conduct in Ireland' (*Natives and Newcomers*, pp. 16, 18). Foster, as though taking Brady and Gillespie's warning against exclusivity to heart, gives a suitably rounded synopsis: 'The strength of the English reaction against Ireland's lack of 'civility' stemmed partly from Protestantism, partly from English nationalism and partly from . . . the repulsion roused by what John Derricke called their "wild shamrock manners" ' – manners which 'coincided with contemporary anthropological ideas of savagery' (*Modern Ireland*, p. 32). Foster's summary is valuable: it suggests that there may be more common ground between the ideologies than their historian-sponsors, who advance them with such exclusive partisanship, allow. And that common ground may well lie in what Foster calls 'English nationalism'.

Indeed, if we examine the claims made for each ideology, we quickly discover that they offer not so much competing explanations for Tudor behaviour in Ireland as complementary ones. Nicholas Canny attributes the changed tempo and ferocity of Englishmen's engagement in Ireland from the 1560s onwards to their assimilation of 'Renaissance anthropology', the discourse of difference which emerged from Europe's – and especially Spain's – encounter with the inhabitants of the New World (*Elizabethan Conquest*, p. 133). With its facile characterisation of 'civil' and 'barbarian', the new anthropology marked a shift in social thinking, away from an older humanist confidence in the potential for civility of even savage-seeming peoples. It introduced more rigid hierarchies of societies, graduated from savage to highly civilised, and implied a 'more cautious notion of man's capacity for self-improvement' (Canny, 'Formation', p. 18). Canny contends that once the English 'had been persuaded that the Irish were barbarians they were able to produce a moral and civil justification for their conquest'. Whereas the Old English regarded the Gaelic masses as contingently barbarous – the benighted but reformable creatures of barbarous rulers – the emerging taxonomy saw them as 'anthropologically inferior', con-genital barbarians (*Elizabethan Conquest*, pp. 128, 131).

But the repercussions of Renaissance anthropology went beyond simply licensing the replacement of reform by a new militarism. Its discourse of difference operated by alienating native practices – dress, agriculture, warfare, sexual mores – from their cultural matrix and interpreting them instead as loathsome residues of older – Scythian, Gaulish, Pictish – barbarisms. It is worth pausing here to qualify Canny's uncompromisingly 'Atlanticist' position by noting that however central the New World was to the emergence of a belief in graduated social evolution, Englishmen's recourse to classical models of barbarism and their reliance on Giraldus Cambrensis, pioneer of the discourse of Irish difference, confirms that Eliza-bethan-style 'new anthropology' was more a reworking of twelfth-century humanists' justifications of the original conquest than an entirely new departure (Gillingham, 'Images of Ireland'; Morgan, 'Giraldus Cambrensis'). This anthropology, more composite than Canny might be willing to grant, worked by denying native culture its own meanings. By subjecting it instead to deprecatory compar-isons, it would not leave language untouched by its operations.

Whereas Canny 'relates the harsh attitudes of the conquerors to the Irish to an intellectual shift brought about by the impact of European colonial expansion', Bradshaw, in a counter-bid for exclu-sive explanation, holds that 'the shift in perspective was brought about by the Reformation' ('Sword', p. 498, fn. 85). His insistence that the radical new policies taking shape from mid-century find their ideological grounding not in 'Renaissance sociology . . . but Protestant theology' stubbornly adheres to the 'single factor' expla-nation so distrusted by Brady and Gillespie. He argues that the Reformation provided 'the intellectual climate which allowed . . .

inhumanity to be perpetrated with a sense of moral righteousness' ('Elizabethans and Irish', p. 47), because Protestantism, especially in its more extreme formulations, drew on a 'radically pessimistic' anthropology ('Sword', p. 497). That pessimism was shaped by Calvinists' conviction that the intellect was blinded and the will enslaved as a consequence of the Fall. Undisciplined, uncivil man exemplified the mark of the Fall to a disturbing degree. Evangelising, far from being able, of itself, to civilise required conditions of civility and obedience before it could operate ('Elizabethans and Irish', p. 48). A position so pessimistic about the possibility of evangelising – of *persuading* – had clear implications for language practices: if the intellect was indeed so darkened, then persuasive language alone was hardly going to lighten it.

But, as Bradshaw acknowledges, the hardline policy did not have the ideological field all to itself: the existence of Protestant humanists on the other side of the argument, who held that the will *was* amenable to enlightenment through education ('Elizabethans and Irish', p. 45), places internal strains on his thesis. This countervailing strain of civic humanism, he argues, influenced by a more optimistic anthropology, remained confident of man's essential rationality. Man, even uncivil man, was the victim of ignorance rather than of wilful or categorical badness and was thus amenable to education and persuasion ('Sword', p. 491). Whereas for radical Protestants civility was a precondition of evangelising, for the humanists it was an outcome: the savage could be led to civility through the word. From these opposed positions, Bradshaw argues, emerged two contrasting strategies: the strategy of the word and the strategy of the sword ('Elizabethans and Irish', pp. 46, 49).

The implications of both these strategies for language in the context of evangelisation is suggestive and will be explored later. What is less compelling about Bradshaw's argument is its bid for exclusivity. For one thing, to attempt to attribute 'harsh attitudes' exclusively to Protestantism and to refuse to countenance the possible influence of the new anthropology is a daring but unconvincing manœuvre: responsibility for the far harsher conduct of the Spanish in America can scarcely be pinned on their Protestantism. Indeed, Bradshaw himself reluctantly acknowledges that 'a certain kind of Counter-Reformation theology' was conducive to a 'rigour' similar to that exercised by the Elizabethans in Ireland ('Elizabethans and Irish', p. 49). If this concession forces us to seek an explanation for 'rigorous' behaviour outside of Protestantism – and it does – then we are already on the way to undoing the binary opposition that he sets up between Protestantism and sixteenth-century colonial anthropology.

Those staking out exclusive claims for Renaissance sociology or Reformation pessimism seem reluctant to countenance that the two perspectives could be complementary. Yet, clearly, the anthropological and theological points of view could be internally coherent. Canny shows that religion was one of the items picked over by the discourse of difference (*Elizabethan Conquest*, p. 125). Under the prevailing anthropological classification, it was regarded as almost axiomatic that Christians were civilised and pagans barbarian (Hodgen, *Early Anthropology*, p. 214). The choice for Protestant colonists in Ireland was self-evident: to acknowledge that the natives were Christian was to concede that they were civil; should they be found to be 'pagan', however, they could be declared barbarous at a stroke (Canny, *Elizabethan Conquest*, p. 125; 'Ideology', p. 586). The religion which the Elizabethans found in Ireland, with its pagan Celtic vestiges, was abhorrent to radical Protestants. The relationship between 'pagan' and 'barbarian' was reflexive and easily made. If we can accept that extreme Protestantism's 'deeply pessimistic anthropology' (Bradshaw, 'Elizabethans and Irish', p. 46) in ways complements rather than overthrows Canny's useful discussion of Renaissance anthropology, we can move on to examine how both have significance for the role of language in the Elizabethan conquest. Far from being binary opposites, the discourses of difference and of Protestant pessimism intersect within the discourse that subsumed them both – English nationalism.

Foster's addition of 'English nationalism' to the reckoning points the way to integrating positions seen by their advocates to be mutually exclusive. Nationalism is a composite ideology rather than a single category; it is constituted by, among other things, a conviction of cultural superiority and religious election. 'Nationalism' is often taken to be an essentially post-Enlightenment phenomenon. Sixteenth-century England, however, represents a precocious anomaly. From as early as the 1530s, England was embarking on a self-conscious project of imagining, representing and, ultimately, vaunting the nation (Hadfield, *Literature, Politics*; Helgerson, *Forms of Nationhood*; McEachern, *Poetics*). Liah Greenfeld shows how a complex of factors – profound social transformation and a new social mobility; Protestantism and its associated literacy; a patriotically motivated literature – worked together to force the emergence of a 'modern, full-fledged, mature nationalism' by the end of Elizabeth's reign (*Nationalism*, p. 70). 'Englishness' was partly defined oppositionally, through counterdistinction with uncivil others (Hadfield and McVeagh, *Strangers*, p. 1); it was confirmed by a sense of religious election (Collinson, *Birthpangs*, p. 5). The ideologies of difference and of militant Protestantism, therefore, should be seen not as competitor ideologies but as complementary strands within the master discourse of Elizabethan nationalism. Foster's synopsis, moreover, recognises that cultural evaluation is central to all three ideologies. All draw on notions of civility and, for the Renaissance, civility was indissociable from language.

Our interest in these ideologies lies not with the archaeology of sixteenth-century justifications – with picking over the bones of old propaganda exercises – but with understanding how the cultural nationalism which they encouraged translated into language policy. Though none of the historians reconstructing these ideologies explores their implications for language, language bubbles close to the surface in all of them. 'Renaissance anthropology', dedicated to parsing the differences between the 'civil' and the 'barbarous', was quickly drawn into making judgements about civil and barbarous tongues. Protestantism, whether in its 'puritan' or 'humanist' incarnation, was committed to the vernacular, either its own or the natives': 'the strategy of the word' implied engagement with the indigenous language, while a Reformation which reified its own vernacular correspondingly sidelined others. Early modern nationalism both housed and was sustained by linguistic chauvinism. Brady argues that the newcomers' 'unearned and wholly unquestioned claims to cultural superiority' not only underwrote their administrative and military incursions but convinced them that military conquest would have to be followed by 'a vigorous campaign of cultural conquest' (*Chief Governors*, pp. xv, xi). And 'cultural conquest' – cultural nationalism – had clear implications for language policy.

THE PLACE OF LANGUAGE IN IDEOLOGIES OF CONQUEST: THE SPANISH MODEL

'Toute colonisation porte en germe la glottophagie' (Calvet, *Linguistique*, p. 84): Calvet's bold assertion invites us to test how ideologies of conquest influence the attendant language encounter: how power takes shape in language, and how language exercises its will-to-power. That exploration is already well under way for other episodes of linguistic colonisation – most notably, into the encounter between Spanish and the languages of the New World which paralleled events in Ireland temporally and massively overshadowed them in scope. The scholarship investigating that encounter is particularly enabling for our purposes because it moves on from where the Irish historians' examination of the ideologies of conquest leaves off: it explores the mechanisms of linguistic colonisation specific to the anthropological discourse of difference, early modern nationalism and militant Protestantism's mirror opposite, Counter-Reformation Catholicism.

To couple the Irish and American situations is not at all to insist on a total correspondence between the two. (Re)conquest of a near neighbour – whose existence was certainly never in doubt – is quite unlike the conquest of a 'new world'. The first altogether lacks the element of the marvellous, the exotic, the utterly unexpected. More-over, the twelfth-century conquest had left behind a linguistic bridge-head in Ireland – the bilingual Old English. So to invoke comparison is not to suggest that English actions or attitudes mimicked Spanish ones. (Indeed, much of the value of comparison lies precisely in exploring divergences between the two.) But, it is useful, as W. D. Mignolo argues in criticising the tendency of postcolonial studies to focus exclusively on 'the legacies of the British Empire', to 'de-colonize scholarship and to decentre epistemological loci of enunci-ation' (*Darker Side*, p. ix). The challenge implicit in Pagden's observation that 'theorists of empire and its historians have remained curiously indifferent to the possibilities offered by comparison' (*Lords*, p. 3) is worth taking up. The comparison not only allows us to explore the dynamic interaction between conquest, ideology and language but also helps us to escape the obsessive Anglo-Irish focus that sometimes narrows Irish literary and historical scholarship.

While the usefulness of the model does not require any a priori demonstration of strict parallels between the two sites, significant connections between them exist. Stated most minimally, both were situations of conquest; both involved a cross-cultural encounter where languages met headlong. But the parallels are not, in fact, so minimal. Spain and England shared the intellectual and philosophi-cal background of Renaissance humanism which influenced both groups' assumptions about language, eloquence and civility. Both were centres of linguistic excitement. Moreover, Quinn, Canny and others have shown that Elizabethan theorists and makers of Irish policy such as Sir Thomas Smith and Sir Henry Sidney – Queen Mary's emissary to Spain from 1553 to 1556 – were familiar with and influenced by the Spanish model of colonisation (Quinn, 'Renaissance Influences'; Canny, *Elizabethan Conquest*, pp. 66, 85). Those lacking direct contact were familiar with the Spanish model through the abundant translations of Spanish travel and promotional literature (Pennington, 'Promotional Literature', p. 179; Steele, *English Interpreters*).[1] Ellis emphasises how emulation of Spain encouraged the development of English colonial policy, awakening 'latent colonialist attitudes' there. In consequence, the older idea of Ireland as a borderland gave way to the idea of it as an 'old colony . . . ripe for plantation in accordance with recent colonial theory', with adventurers like Humphrey Gilbert increasingly coming to see Ireland 'as a New World ripe for colonisation on the Spanish model' (*Tudor Ireland*, pp. 249, 255). Moreover, Englishmen consciously drew parallels between the Irish and native Americans (Muldoon, 'Indian as Irishman'). When Shane O'Neill entered the court of Elizabeth with galloglasses attired in saffron shirts and 'rough hairy Clokes', the courtiers 'admired no lesse, than they should at this day to see those of China, or America' (Camden, *Annales*, p. 90). The author of 'The Newe Metamorphosis' opined that 'like brutish Indians, these wylde Irish live / . . . cruell and bloody, barbarous and rude' (Lyon, p. 76); Fynes Moryson imagined Ireland as an 'Island in the Virginian Sea' (*Itinerary*, pt 3, p. 156); Richard Boyle, newly arrived in Cork, marvelled at being 'dropped here into a New World' (Canny, *Upstart Earl*, p. 11). The shared intellectual background of English and Spanish colonial planners ensured that, for all the dissimilarities between Munster and Michoacán, there were notable coincidences – as well as interesting variations – in both powers' attitudes to language and its management in a colonial context.

Moreover, by the century's end, men who had cut their teeth in the Munster plantation graduated from colonial apprenticeship there to direct competition with the Spanish in the New World, thereby opening a decisive chapter in European linguistic expansion. The Argentinian Mignolo's anxiety to inscribe Spain's contribution to 'the darker side of the Renaissance' into the mainstream of postcolonial discourse prompted him to write his book of that title in English. To write in Spanish, he avers, 'means, at this time, to remain at the margin of contemporary theoretical discussions' (p. viii). The implication is that the great colonising language of the sixteenth century enters the twenty-first intellectually marginalised by the language which, four centuries earlier, was, almost unnoticed, rehearsing in its small-scale Irish venture the manœuvres of linguistic expansion that it would soon extend to America and beyond.

Christopher Colombus made landfall, on 12 October 1492, on a small island which he immediately christened San Salvador. The linguistic – and, of course, territorial – conquest of the New World begins with naming. Calvet identifies this *droit de nommer* as an unfailing gesture of all imperialisms (*Linguistique*, p. 57). The expedition's interpreter, Luís de Torres, recruited for his command of Hebrew, Aramaic and Arabic, came face to face with the limits of the Old World's languages when he tried to parley with the Arawak-speaking Tainos. America, especially South America, is remarkably diverse linguistically: 170 major language families subdivide into an estimated 2,000 distinct tongues (Martinell Gifre, *Aspectos*, p. 108).

From the outset, language difference was bound up in the discourse of difference which guided Europeans' interpretations of the New World. The 'brave new world' that the Spanish had discovered was, in almost every way, an altogether strange and unfamiliar one. In Mexico and Peru, they confronted dazzling empires at the height of their powers. But the Spanish had not come to learn from, much less admire, the unexpected continent which their mariners had chanced upon: they came to build 'Nueva España', 'Nueva Granada'. To justify the overthrow of the existing civilisations and their replacement by Spain's brand of Christianity and capitalism, strangeness and difference could not be surveyed neutrally. What was different had to be adjudged imperfect, inferior and savage. Then it could be transformed – or destroyed.

The colonial discourse of difference – the discursive reflex of 'renaissance anthropology' – is possible only when the boundaries that separate self and other, and recognise the integrity of that separation, are transgressed. The colonist, no longer content to acknowledge the autonomy of the other's discourse, extends the bounds of his discursive space and presumes to include – and evaluate – the other and his cultural attributes according to the values of the metropolitan culture. That annexation sets in train a whole sequence of evaluations – including the evaluation of language. Affergan traces the process that draws the other away from autonomous individuality, from evaluation on his own terms, into the colonist's system of classification and meaning. The radically distinct other is ontologically resistant to any attempted reductive appropriation and stands apart, 'irrepérable, ni adversaire, ni colonisé, ni dominant, ni dominé, ni assimilable, ni modèle' (*Exotisme*, p. 85). But the colonial impulse is to classify such an entity according to a scale of likeness and difference, in what Affergan calls '[la] réduction forcée de l'altérité en différences' (p. 78). The discourse of difference operates by simultaneously devaluing the other and – in an impulse that joins cause with nationalism – validating the self. The distinctness and opacity of the other is denied; it is translated into a system of differences that domesticates him and, in calibrating his points of resemblance or deviation, prepares for his assimilation or conquest. The discourse builds up a pattern of paired contrasts, pitting the perfections of the self and his civilisation (taken, in a manner guaranteed to fix the results, as the standard) against the – thereby inevitable – imperfections of the other.

Once set on a European-graduated scales, the Indian could be measured – and found wanting. Judgement was delivered as a label – 'barbarian', 'cannibal', 'savage' – which undid the selfhood of the other. The labelling, the (mis-)naming involved in this reductive classification, was an eminently linguistic act: behind the name stood a colonial language strategy, not an individual. And a key term in the colonial classification was language: the barbarian's tongue. Judgements about language were central to the discourse of difference. To meet the impenetrability of a foreign language is to face otherness in one of its most intractable manifestations. Until race emerged, in the seventeenth century, as the standard measurement of difference, religion and language were its markers: differences in them 'touched the Renaissance European to the quick' (Hodgen, *Early Anthropology*, pp. 418, 214). Caught up in the discourse of difference, indigenous speech was subjected to a kind of colonially skewed comparative linguistics. It was evaluated not on its own terms but as an index of otherness – and of deficiency.

By the time the Spanish came to judge the Amerindian languages, they could draw on a tradition of thinking about language that represented the merging and continuing elaboration of Greek and

Judeo-Christian theories of language. Europe had long practice in attaching the epithet 'barbarous' to 'tongue' and, through that pairing, making language a key term in defining 'barbarism'. Far from being just another item in the classification, language was central to bringing the discourse of difference into being. Barbarism itself, etymologically rooted in *barbaros*, the babbling outsider unable to speak Greek, is 'a concept grounded in linguistic difference' (Pagden, *Fall*, p. 179; cf. Hall, *Inventing the Barbarian*). Without the barbarous tongue, there was no barbarian. The Judeo-Christian tradition, brooding on the legacy of Babel, brought a more systematically pessimistic conception of language. Babel begot not just linguistic confusion but linguistic degeneracy. Classical and biblical views of language had merged by the late Middle Ages (Jones, 'Image', p. 389). In providing the founding myths of Renaissance linguistics, they placed strong associations between language and notions of degeneracy and barbarism at the heart of European thinking about language.

The concept of the 'barbarous tongue' presupposes, at a stroke, a hierarchy of both languages and societies. There are, it suggests, civil societies with civil tongues and barbarian societies with barbarous tongues. The connection is seen as causal. The belief that civil tongues begot civil societies was widely accepted from antiquity onwards. Cicero argued that eloquence led men from native savagery to civility (Greenblatt, 'Learning to Curse', p. 565). For Aquinas, only *communicatio*, civil and persuasive exchange, could build a civil society. Barbarians, by definition defective in such conversation – Aquinas held that they did not speak a systematic language – were correspondingly cut off from sophisticated social organisation (Pagden, *Fall*, pp. 23, 127; Borst, *Medieval Worlds*, p. 9). Once the equation is made between the level of communication practised by a society and that society's stage of development, it becomes possible to use communication itself as a yardstick for ranking societies: the first becomes an index of the second. Although, ostensibly, Aquinas' theory credits language with bringing civil society into being, the attribution – especially as it was later exploited by colonial apologists – is somewhat disingenuous. The real cynosure is not civil language but civil society. The flattering of its language works by back formation. What is being vaunted is reality, a European reality. Mignolo points out that sixteenth-century Spain enjoyed 'the economic and political power that made possible the universalization of regional values' (*Darker Side*, p. 19). Language at its fullest development will be commensurate with that – purely regional – reality and will express it adequately.[2] Conversely, a language will be found defective if it fails to correspond with that reality. This equation was grounded in the theory – or theories – of language which governed Renaissance Europe's understanding of the connection between language and 'reality'.

That connection was, according to Foucault's sweeping characterisation of the sixteenth-century episteme, one which indentured language to the world through analogical correspondences (*Order of Things*, p. 35). Only in the seventeenth century, runs the necessary companion-piece to this argument, is language 'discovered' as a maker of meanings (Cohen, *Sensible Words*, p. 25). Such dichotomous thinking, however, obscures the dynamism with which language was being re-imagined by both theorists and practitioners well before 1600. True, sixteenth-century Europe's inherited paradigm of how language worked was referential. Meaning was transcendent; language was nomenclature: words simply named pre-existent meanings. Nonetheless, the age of lexical exuberance and prolific inventiveness that runs from Rabelais to Cervantes anxiously fretted that words were spinning free of extra-linguistic correlatives. A loss of confidence in the power of words to connect with a priori meanings meant that 'words, words, words' – and not just Hamlet's – were haunted by a sense of 'vacuité sémantique' (Dubois, *Mythe*, pp. 40–1). Intellectuals like Richard Hooker were coming to recognise that, far from inhering in language, meaning was conventional and cultural (Shuger, *Habits of Thought*, pp. 30–7). A gap was being prised open between *res* and *verba*.

In *Language and Meaning in the Renaissance*, Richard Waswo shows how humanist philology set in motion a process which destabilised the relationship between word and thing to produce 'a generally altered consciousness of language' (p. 113). By uncovering the flux of Latin in time, Lorenzo Valla had effectively demonstrated that language was the socio-historical construct of a speech community. Valla's realisation that language was 'cognitive, contingent, and semantically constitutive' (p. 102) sparked off what Waswo calls the 'Renaissance semantic shift' (p. 60). Comparative linguistics, too, was pointing up the agency of individual tongues in making culturally specific meanings. In demonstrating that seeming synonyms like '*homo*' and '*anthropos*' signified subtly different things, Juan Luis Vives was implicitly showing that different languages functioned differently (p. 124). But the shift from referential to relational semantics – from seeing language as representing 'Reality' to seeing it creating *a* reality – was faltering and produced only what Waswo calls an 'abortive intellectual revolution': the historical constructedness of language was accepted empirically by comparative philologists and translators when working with real languages but it remained irreconcilable, as a theory, with the prevailing ontological metaphysics (p. 132). This produced an often creative 'tension between language *treated* as creating meaning and *conceived* as but containing it' (p. 125).

Both the dominant and the emerging conception of how language worked gave considerable latitude for judgemental comparisons between languages – but they fixed the limits of those evaluations very differently. Du Bellay's unquestioning assumption that words simply named a reality that anteceded them places him firmly among the referentialists. Nonetheless, his espousal of the essential equality of all languages did not stop him recognising the untranslatable 'je ne scay quoy' of each or acknowledging that some languages had, with time and cultivation, become 'richer' than others (*Deffence*, pp. 36, 13). Comparison could be competitive. Lascari, one of the participants in Speroni's 'Dialogo delle lingue', held that 'Diuerse lingue sono atte à significare diuersi concetti' (different tongues are fitted to express different concepts), some learned, some not (*I Dialogi*, fo. 125v). Criteria for adjudication were to hand. Godfrey Goodman, James's I's chaplain, had clear 'heads' – pronunciation, lexical adequacy, cognitive patterns – for judging 'base and barbarous' tongues:

some of them [are] very harsh in pronunciation, that a man must wrong his owne visage, and disfigure himselfe to speake them: others without grauitie or wisdome in their first imposition, consisting only of many bare, and simple tearmes, not reduced to any certaine fountaines, or heads, which best resembleth nature: Many of them hindring mans thoughts, and wanting a sufficie[n]t plentie of words, cannot significantly expresse the quicknes of inuention, or liuelily expresse an action: some giuing way to fallacies and sophistrie, through Tautologies, ambiguous words, darke sentences; others inclining to ribaldrie, and luxurious speech. (*Fall of Man*, pp. 293–4)

Goodman's subscription to the traditional semantics, however, meant that while he acknowledged 'fallen' languages' imperfections and inequalities, he remained convinced of their common origin and perfectibility. Referential semantics with its faith in the existence of universal meanings and a common Adamic origin set limits on the differences conceivable between languages. No such limits were set by relational semantics. If a language mapped not the divine order of things but the mental and cultural world of its speakers, its scope for singularity and divergence was considerable. To encounter an unknown language was to journey into an alien world. Evaluation conducted under the sign of relational semantics opened up the possibility of finding not a deep-down similitude guaranteed by transcendent meanings but an unsettlingly different universe of meanings. Waswo confines his exploration of the shift from representational to relational semantics to the major European languages. But, if historical and comparative philology within Europe challenged confidence in the existence of a unified meaning beyond – but accessible through – language, the 'langages pellegrins' far to the west could only undermine it further. As we shall see in Ireland, too, the encounter with language difference and the evaluations it provoked would challenge and re-shape colonial intellectuals' understanding of how language worked.

Our immediate concern lies with how Europeans' contradictory ideas about the way language *meant* influenced their evaluation of New World languages. On the one hand, a correspondence theory oriented evaluators towards measuring the adequacy of native languages to express meanings understood to be universal; its focus was on *copia* and precision. On the other hand, an inchoate recognition that language itself created meaning placed evaluators in the position of judging not just the adequacy of a language to articulate 'reality' but also the potential of such languages anarchically to make their own heterodox meanings. In Europe, as Waswo shows, the line between whether language represented meaning or constituted it was never clearly drawn: a discursive practice that recognised the instrumentality of words in generating meaning remained hitched to a theory that saw meaning as transcendent (*Language and Meaning*, p. 153). In evaluating the languages of others, too, I suggest, the two positions criss-crossed. Europeans' almost unquestioned theoretical subscription to an isomorphic view of language, allied to their robust conviction that their language was in perfect alignment with reality, left space only at the margins for indigenous languages. Lacunae in native languages' correspondence to European meanings were inevitable. But while Nahuatl's 'lack' of a word for 'angel' could be taken as proof that the Mexica's language had an incomplete grasp of reality – that it was referentially inadequate – the evidence could equally suggest that Nahuatl fashioned its own, different reality. With 'exquisite confusion', both perspectives could even work together. That Castilian had no equivalent for '*kwawxochipixkeh*' could confirm both that Spanish conformed to 'reality' – there were no 'demon lovers' among the Platonic forms – and that Nahuatl constructed a false reality where there were. The European language is the mirror, referentially reflecting reality; the other's is a lamp projecting fantasies. Angels exist; *kwawxochipixkeh* do not – but, disturbingly, they can be conjured up in language. But whether condemned for being referentially inadequate (as lacking words for 'real', Christian, things) or for being relationally disquieting (summoning heretical fantasies into being) both theories of language coincided in inclining their subscribers to find native languages barbarous.[3]

Language in the New World was a key criterion for judging the native. 'Not only was the concept of barbarism in origin a linguistic one but . . . the evaluation of Indian languages played a crucial role in assessing the status of their users' (Pagden, *Fall*, p. 70). The polysynthetic, agglutinative languages of the Indians gave the Spanish rich pickings for their judgemental evaluations (Gonzalbo, *Historia*, p. 67). We can extrapolate the categories which sixteenth-century philologists employed to judge native languages by identifying the criteria invoked by commentators like José de Acosta and Bernardo de Aldrete. Acosta reviewed the Inca lingua franca, Quechua, in *De procuranda indorum salute* (1588), his monumental missionaries' handbook. His evaluation exemplifies how far judgement was conditioned by ideology and episteme. Ideologically, Acosta's analysis answered to the pragmatics of evangelisation and the need to allay missionaries' qualms about the difficulty of learning Quechua. Epistemologically, he worked within the paradigm of referential semantics, assessing Quechua's adequacy as a vehicle for conveying Christian meanings. Praise is held in check by the ideology which guided his analysis: for all its admirable effects, he opined, Quechua is not a language of culture and is, in respects, barbarous. It can be ranked only midway in the hierarchy of languages, just as its speakers rest mid-way on the scale of civility (Mustapha, 'Langue', p. 240). Acosta's analysis is cursory and unsystematic but his focus on the sound, lexicon and grammar of Quechua and the cognitive functions which, he thereby inferred, it permitted its speakers allows us to identify the main criteria for linguistic evaluation in the sixteenth century and beyond. These are the terms through which a discourse of difference was brought to bear on language. Though far more haphazardly, the Elizabethans worked within the same parameters when evaluating Irish and I reuse the framework in chapter 3 to structure my analysis of them.

Pronunciation/phonetics

Acosta began his analysis with a verdict on Quechua pronunciation which he found 'ciertamente bárbara en gran parte' (certainly barbarous on the whole), a judgement complicated by his concession that its phonetics had considerable affinity with Spanish (*De procuranda*, p. 362). Acosta could join sense to sound when judging Quechua phonetics. But the uncomprehending, too, could hazard judgements from sounds. In the absence of sense, we register only a jumble of clicks, consonants, aspirants, tones, rhythms, glottal stops. Once sense is added, these sounds acquire the entirely different import that meaning brings. A judgement purely from sound is, by definition, a judgement from ignorance. To say what something *sounds like* is to invite judgement by analogy. To Ortiz de Hinojoso, the Indian languages sounded like 'voces illyteratas de páxaros o brutos . . . que no se pueden escribir ni apenas pronunciar' (the unlettered voices of birds or beasts . . . which cannot be written nor scarcely pronounced) (Gonzalbo, *Historia*, p. 102). Description by analogy gives freedom to the listener who wields it; the analogy chosen registers more the prejudices projected by the hearer than it reflects on any intrinsic qualities of the language itself.[4]

Semantic adequacy

In an episteme which saw meaning as fixed and universal and words as a corresponding set of well- or ill-matched names, the adequacy of a language's lexicon assumed crucial diagnostic importance. Put to the test, Indian languages were found wanting. When they failed to correspond isomorphically with European concepts presumed to be universal, the gap was taken as evidence of impoverishment. While Acosta admired the expressiveness, elegance and 'concisión admirable' of Quechua, he complained that it suffered from a 'gran penuria de palabras, porque como bárbaros caracían del conocimiento de estos conceptos' (great poverty of words because, as barbarians, they lacked the knowledge of these concepts) (p. 363). The missionaries found to their dismay that the indigenous tongues had words for neither 'God', 'demon' nor 'fiesta' (Baudot, 'Dieu', p. 145; Husson, 'Contresens', p. 264). By identifying the Christian particular with the universal, the missionaries could find only deficiency in what was simply difference. The Indian languages were alarmingly lacking in the vocabulary of Christian theology; they were not Christian tongues: a statement of the obvious was elevated to a verdict.[5]

The – predictable – poverty of American languages in words for a European piety was used to justify the extension of Spanish. Philip II's Royal decree of 1596 gave voice to a belief widespread among the Spanish that indigenous languages were inadequate to express 'the mysteries of the faith', declaring that 'en la mejor y más perfecta lengua de los indios no se pueden explicar bien ni con propriedad los misterios de la fe, sino con grandes absurdos e imperfecciones' (even in the best and most perfect of the Indian languages one cannot express the mysteries of the faith well or appropriately without considerable absurdities and imperfections) (Clément, 'Créoles', p. 121).

Grammar

Acosta was at pains to insist that, grammatically, Quechua was less difficult than Latin or Greek; it was 'más sencillo y tiene poquísimas inflexiones' (simpler and has very few inflections) (*De procuranda*, p. 362). 'Excessive' complexity was seen as a defect (Pagden, *Fall*, p. 183) – and an impediment to vernacular evangelisation.

Cognitive range

Referential semantics conditioned evaluators to believe that the nature of a given language determined the cognitive range of its users by controlling their access to meaning. To judge a language was to judge the habits of thought which it permitted.[6] The link forged between reason and eloquence implied a consequent equation between defective tongues and defective thinking. The relation between eloquence and the wisdom which it expressed – or created – was one of the points where the unresolved tension between referential and relational semantics showed up most sharply. While the relationship was theorised as being merely metonymic, in practice rhetorical forms were handled as though they were semantically constitutive (Waswo, *Language and Meaning*, pp. 190–6). The resistance of Indian languages to concepts like the Trinity which relied on paradox was taken as evidence of their deficiency (Pagden, *Fall*, p. 182). Conveniently, of course, languages ill-fitted to philosophy or theology invariably proved adequate to issuing orders to a captive workforce. This disabling division of labour, which also willingly conceded passion and poetry to languages judged unequal to higher thinking, was well established by the sixteenth century. Many of those alleging rational deficiencies in Indian languages were quite willing to allow them the consolation of being, at least, rich in metaphor and subtle in phrasing (Duviols, 'Langue et évangélisation', p. 280).[7]

Writing

Writing was treated as a crucial indicator of a people's level of civilisation. When Acosta classified 'barbarians' hierarchically for the purpose of matching evangelising strategies to different barbarians' levels of development, he used writing as the deciding variable. The Chinese and Japanese came closest to *recta razón*: they had 'el uso y conocimiento de las letras, porque dondequiera que hay libros y monumentos escritos, la gente es más humana y política' (the use and knowledge of letters, because wheresoever there are books and written monuments, the people are more human and civil). Next came nations like the Incas who, though they did not have writing, compensated ingeniously for its absence – 'suplieron su falta' – with their quipus. Bringing up the rear were 'los salvajes semejantes a fieras, que apenas tienen sentimiento humano' (savages like wild beasts who scarcely have human feeling). Lettered barbarians could be evangelised through preaching; the entirely unlettered could be 'cazados como bestias y domados por la fuerza' (hunted like beasts and tamed by force) (pp. 46–7). 'A celebration of the letter' as a sign of civility was central to the Renaissance philosophy of language (Mignolo, *Darker Side*, p. 29). Writing was credited with fixing language, thereby holding degeneration at bay, and with preserving memory and the glories of the past (Mignolo, 'Teorías', pp. 177, 181). Given Renaissance Europe's reverence for alphabetic writing, it is unsurprising that the Spanish looked contemptuously on the native American hieroglyphic codices which they burned with such energy. To possess writing was to be on the highest rung of language's evolutionary scale. To lack it, argued Aldrete, was to lack *scientia* and *policía* – civility – and to live in the manner of beasts (*Del origin* I, p. 148; cf. Mignolo, 'Literacy and Colonisation', p. 78).

Genealogy

A language's supposed ancestors could also be called upon to take the stand. 'Fabricating genealogies was a major intellectual activity in the sixteenth and seventeenth centuries' (Ryan, 'Assimilating New Worlds', p. 532). The lineage of a language was a sure indicator of its nature. The uncovering or, more commonly, the invention of a family tree allowed for an unfamiliar language to be fitted into a familiar schema and to be judged by association. There was a tendency to see in particularly 'confused' tongues the clearest mark of Babel and descent in direct line from Nimrod (White, *Tropics*, p. 161). The origins of the Indian tongues excited much speculation. Their multiplicity bore all too clearly the sign of Babel's confusion and was taken as an index of barbarity. Given the weight which contemporary theories of language placed on *communicatio*, a diversity which hindered it was seized upon as confirmation of rudimentary social development (Mannheim, *Inka*, p. 36). The Spaniards' corresponding insistence on seeing all native languages as dialects played out a well-established colonial reflex: the colonist speaks a 'language', the colonised a mere 'dialect' – an invariably loaded distinction (Calvet, *Linguistique*, p. 54).

Evaluation of the other's language, like the discourse of difference under which it is conducted, is in important ways simply the obverse side of the colonist's confident estimation of his own language. At a certain point, the apparently separate strands of the discourses of difference and of early modern nationalism come together: in a binary world, an uncivil tongue presupposed its opposite. There are two languages involved in colonial-style comparative linguistics. The language of the victor is always the implicit linguistic gold standard from which the other deviates; the colonist's confidence that his is a civil tongue is the linguistic correlative of his nationalism. If Babel's multiplication of tongues marked language's degeneration from the perfection of the divine *Ursprache*, clearly some had degenerated rather more grievously than others. Comfortingly for the representative of the expansionist society, surveying the sorry legacy of Babel, his is the civil society, his the eloquent tongue. He is the categorical opposite of the Wild Man, whose muteness marks him as occupying the antipode to civic eloquence; he also stands apart from speakers of 'primitive' tongues. The sense of superiority conferred by this conviction is the enabling perspective of sixteenth-century nationalism. The sixteenth century is not only the period when Spain conquers Central and South America; it is also the *Siglo de Oro* of its literature. Castilian, systematised by grammarians like Nebrija and caught up in the excitement of humanistic learning, is, as Heath remarks, 'a vigorous tongue – the cultural and political instrument of a self-proclaiming society' (*Telling Tongues*, p. 7).

Linguistic chauvinism went hand-in-glove with nationalist confidence and it inclined colonists to impose their language as a stamp of their superiority and as a right of conquest. 'Siempre la lengua fue compañera del imperio' (language was ever the companion of empire): the formula, from the prologue of Nebrija's *Gramática castellana*, published with uncanny aptness in 1492, is often taken as the classic expression of Spanish linguistic imperialism. Nebrija's assertion drew on Valla's *Elegantiae*, which argued that Latin had given the Roman empire its coherence and endurance (Asensio, 'Lengua compañera', p. 400). Indeed, when quoted in full – 'siempre la lengua fue compañera del imperio i de tal manera lo siguio que juntamente començaron, crecieron i florecieron, i despues junta fue la caida de entrambos' (language was ever the companion of empire and in such a way it followed that together they began and grew and flourished and afterwards together they fell) (Aldrete, *Del origin* II, p. 39) – Nebrija's observation, penned before Columbus sailed, reads more like a timeless contemplation of the correlation between the grandeur and decadence of languages and empires; it is as much nostalgic as it is prophetic or prescriptive. Yet this was a backwards glance that could prompt future emulation. Maybe, Milhou teasingly remarks, Nebrija was proleptically including 'ces peuples asiatiques que Colomb, qui n'était pas encore parti, s'apprêtait à decouvrir' (these Asiatic people whom Columbus, who hadn't yet departed, was preparing to discover) (*Langue et identités*, p. 15).

Sixteenth-century Spanish humanists took up Nebrija's clarion call. Medina, writing in 1580, urged that 'the majesty of Spanish be extended to the furthermost provinces penetrated by the banners of its victorious armies' (Pérez, 'Nueva conciencia', p. 5). The title to chapter II of Aldrete's *Del origin y principio de la lengua castellana* proclaimed that 'Los vencidos reciben la lengua de los vencedores, rindiendola con las armas, i personas' (The defeated receive the language of the victors, surrendering [their own] along with weapons and people). Nebrija himself approvingly quoted the Archbishop of Granada who argued that Spain's recent victory over the Moors and the *guanchos* of the Canaries – 'pueblos bárbaros e naciones de peregrinas lenguas' (barbarous people and nations with exotic languages) – meant that they must accept the laws which the victor imposed 'e con ellas nuestra lengua' (Milhou, *Langues et identités*, p. 15).

For all the rhetoric of linguistic expansion, language policy in Spain itself was measured. In the sixteenth century, one Spaniard in six spoke a language other than Castilian and no official attempt was made to impose Castilian as the national language. But tolerance had limits: Arabic, because it, unlike Catalan, Galician or Basque, housed religious and cultural beliefs alien to the rigorously imposed Christian orthodoxies, was remorselessly stamped out (Milhou, 'Politiques', pp. 31–3). A language threatening conformity would not be countenanced. Moreover, as the Archbishop of Granada's remark had shown, 'pueblos barbáros e naciones de peregrinas lenguas' were in a different relationship with the metropolis; conquest changed the rules. The Spanish arrived in the New World 'armed with the conviction that languages were implanted by right of conquest' (Mannheim, *Inka*, p. 34). The legislative record proves, according to Mignolo, that throughout the colonial period, 'the aphorism *la lengua compañera del imperio* was a concern of the Crown and a reality at the level of the norms' (*Darker Side*, p. 53) – though demographics and the practicalities of evangelisation precluded the all-out pursuit of hispanicisation. The peninsular example showed that linguistic diversity would be tolerated – but only as long as all, in effect, sang from the same hymnbook. Indian languages, however, were feared as repositories of pagan thought. As Mannheim grimly observes: 'Language was the source and pillar of cultural memory in a political context that called for forgetting' (*Inka*, p. 69). Aldrete recognised that conquest would be consolidated only when linguistic contours mapped territorial ones, with shared memories stored in a common language (Mignolo, *Darker Side*, p. 33). Meanwhile, the indigenous language could be made to serve the Spanish instrumentally in a way that led to 'amnésie culturelle' (Duviols, 'Langue et évangélisation', p. 283). Language is caught up in the world of shrunken choices characteristic of colonial situations: it can either parrot the master's voice, assimilated into a likeness that compromises its unique identity – or it can resist and be silenced.

The manner in which Spanish became the dominant language of

Latin America while the indigenous languages shrank into subordi-
nate status or ceased to be spoken at all seemed to owe less to
singleminded policy – the triumphalist raising of linguistic banners
as urged by Medina – than to the more indirect operation of power
which seeped into all quarters of native life, including language.
Nebrija's more subtle formulation better captures the process:
language is the discreet, often self-effacing but insidious companion
of empire, gaining a toe-hold everywhere the agents of empire turn –
even when those agents are evangelists speaking in indigenous
tongues.

Evangelists bring us to the third ideology identified as shaping the
Elizabethan conquest, the Reformation. As well as raising questions
about the relative importance given to evangelisation – and the
vernacular of the evangelised – by the Reformation and the
Counter-Reformation, the linguistic conduct of the Counter-
Reformation in Ibero-America throws an interesting, oblique light
on how reformation and language intersected in Ireland. Both the
strategy of the sword and the strategy of the word had implications
for language. The strategy of the sword, promoted by men confident
of their election and the rightness of imposing concepts of civility
sanctioned by their own society, is an expression of nationalistic
certainty. Linguistically, it would never compromise its civil tongue
by embracing indigenous languages which it was predisposed to
disparage. Strategists of the word, however, willingly embraced
vernacular evangelisation. The value of the Spanish model is to show
that all engagement with the language of the other conducted under
the disequilibrium of conquest entailed its own measure of linguistic
colonisation.

The Spanish conquest of America operated on two fronts: materially, this was a conquest of territory and of the sources of wealth,
conducted with ruthlessness and cupidity; spiritually, it was a
conquest of souls for a Christian god. Indigenous language was an
obstacle to both enterprises, a barrier to commands and catechisms.
The *conquistadores* rarely bothered to learn indigenous languages,
relying instead on interpreters. But, 'ce qui n'était pas nécessaire
pour conquérir les terres l'est devenu pour conquérir les âmes' (what
was not necessary for conquering land became so for conquering
souls) (Kozinska-Frybes, 'Plurilinguisme', p. 174). As Kozinska-
Frybe's elegantly balanced formula reminds us, the missionary effort
was as much a work of conquest as were the military campaigns

which partnered it. Therefore, if the linguistic emphasis of the missionaries was often at odds with that of the civil and military administration, the overall valence of the encounter is not as distinct from the wider colonial one as some scholars are inclined to believe (Kobayashi, *Educación como conquista*, p. 266; Hernández de León-Portilla, 'Santa Cruz'). The distinction is more one of means than of ends. A policy of 'soft assimilation' served 'a politics of social subordination' just as surely as a 'hard assimilationist' one did (Mannheim, *Inka*, p. 77). The inescapable truth was that Catholic evangelising sanctioned colonisation.

Spain's legal entitlement to exploit the Americas rested on the bull *Inter caetera* issued by the Spanish pope, Alexander VI, in 1493; the bull made that right provisional on the Spaniards' preparedness to evangelise (Gonzalbo, *Historia*, p. 21).[8] While castilianisation might serve the secular conquest, it was less suited to the spiritual one. Charles V's *cédula* of 1550, in propounding that Spanish was 'el gran medio de conversión y el camino más fácil para exponer y comprender el dogma' (the great medium of conversion and the easiest route for explaining and understanding dogma), was stating what all, legislators and missionaries alike, held to be self-evident (Clément, 'Créoles', p. 121). But the ideal had to yield to demographic reality. There was a huge numerical imbalance initially between speakers of indigenous languages and hispanophones. (It was running at 50:1 in sixteenth-century Mexico.) Figures rather than philosophy determined that evangelisation would be conducted in the indigenous languages (Milhou, 'Politiques', pp. 23–4). The missionaries' adoption of these languages as the medium of spiritual conquest was consistent with the Crown's ultimate aspiration to see Castilian widely diffused. Provincial councils which advocated the use of native languages for conversion also unfailingly recorded their belief that Spanish was the ideal – though not immediately practical – medium of religious instruction; using native languages was therefore seen as an essentially interim measure, however drawn out that interim might be (Castañeda Delgado, 'Iglesia', pp. 37–9). 'La lengua castellana bien podría ser la compañera del imperio, pero no era el mejor medio para lograr sus fines' (Spanish might well be the companion of empire, but it was not the best way of achieving its ends), as Mignolo dryly notes ('Teorías', p. 189).

A Catholic Church which had always drawn on multilingualism was comfortable with vernacular evangelisation. The Council of

Trent (1545–1563) placed preaching in the mother tongue at the heart of the Counter-Reformation by authorising the promulgation of pious texts in the vernacular. The Missionary orders like the Dominicans subscribed enthusiastically to vernacular evangelisation; the Jesuit Constitutions stipulated that no postulant could take his fourth vow until proficient in the language of his mission (Tardieu, 'Jésuites', p. 194). The missionaries' option for the vernacular unleashed a remarkable project of language-learning, translation, lexicography and grammatical studies. By the end of the century in Mexico alone, catechetic works had been produced in fifteen languages (Kozinska-Frybes, 'Plurilinguisme', p. 174). The decision of the Fourth Provincial Council in Lima to preach in the Andean languages was followed by the publication of *Doctrina christiana* in a trilingual – Spanish–Quechua–Aymara – edition (Husson, 'Contresens', p. 260); its thirty-one sermons were carefully marked to enable the language-learner to deliver the material with the correct intonation and phrasing (Mannheim, *Inka*, p. 138).

The feat of the churchmen in mastering the Indian languages was, at times, breathtaking. But it was a colonising mastery which sought to control rather than to empower native languages. This was linguistic colonisation in the sense of circumscribing a language both internally, by regulating its concepts and lexicon, and externally by fixing boundaries to its field of operation. Internally, it colonised by infiltrating Christian and European concepts into American tongues – what Gruzinski calls 'la colonisation de l'imaginaire'. Missionaries planted Christian concepts inside the chosen *lenguas generales* by loaning Spanish words and exploiting the pliable nature of agglutinative languages to mint a new Christian currency (Husson, 'Contresens', p. 265). Duviols' study of the Jesuits' use of Guarani in the Paraguayan missions shows that the indigenous language was alienated from its speakers by the missionary-translators, endowed with an unfamiliar lexicon, infused with egregious concepts and systematised according to the alien grammar of Nebrija's *Gramática Latina* ('Langues et évangélisation', p. 283). While the totalising intentions of the missionary-colonists might at times be subverted through the agency of native speakers (Rafael, *Contracting Colonialism*, p. 211), the great philological labours of the religious were part of a wider politics which placed the native languages in a position of subordination that exactly mirrored the colonial pattern of domination. The colonial administration circumscribed native languages, instituting hierarchies of language which marked some, the *lenguas generales*, for survival – and service – and others, the *lenguas particulares*, for marginalisation and, often, extinction.

A remorselessly Christianising and Europeanising impulse distorted the 'dialogue' between the indigenous languages and Spanish. The blindspots and rigidities of the Europeans led to misunderstanding and the subjugation of the native languages; it did not bring communication. At the heart of the encounter lies a profound incomprehension. Words are glossed, but meaning remains fugitive. The failure of understanding at that deep level makes Todorov see in the meeting of Spaniard and native American only 'la méconnaissance' and 'l'incompréhension totale' (*Conquête*, pp. 67, 44). Husson's survey of linguistic practices in Peru leads him to echo Todorov's dark conclusion: between the two sides, there was 'incompréhension globale' and, even at the most banal level, 'l'impossibilité de communiquer par la parole' ('Contresens', p. 257).

Bartolomé de las Casas's *Brevísima relación de la destructión de las Indias* passionately denounced the colonial brutality that distorted the dialogue between Spanish and the Amerindian languages. It opens with an unbearably explicit depiction of the conquistadors' extermination of the Tainos on 'Hispaniola'. These Arawak-speakers yielded up to the European languages more loanwords – *barbacoa, batata, canoa, hamaca, iguana, maiz, papaya, tabaca* – than did the speakers of almost any other American language. They numbered roughly three million in 1492; by 1568, only thirteen remained (Chiarelli, 'Commémoration', p. 225). Then the islanders, whose *habla dulce*, sweet speech, Columbus had admired on his first landfall, fell silent. Las Casas's humanity and empathy vibrate in the respect he accords their language; he honours its dead speakers with his insistence that their names be spoken correctly: 'Guacanagarí, vltima aguda' (Guacanagarí, last [syllable] stressed) (para. 32). One M. M. S. translated the *Brevísima relación* into English in 1583, under the significantly modified title, *The Spanish Colonie*. With his sights fixed on the imperial competitor rather than on its victims, he rode roughshod over Las Casas's linguistic scrupulousness. Blind to the deference they implied, he silently dropped – and disobeyed – Las Casas's pointers to pronunciation: 'Guarionex, which had vnder him his Uassals . . .' (fo. A.4v).

The switch from Las Casas's attentiveness to M. M. S.'s elision is suggestive of a divergence in the way that the agents of their respective nations engaged with indigenous languages. That divergence gives the Spanish comparison a threefold usefulness: it throws the particularity of English linguistic colonisation into relief; it supplies coordinates for uncovering the more occult manœuvres of the English variant; and it offers us a way of moving from the historical events and ideologies with which we began towards understanding how the colonial enterprise and the philosophies underpinning it shaped language policy in Ireland.

In the English writing of the Elizabethan conquest, there is a peculiar tension between the absence of Irish textually, as either an autonomous language or an impediment, and its implicit presence as a threat that required its replacement by English. Whereas the Spanish gave prominence to language as an item of difference and parsed those differences forensically, the English, for the most part, repressed linguistic difference, declining to investigate or thematise it. That repression shows up in the English texts as what might almost be styled 'a discourse of sameness': that ideologically-inflected refusal to recognise the reality of the language barrier is explored in the next chapter. But, as the impulse to expunge Irish textually and excise it legislatively demonstrated, Irish was *not* the same. Though never as explicitly as were the Amerindian languages, Irish, too, was caught up in a discourse of difference. Beneath the studied inattention, Irish was noticed and, as an item of difference, evaluated. Familiarity with the forthrightness of Spanish evaluations enables us to draw the more shadowy English evaluations of Irish into the light. Similarities can help us to recognise recurring patterns. Englishmen and Spaniards were at one in subscribing to the discourse of civility and in feeling the stirrings of linguistic nationalism. At other times, differences prove more instructive. The contrast between Spanish evangelists' option for the vernacular and their English counterparts' aloofness from 'the strategy of the word' helps us to pin down the specific cast which Anglicanism gave to linguistic colonisation. Thus primed, we can move on to explore the particularity of the language encounter conducted under the shadow of the Elizabethan adventure in Ireland.

CHAPTER 2

'A bad dream with no sound': the representation of Irish in the texts of the Elizabethan conquest

You're a bloody English bags, says your man in Irish.
Flann O'Brien, *At Swim-Two-Birds*, p. 86

Matched against the general volubility of Irish history, the Elizabethan conquest can seem strangely silent. It is visually arresting – Derricke's wood-kern feasting in the bracken, the half-dead crawling out of the woods and 'glyns' after the Desmond rebellion, the 500 'goodly personages' lying slain on a small promontory at Smerwick – but the picture is transmitted largely without sound. The sound of voices speaking Irish is scarcely heard at all. There is an outflow of *Views, Discoveries, Descriptions, Images, Platts, Anatomies* but, as the relentlessly visual register of these titles insists, Irish-speakers are looked at rather than heard. Their story is told almost without quotation marks.

This chapter examines how Englishmen serving in Ireland between roughly 1558 and 1607 represented the Irish language in their writings. The Spanish-American material reviewed above might lead us to expect that language would be foregrounded by the encounter, that the indigenous tongue would loom large both as a material reality and as a category for evaluating – and disparaging – the other. Coming to these texts from the linguistic excitement of the Spanish *conquista*, we are altogether unprepared for the silence that meets us. We pass from a discourse where language was over-determined to one where it is blanked out.

Late sixteenth-century Ireland was, as the English writers chronicling it complained in chorus, endlessly 'clamorous'. Most of that clamour was made *as Gaeilge*. The Elizabethan texts buzz with reports of battlecries, oaths, insults, parleys, submissions, defiances, deceptions, rumours, curses. Yet, at the heart of these reports from a noisy island, there is a paradox: the language that made most of the

noise is almost never heard. English texts use their linguistic mono-
poly to construct the illusion of a monophone island; 'voices off' are
kept there. It is necessary to realise just how overwhelmingly Irish-
speaking the island was on the eve of the Elizabethan conquest in
order to appreciate the remarkable bravura with which the illusion is
sustained – and the force of the ideological imperatives to which it
answers.

THE LINGUISTIC DEMOGRAPHY OF ELIZABETHAN IRELAND

While the hibernicisation of the original colonisers was never as
complete as the old *Hibernicis ipsis Hiberniores* formula complacently
suggested, there is no doubting that in the fourteenth and fifteenth
centuries Irish seeped back into areas which had been won for
English after the Norman Conquest in 1169. The drift back to
England of the smaller tenants, the toll taken by the Black Death in
the Pale, the deflection of English attention by wars at home and in
France weakened the colony's resistance to Gaelicisation. While
Curtis points out that 'English had a hold upon Ireland which it
never lost, and even when Irish was most triumphant it had always
been the second language', he also suggests that the repeal of the
language provision of the Statutes of Kilkenny in Poynings's parliament of 1495 was an acknowledgement of 'the complete triumph of
the native tongue' (Curtis, 'Spoken Languages', pp. 241, 252; cf.
Cosgrove, 'Hiberniores', p. 14; Cronin, *Translating Ireland*, p. 23). The
vitality of English within sectors of the Pale shows that the 'triumph'
was never entirely 'complete', but there was no doubting the
ascendancy of Irish at Elizabeth's accession. Even the most loyalist
Old English magnates were bicultural: they spoke both languages
and patronised Gaelic poets who adapted their panegyrics to the
political and cultural orientation of their newer patrons (Simms,
'Bards', p. 180; O'Sullivan and Ó Riain, *Marcher Lords*, p. xvii).

The early sixteenth-century reformers bemoaned the linguistic as
well as the administrative decay of their colony. 'The State of Ireland
and Plan for its Reformation' (1515) surveys the colony at its lowest
ebb: disorder reigns; 'greate captaines of thEnglyshe noble folke . . .
folowyth the . . . Iryshe ordre'. In 'halff' of Louth, Monaghan,
Dublin, Kildare, Wexford and in all of Kilkenny, Munster, Connacht
and Ulster, 'thEnglyshe folke . . . ben of Iryshe habyt, of Iryshe
langage, and of Iryshe condytions, except the cyties and the wallyd

tounes' (*SPH8* II, p. 8). Sir William Darcy warned Henry VIII that in Desmond and Ormond, 'the lords and gentlemen . . . be in no better case than the wild Irish, for they use Irish habit and Irish tongue' (*CCM* I, p. 7). 'The Lorde Deputes Boke' confirmed that the 'Englyshe marche borderers use Iryshe apparell, and the Iryshe tounge . . . oneles they come to Parlyament or Counsayll' (*SPH8* II, p. 479). In 1542, Kilkenny Council nonchalantly decreed that when a portreeve who 'can not speak englishe nor order him self after the english sort and fashion' was appointed, he should nominate an English-speaking deputy to stand in for him in court; the Council would 'moderate the said wadges reasonably' (Gilbert, *Facsimiles* IV.2, plate xlvii). John Alen told the king, in 1533, that the writ of English law and language extended scarcely 20 miles outside Dublin; beyond lay 'the grete decaie of this lande, which is so farre fallen into myserie . . . that noither the Inglishe order, tonge, ne habite been used' (*SPH8* II, p. 162).

Even within the Pale '[a]ll the comyn peoplle . . . for the more parte ben of Iryshe byrthe, of Iryshe habyte, and of Iryshe langage' and reformers linked the colony's decline to the encroachment of their language (*SPH8* II, p. 8). In 1537, Robert Cowley condemned the infiltration of Irish tenants into 'the hart of the English pale . . . whiche neither can speke thEnglishe tonge, ne were capp ne bonet' (*SPH8* II, p. 449). In 1577, Richard Stanihurst looked back nostalgically to a time when English flourished in the colony – before vigilance slipped, leaving Irish 'free dennized in the English pale: this canker tooke such deepe roote, as the body that before was whole and sounde was by little and little festered, and in maner wholy putrified'. Irish had crept back, even into Wexford, which had once been 'so quite estranged from Irishry' that if a stranger turned up speaking Irish,

the Weisfordians would commaunde hym forthwith to turne the other ende of his tongue, and speake Englishe, or else bring his trouchman with him.

But, by dropping their guard against Irish, the Wexfordmen

haue made a mingle mangle or gallamaulfrey of both the languages, and haue in such medley or checkerwyse so crabbedly iumbled them both togyther, as commonly the inhabitants of the meaner sort speake neyther good English nor good Irishe (*Chronicle*, p. 14).[1]

In *De rebus in Hibernia gestis*, Stanihurst's proud insistence that the towns had held fast to English is qualified by a reluctant concession:

the townspeople 'speak English, and Irish also because of their daily commerce with their Irish neighbours' (p. 145). Only in Dublin itself was English holding out: Cowley, canvassing for the appointment of a noble Lord Deputy in the early 1540s, could boast that the hawking nearby was good and that the citizens 'speke but English' (*SPH8* III, p. 347). But even Dublin was more diglossic than its spokesmen cared to admit. When Margaret Barnwall, a Dublin gentlewoman and defiant recusant, fled to St Malo, her first words – to quell the city's guard-dogs – were 'in lingua Hibernica' (Moran, *Spicilegium*, p. 108). In 1578, Lord Chancellor Gerrard noted that all the Old English 'and the most part with delight, even in Dublin, speak Irish' (*CSPI* 1574–85, p. 130).

If Irish was 'almost general' even in the Pale (*CSPI* 1598–9, p. 507), it was sovereign beyond it. Sir Henry Brouncker, writing from Munster in 1606, conceded that the Reformation of religion could be attempted only in the towns, where English was understood, 'for there are few or no Irish preachers, and the country people understand little English' (*CSPI* 1603–6, p. 543). Archbishop Brown wrote to Cromwell in February 1539 announcing that 'I entende to travaile the countrey so ferr as any Inglish is to be understanded'; beyond, his suffragan, Dr Nangle of Clonfert, would take over (*SPH8* II, p. 123). The Archbishop, it is safe to conclude, did not go far.

The great Anglo-Norman families never forsook English completely. Travelling through South Leinster and Munster in the autumn of 1535, Stephen Ap Parry gave his correspondent, Cromwell, a sense of the linguistic patchwork of the region. In Dungarvan, he and his anglophone companion, James Butler, visited Butler's brother-in-law, Garret MacShane, who though he could 'speak never a word of English . . . made us very good cheer'. Another brother-in-law, Sir Thomas Butler, 'can speak very good English'. One Cormac Óg introduced Ap Parry to Sir John of Desmond's nephew and challenger; the young pretender spoke 'very good English, and keepeth his hair and cap after the English fashion'. Old Sir John himself is shown to speak 'very good' – if rather demotic – English: 'Let me have that Irish whoreson Cormak Oge'! (*CCM* 1, pp. 76–8). Ap Parry's employment as a jobbing interpreter (see p. 191 below) made him unusually alert to patterns of language use. That encounters with English-speakers were worthy of note, however, only confirms the secondary status of English in a world where Irish was needed even for talking to Old English brothers-in-law. Lord Deputy Sidney spent six weeks in Munster, in 1575, attended by the principal lords, Desmond, Thomond, Cloncare, Barry, Roche, Lixnaw, Dunboyne, Barry Óg and others. Among his entourage was Lord Louth, who 'did great Good amongst great ones; for being of this Countrye Birthe *and of their Language* . . . did . . . moche perswade theim to leave their Barbaritie' (Collins, *Letters*, p. 91; my emphasis). Clearly, in the Lord Deputy's judgement, however much English these lords knew, 'their Language' was Irish. (English writers' customary and unquestioning use of the definite article when referring to Irish – 'the language' – is the closest they ever come to recognising it as the vernacular.)

Irish was even more unchallenged in Connacht where, according to Governor Bingham, the old colonists had 'growne to suche barberous, disordered manner and trade of life' that they had become entirely 'irishe in speech' (PRO SP 63/135/80). In 1569, the Irish Council petitioned Queen Elizabeth to fund a grammar school in Galway, arguing that 'the careless education of the nobilitie and gentilmen of those partes' meant that even

the brothers of the erle of Clanricarde, yea, and one of his uncles and he a bysshop can neither speake nor understande in maner any thinge of ther princes language. (Hogan, *English Language*, p. 35)

The Lord Mayor and Council of Galway implicitly conceded as much when they wrote to the Lord Deputy, in 1602, seeking the appointment of the noted Irish-language preacher, Rowland Lynch, to Clonfert: they explained, with delicate ambivalence, that 'we knowe not any in our province more fytt to instruct vs in our vsuall Language' (PRO SP 63/210/59). English had made least headway in Ulster. Travelling through it at the end of the Nine Years War, Moryson found that all the gentlemen and commoners 'and the very jurimen putt upon life and death and all tryalls in law, commonly spake Irish, many Spanish, and fewe or none could or would speake English' (*Shakespeare's Europe*, p. 214).

The dominance of Irish meant that Elizabethans entered a world populated largely by monophone Irish-speakers. Few newcomers acquired Irish (see chapter 3). At mid-century, many of the lords they were dealing with knew little or no English. Con O'Neill gave thanks 'in his language' when invested as Earl of Tyrone at Greenwich in 1542 (*CCM* 1, p. 199). Shane O'Neill would not 'writh his mouth' to speak so 'clattering' a tongue as English – though, as the preamble to his 1562 submission shows, he was aware of his consequent vulnerability: 'Because my speech being Irish is not well understood, I caused this my submission to be written both in English and in Irish' (Holinshed, *Chronicles* VI, p. 6; *CCM* I, p. 312). There is no evidence that Turlough Luineach spoke English. Nor did Hugh O'Donnell, as Sir Robert Gardiner and Anthony St Leger discovered during negotiations with both Hughs. When O'Neill moved apart, leaving them alone with O'Donnell, the Commissioners 'conceived [that] although he did understand English yet could hardly speak it' and so they 'called Sir Henry Duke to interpret his speeches' (*CSPI* 1592–6, p. 224). Even those who had acquired some mastery of English did not always feel completely at home in it. In 1600, while her husband was held captive by Ony MacRory, Hugh O'Neill wrote to the Countess of Ormond, the English-born Elizabeth Sheffield: 'Madam, I have written to your Ladishippe before, for want of opportunitie, in myne owne natural language, which I thinke you did not so well understand, as you might conceave my full meaninge' (Graves, 'Ormonde', p. 425). In a sentence, O'Neill conveys the confused amalgam of pressures and sentiments bearing in on those for whom recourse to English was increasingly necessary. There is ease as well as O'Neill's characteristic *hauteur* in his reference to 'myne owne natural language', a sense of the 'inopportuneness' of having to use another and resignation to the overriding imperative to be understood.

A 'DISCOURSE OF SAMENESS' AND THE ELISION OF IRISH

Almost nothing of this complex linguistic texture finds its way into Elizabethan accounts of Ireland. Throughout the predominantly Irish-speaking island, the meeting of native and newcomer implied an inevitable linguistic corollary: hibernophone met anglophone. Yet the reality of that encounter with its inevitable verbal and gestural fumblings – the sign language, the pidgin phrases, the macaronics of the new speaker, the mispronunciations and misunderstandings, the staggered exchanges mediated by interpreters and their variously unreliable glosses, the whole drama of language in flux – is blacked out. English writers consistently erased the majority language, reducing Irish-language utterances to English paraphrases. In a colonial context, the elision of the native language is more than just a narrative short-cut; it is an ideologically-motivated strategy.

Brady, attempting to account for the reason that the Tudors were so 'remarkably incurious about Gaelic Ireland', concludes that their inattention represented 'a quite deliberate decision to minimise the distinctiveness of Gaelic culture as an entity in itself' (*Chief Governors*, p. 245). In Latin America, the native languages fitted naturally into a discourse of difference. Canny demonstrates that in Ireland, too, certain aspects of native culture – agriculture, diet, dress, law, religion – were similarly evaluated (*Elizabethan Conquest*, pp. 125ff.). But the Elizabethans' representation of Irish suggests that, when it comes to language, the model requires some qualification. Rather than being easily accommodated within a discourse of difference, the Irish occupied a position of 'imperfect otherness' (Murphy, 'Shakespeare's Irish History', p. 40). The 1541 Act which brought Ireland directly under the sovereignty of the king allowed Englishmen to view Ireland as an integral part of the Tudor kingdom. Their Ireland was a domestic rather than a foreign affair, a border province in revolt from central government rather than a separate polity resisting annexation. Under the new judicial arrangement, what was different was merely deviant and would be refused recognition on its own terms. In a context where the legitimacy of separatist claims was inconceivable, the rebel's tongue would be heard as a dissident *patois* rather than as an autonomous foreign tongue.

The erasure of Irish is not simply another instance of the propensity of educated classes in the early modern period to ignore 'the culture of the inarticulate' (Burke, *Popular Culture*, p. 49); it represents, rather, an attempt to render a volubly contestatory culture inarticulate. If a discourse of difference served the Spanish in justifying their intervention in America, a discourse which downplayed demonstrations of autonomy and difference was, at times, more useful to the Elizabethans. That the natives happened not to speak English was better ignored than thematised in the way it would be when colonists like Ralegh graduated from Ireland to the New World. Yet this implicit 'discourse of sameness' was under constant strain. Culturally, Ireland was different and its difference anathematised; that difference was encoded in the very language which the Elizabethans seemed intent on ignoring. Irish, therefore, occupied a complex place in colonial discourse. For much of the time it was denied, repressed through a discourse of sameness. But its otherness was ultimately inescapable: as an item of difference, it was evaluated and literally repressed, legislatively and militarily. Its literary denial is the subject of this chapter; the next two chapters explore the consequences for Irish in its other incarnation, as an item of difference.

The colonial writers whose representations – and repressions – of Irish we are about to examine all spent time within earshot of the language. Most participated in the military campaigns which they chronicled. Sir James Perrott was both the son of a Lord Deputy and a captain under Chichester. Thomas Churchyard served with Humphrey Gilbert in Munster. Captain Tom Lee saw action in Ulster and Leinster and described himself as a 'bedfellow' of Hugh O'Neill (Lodge, *Desiderata*, p. 115). Sir John Harington spent part of 1586 as an 'undertaker' in the Munster plantation and returned to Ireland with the second Earl of Essex in 1599 as a captain of horse (Harington, *Short View*, p. 2). Dymmok, too, served under Essex. Fynes Moryson was Mountjoy's secretary at the height of the Nine Years War. Richard Beacon was Her Majesty's Attorney in Munster. They chronicle wars where skirmishes are muddled and inconclusive, where even the great set-pieces like Kinsale are anti-climactic. Far from language being drowned out by the clash of swords or the bluster of arquebusses, the 'business' of Ireland is as much a highly developed communications exercise as it is a military 'hurly-burly'. The colonial texts hum with accounts of parleys, petitions, negotiations, spying, codebreaking; letters between Ireland and the Court – Mountjoy writes to Cecil 'from the camp amongst the rocks and the woods in these devils' country' (*CCM* 4, p. 2) – flow constantly. The Irish lords, too, are busy communicating. Rich notes that they all have messengers 'to run about the Countrey with Letters' (*New Description*, p. 38). Above all, these networks of communication constantly intersect. O'Neill and O'Donnell, cut off from the Spanish by Mountjoy's forces, keep their lines open: 'they practysed daylie by secreat messengers and letters passing too and froe'; more open than they wished – Mountjoy 'had prevy advertisments of all their private practices' (Farmer, 'Chronicles', pp. 122–3). It is precisely because communication was so central to the enterprise that the silence which wipes Irish from the record, muffling and distorting the encounter, is a particularly self-serving 'oversight'. The contrast with the scrupulous documentation of language usage earlier in the colony's history confirms that the denial of language difference was not just accidental. The late fourteenth-century account of the Irish lords' submission to Richard II in 1394, for example, reads like a drama of translation: John Malachie, a Dublin clerk, interpreted, 'in English', for Donough O'Brien while Thomas O'Lochran translated for Juvenis O'Nel (*CCM* 5, p. 379–80; cf. Bullock-Davies, *Interpreters*, p. 24).

The colonial writers regularly complain of the 'plashings' that blocked their passage through the woods (Dymmok, 'Treatice', p. 35; Gainsford, *Glory*, p. 144) but say nothing of the linguistic plashings over which they stumbled. Instead, reports from the language frontier abstract the message from a medium that is always vague, unspecified, mystified. By excluding the mechanics of translation from their coverage, they create an illusion of transparency, which is nothing less than the illusion of linguistic hegemony. This textual anglicisation parallels the wider political and military project of anglicisation in which these writers participated. Events which are above all language events are stripped in the telling of their language dimension and presented as exchanges from an uncomplicatedly monophone English world. Drury gets information on the Desmond rebellion by, as he blandly remarks, 'examination of one or two of the rebels company which are apprehended in Kerry' (Hogan and O'Farrell, *Walsingham Letter-book*, p. 104). The euphemism, 'examination', mystifies both the method and the linguistic medium employed. Moryson is less coy about the first: after capturing Dunboy, the English keep twelve men back from the general execution 'to be examined under torture' (*History* II, p. 287). It seems highly unlikely that one Neile Oge himself confected his obsequious submission – 'I silly worm do . . . feel to our smart, what it is to stand against her majesty's force' – but all trace of the ghostwriter has vanished (Lodge, *Desiderata*, p. 84).

The State Papers burst with detail but consistently ignore the language barrier. Such recognition as Irish gets is offhand and almost accidental. In September 1580, Sidney briefs his successor, Lord Grey. The advice is wide-ranging – Sidney includes tips on exercise and physicians – and seems comprehensive. Yet he never mentions language (Grey Egerton, *Commentary*, pp. 68–74). Perrott's own 'Orders to be observed by the justices of peace within their several limits throughout the realm' overlook nothing – parishes must make 'butts . . . for the exercising of archers', cattle must be branded or given an 'ear mark' (Lodge, *Desiderata*, pp. 22–3) – nothing, that is, apart from the language through which most of that business would be transacted. English reluctance to part with money for Irish campaigns is reflected in the accounts, reckonings and inventories that punctuate many of these texts. Everything is costed – sums paid to bowers, fletchers, trumpeters, messengers (Longfield, *Accounts*). But only rarely do we find a reference to a singularly elusive figure: '27l. 7s. 6d. the Irish interpreter' (Moryson, *History* I, p. 68).[2] Inattention to language must have led, at times, to almost comic incomprehension. Surveying lands in Munster as a prelude to plantation, Commissioner Peyton complained that the 'transmission of information was sometimes not easy', adding that the want of an interpreter hindered matters. McCarthy Morrogh wryly concurs, 'This would seem to be a fine understatement considering that the survey was conducted largely by the examining of locals' (*Munster Plantation*, p. 12).

Richard Beacon's *Solon his Follie* is representative in viewing Irish as an index of political recalcitrance – it confirms the natives 'in their disobedience and savage life' (p. 94) – and in then ignoring the practical implications of language difference. So when Epimenides coaches Solon on 'the art and skill of perswading' the people of Salamis/Ireland to reform (p. 29), he rehearses all the tricks of *ars rhetorica*, neglecting only to acknowledge that persuasion presupposes a shared language. The only 'translation' envisaged by Epimenides – that of euphemism – is internal to English. He advises Solon to revive his attested skill in clothing 'things bitter and vnpleasant, with pleasing names; calling taxes, contributions; garrisons, gardes; prisons, houses' (p. 32). Playing with English synonyms in a context that called for a more radical translation, Beacon skips over the fact that 'taxes' would have to be called '*cánacha*', not 'contributions' if they were to make sense to Solon's Munster audience. Epimenides' is merely a rhetorical excursion into the arts of persuasion: for Beacon, real reform can be achieved only through force and 'a severe and stout Magistrate' modelled, ominously, on Lord Deputy Grey and Bingham, the repressive governor of Connacht (p. 59).

Taut with denial, the English text is stretched across meanings more plural and inaccessible than it is prepared to grant. Inevitable strains and unravellings show up in its texture, through which the unacknowledged presence of Irish can be glimpsed. James Perrott wrote two biographies of his father, the Lord Deputy. In both, Sir John's progress through Gaelic Ireland is narrated as a feat of communications: friars recant, lords swear loyalty, rebels sue for grace. Nowhere is there the least hint of a language barrier. Paradoxically, we become aware of the unacknowledged presence of Irish only when the mute routine is interrupted by two bold snatches of colloquial English. Perrott's *Chronicle*, which otherwise carries no quotation marks from the battlefield, mentions that Samuel Bagenal, ambushed outside Newry, is challenged by a hardy rebel who 'speakinge in English, cried: "Have at your golde jerkine!"' (p. 168). We must surmise that the incident is recorded for its curiosity value rather than for the intrinsic merit of the repartee. By flagging what was so clearly an unexpected burst of English from the lips of this cheeky rebel, Perrott is implicitly signalling that rebels otherwise speak something else. Similarly, in the *History of Sir John Perrott*, the Lord Deputy encounters a Scottish captain at the siege of Dunluce who 'refused Parley, and answered (speaking very good *English*) That they would keepe it to the last Man' (Rawlinson, p. 159). By then Perrott had travelled the four provinces, but only here is a speaker heard or his language identified. Whereas the encounter with an English-speaker is sufficiently unusual to provoke comment, Irish, it appears, is a norm so absolute and self-evident that it becomes, paradoxically, inaudible, entering the text only as a pervasive background absence.

Only a handful of times in all these pages is the illusion that these are reports from an anglophone island suspended even for an instant. Irish was usually admitted only when disclosure was strategically useful. Turlough Mac Henry O'Neill, chieftain of the Fews and Hugh O'Neill's half-brother, inclined to the English during the Nine Years War and its aftermath. Mountjoy entertained him at a St George's Day banquet in 1601; he served as an army captain and was later knighted. He was a member of the 1609 plantation commission and visited London in 1610. In 1613, he stood for election to the Irish parliament. During the years of his usefulness, no reckoning was made of the language he spoke.[3] But when the now-redundant ally prejudiced the advance of a New English parliamentary candidate, it became opportune to trumpet the language difference which it had once been prudent to occlude: Sir Turlough was disqualified – because he spoke no English (Ó Fiach, 'The O'Neills', pp. 45–59).

Fynes Moryson's *An History of Ireland*, the second part of his three-part *Itinerary*, runs to more than 700 pages. Irish makes clandestine appearances but never once does Moryson openly advert to a native language. In Part 3 of his *Itinerary*, however, he 'revisits' Ireland, now writing more as a colour writer than as Mountjoy's erstwhile secretary. Here, for the first time, the linguistic demography of Ireland enters the record: 'at this tyme whereof I write [i.e. 1599–1603], the meere Irish disdayned to learne or speake the English tounge'; not only that, 'the Irish English altogether vsed the Irish tounge, forgetting or neuer learning the English' (*Shakespeare's Europe*, p. 213). This is the reality that the Elizabethan texts occlude; this is the reality that insists, nonetheless, on intruding.

The veil is inadvertently lifted by Sidney's bumbling protegé, John Derricke. In his account of the Lord Deputy's parley with 'wood-kern', visual supplement contradicts textual assertion. The text is party to the fiction that meanings travel 'worde for worde', without impediment, between the two sides:

> The messenger he trotteth forth,
> to knowe the Rebells minde.
> Who makes his backe retourne,
> With answere of the foe:
> *And worde for worde as he did speake,*
> *he doeth relate it soe.*   (*Image*, p. 61; my emphasis)

The engraving which supplements this account bears, however inadvertently, dissenting witness (fig. 1). Plate VII depicts an English camp, with cavalry and foot in battle array. Sidney, on horseback, inclines towards a figure whose shaggy locks mark him as Irish. Both have a hand to a sealed letter which is being passed from one to the other. According to Sir Walter Scott, Derricke's first editor, Sidney is 'delivering a letter to an Irish Karne'. (D. B. Quinn, more circum-spectly, has Sidney 'handling' the letter.) But an inscription beneath his feet identifies the 'Karne' as 'Donolle obreane the messenger' and the word coming from his mouth brings the fiction of trans-parency up short with sibilant obduracy: 'Shogh'. In English, 'shogh' yields no meaning beyond perhaps a sound-effect caught between cough and sneeze. But listened to as Irish, it makes sense as a reasonable transliteration of *seo*: Sidney 'is delivering' nothing; rather, O'Brien addresses Sidney in Irish, handing over his letter with a peremptory 'here'. If anything is 'worde for worde' in this exchange, it will only be the translation. Once avouched-for literal-ness has been exposed as a rhetorical trope, we begin to see that assurances like 'for so he termed it', 'even with these words', 'for so they call it' which seem to guarantee *oratio recta* actually signal a switch to surreptitious translation.[4]

Figure 1 The exchange of a sealed letter between O'Brien the messenger and Sir Henry Sidney

An entry in *The Walsingham Letter-book* casts a valuable sidelight on the textual strategies which erased Irish by simultaneously enacting and unmasking them. 'The declaration of Charles Egerton, taken before the Council in Ireland: 25 September, 1579', relates a series of exchanges between some citizens of Carrickfergus and Turlough Luineach O'Neill. All the action is verbal and is narrated as though transacted, without a hiccup, in English. But it is clear from the context, if nothing else, that these exchanges cross the faultline between the two languages. The first crossing is made by Mr Sackford, a townsman who, to have understood 'by the common brute of speeches of people' in an overwhelmingly Irish-speaking locality that Turlough has been retained as Commissioner for Ulster, must have moved between the two languages. Bringing back tidings from his foray into Irish, Sackford convinces the town council 'to send a messenger with a lowly letter' to Turlough craving his assistance in recovering a hundred head of cattle. No indication is given of the language used but the letter successfully fords the divide, as does Turlough who, crossing in the other direction, 'sent an answere to Mr Sackford' agreeing to a meeting in Belfast with the proviso that the citizens bring him 'a hoggeshead of stronge beere, two hoggesheades of clarett wine, and some sacke and some aquavitie'. In addition, he entrusted his messenger with a threat to be relayed 'by word of mouth' (Hogan and O'Farrell, pp. 188–9).

When the two sides meet, exchanges are reported in a mixture of direct and indirect speech:

Then hee [Turlough] asked what they had brought him, one tould him both beere and wyne; it was well for them said hee that they have done so, yf they had not come my horses should have eaten their corne, my men their beefes, and their towne should have been burnt.

The two sides parley, seated in a circle on the ground in Turlough's camp. O'Neill launches with equal extravagance into drink and speechifying, making 'manie more badd speaches', reported by quotation and paraphrase. Sackford retires, hoping that it was 'the druncke had spoken thus' but the next morning, though then 'fresh and fasting', Turlough 'entred into his former speeches'. Sackford slips back across the language line to the quiet of his own cabin, but must have had to recross it when a drunken gallowglass entered demanding wine with 'threatneng words' (pp. 189–90).

These conjectured crossings are invisible in a narrative where all the characters speak English with an almost baroque fluency. Indeed, the text might force reconsideration of the extent to which English had penetrated Ulster were it not for its very last sentence, which throws all the crisscrossings that preceded it into relief: 'All theis speeches were interpreted by Nicholas Wylles, Mayor, and William Piers, junior, William Doben, Alderman, and Michaell Savage, Sherife, and John Trondell, lieutenant to Brewerton' (p. 191). There is more than narrative convention at stake here. The stranglehold on mimetic circulation is absolute (cf. Greenblatt, *Marvelous Possessions*, p. 139). The text represses not only the language of Turlough's speeches but their real political content. Branded 'badd speaches', what is admitted into the text, filtered through hostility, translation and reconstructed paraphrase, survives merely as caricature and distortion. Through such manœuvres, ideology takes up residence in narrative conventions which serve as much to circumscribe expression as to advance the telling. The native's medium, message and voice are denied or traduced through three narrative strategies which merit closer examination: occluded translation, ventriloquism and spectacle.

NARRATIVE STRATEGIES OCCLUDING IRISH

Unacknowledged translation

The first strategy, unacknowledged translation disguised as paraphrase or quotation, consistently denies the materiality of the language barrier – and the existence of the indigenous language. The 'fluent' strategy traditionally favoured by English translators means that even where acknowledged, translation irons out and assimilates difference.

By producing an illusion of transparency, a fluent translation masquerades as true semantic equivalence when it in fact inscribes the foreign text with a partial interpretation, partial to English language values, reducing if not simply excluding the very difference that translation is called on to convey. (Venuti, *Translator's Invisibility*, p. 21)

In colonial contexts, 'fluent' translation additionally represses 'the asymmetrical relations of power that inform the relations between languages' (Niranjana, *Siting Translation*, p. 60). When the fact of translation itself is repressed, however, the scope for traducing native meanings and denying the native's alterity is even greater.

Irish abounds in these texts but by implication only. It is almost always dubbed: 'What shall I be the better for the country, when you leave me nothing in it, but the bare land desolate and destroyed?', fulminates Niall Garbh O'Donnell with implausible fluency, in Docwra's account of one meeting. Docwra's claim that O'Donnell spoke 'even with these words' – a notoriously unreliable assurance – is undermined by his own previous demonstration that the Irishman spoke little English. Reporting on an earlier meeting, Docwra had explained that O'Donnell, in one of his 'humours', 'began with his own little broken English' but could continue only with 'the help of Captain Willis to interpret for him'. But the crack which allowed the reader to surmise the existence of another, unidentified, tongue is quickly resealed. Docwra reverts to reproducing translated speech as reported speech: he recasts the bilingual trialogue as a monophone English dialogue, camouflaging the hectic activity of the interpreter and repressing the language – other than 'broken English' – which O'Donnell actually spoke (*CSPI* 1600–1, pp. 327, 289). When Bishop Jones and his fellow Commissioners met Hugh O'Donnell, along with Hugh O'Neill, in March 1598, they encountered a difference of which language – given that O'Donnell spoke no English – was one of the most inescapable signs. Yet Jones chose to report the exchanges as though no linguistic impediment existed. ' "Tush", says Tyrone', as indeed he could have done; but Jones's O'Donnell, too, is impossibly fluent in English: 'I will allow no Englishman either to dwell in my country, or to have any government in any of the lands that I challenge' (*CSPI* 1598–9, p. 119). Interestingly, an Irish-language account of O'Donnell's negotiations also exists and its incommensurability with the English telling illustrates the force of political imperatives in determining rhetorical strategies. O'Donnell's biographer focused on his subject's motivation in order to legitimate his actions. He, therefore, reconstructed not the exchanges themselves but the internal narrative of recollection that drove O'Donnell's tactics (Ó Clérigh, *Beatha*, 1, p. 28; Mac Craith, 'beathaisnéis').

However omnipresent in reality, the interpreter is consistently airbrushed from the colonial texts. This erasure mystifies and occludes the materiality of the original language exchange. In Farmer's version of a story that enjoyed some currency at the end of the Nine Years War, the interpreter exists only by inference. Sir Arthur Chichester is riding through a wood when his party 'felt a great

savour'. (Synaesthesia is common in these texts: speech is regularly
seen, not heard.) He sends his soldiers to investigate. They find five
children roasting the thighs, arms and sides of their dead mother
over a slow fire. Chichester goes, predictably, 'to *see* it' but then sight
gives way to speech: he 'demanded of them why they did so; they
answered they could not get any other meat' ('Chronicle', p. 129; my
emphasis). But the passive voice that then takes over – 'It was
demanded where their cows were . . . it was demanded when the
wod kearne were there . . . It was asked of them . . .' (pp. 129–30) –
signals the moment where the interpreter slips, invisibly, in. Only
such a figure can explain the seemingly fluent catechesis otherwise
implausible in an area – Killoltagh in Ulster – where even the
jurymen knew no English (Morley, *Ireland under Elizabeth*, p. 363).

A similar pattern emerges in Hooker's account of Ralegh's
encounter with a band of Gaels outside Rathkeale. Knowing that
kerns came to scavenge once the English struck camp, Ralegh stayed
behind to waylay them. Among the foragers who duly turned up
was a man carrying withy halters. Hooker's text ignores the
language impediment, yet preserves the trace of its presence and its
management. Campaigning in Munster in the 1580s, where English
was almost unknown outside the cities of Limerick, Cork and
Waterford, Ralegh would have relied on interpreters much of the
time[5] – as he seems to do here: the halter-bearer is seized 'and *being
demanded* what he would doo with them, and whie he caried them;
gaue answer*, that they were to hang vp English churls; for *so they call*
Englishmen'. The awkwardly interposed passive – 'being demanded'
– and the concealed identity of the agent there and in 'gaue answer'
hint at the intervention of an interpreter. Tellingly, the only character to speak inside quotation marks is Ralegh: '"It is so (quoth the
capteine) well, they shall now serue for an Irish kerne"' – and the
withy-halter is promptly translated into a noose ('Historie', p. 437;
my emphasis).

One peculiarity of this occluded translation was that while the
English texts never directly acknowledged that the Irish were using a
different language, they condescended to the pretence that they used
a different set of *English* words – a back-handed concession which
restricted native linguistic autonomy to English synonyms. Stanihurst
mischievously recounted how a newly arrived English Commissioner
imagined that he was mastering Irish when he was merely cracking
'sometyme a worde, other whyles a sentence' of Wexford-accented

English (*Chronicle*, p. 14); and for many other newcomers, too, Hiberno-English functioned as a kind of surrogate Irish. So when Hooker declares that the Irish call the English 'churls' ('for so they call Englishmen'), he reduces the gap between two languages to merely an internal option within English. In reality Irishmen, operating in a language independent of English tautology, called 'English churls despitefully' – as Campion, schooled by 'daly table talke' with the Stanihursts, points out – *boddai sassonis* and *boddai Ghalt* ('Saxon chuls', 'foreign louts') (*Two Bokes*, p. 20; cf. *CSPI* 1598–9, p. 440). 'Churl' was foreign to Irish but current in the speech, archaic-seeming to metropolitans, of the Old English (Maley, *Salvaging Spenser*, p. 41). Moryson likewise reduces the distance between two languages to a matter of internal variations within English when he reports that the Irish are 'great swillers of Spanish sacke' which, according to him, they 'merily called the king of Spaynes Daughter' (*Shakespeare's Europe*, p. 224). The actual Irish metonym, *iníon Rí na Spáinne*, is thereby suppressed and recast as a colourful dialectal variant of English.

Ventriloquism

The second strategy for repressing Irish went beyond translation to simulate linguistic – and ideological – compliance textually. Those who spat out 'badd speaches' in the flesh could be made, on the page, to mouth fantasies of submission in a language they did not speak. In her analysis of colonial discourse in eighteenth-century Africa, M. L. Pratt shows that 'indigenous voices are almost never quoted, reproduced or even invented' (*Imperial Eyes*, p. 52). In Spanish America, when words *are* invented for the native, his utterance is turned into 'an echo of the voice of the invader' (Pastor, 'Silence and Writing', p. 152). Derricke turned those whom his patron, Sidney, had difficulty controlling in actuality into models of compliance through doggerel prosopopoeia. In the third part of *The Image of Irelande*, he scripts Rory Óg O'More as a paragon of show-trial auto-denunciation: 'I *Rorie Ogge*, inhabitaunt of *Leaske*, / A rebell false, against my (soueraine quene)' (p. 71). The narrator affects to retreat to the margins of his text from where he offers comments: 'Rorie is here a very penitent persone' (p. 73). The pose of disinterested onlooker creates the illusion that Rory is confessing, unprompted:

> I vilaine vile, and craftie as the Foxe,
> Yea like the Wolfe, whiche doeth extortion vse,
>
> . . .
>
> My wicked life, I needes must now confesse.   (pp. 71–2)

Similarly, the sentiments of 'noble cheualrie' which Derricke's
Turlough Luineach spouts in his 'protestation . . . to the Lorde
Deputie' (p. 89) – are as implausible linguistically as they are
politically. But they flattered a patron whose own engagements with
Turlough had produced a more muted outcome.

Ventriloquism touches against the terrible paradox that lay at the
heart of linguistic colonisation in sixteenth-century Ireland: the
grafted tongue followed after the severed head. Derricke captures
this concatenation of violence and language change when he turns,
for a second time, to put words in Rory's mouth. O'More, long a
thorn in the administration's side, was finally slain and his head
displayed on the wall of Dublin Castle. As poet's dummy, O'More
can be made to mouth fantasy recantations in an act of necro-
ventriloquism. Derricke invites the reader to

> suppose that you see a monstrous Deuill, a truncklesse head, and a hedlesse
> bodie liuyng, the one hid in some miskin & donghill, but the other exalted,
> yea mounted vppon a poule (a proper sight, God wot, to beholde) vanting it
> self on the highest toppe of the Castell of Dublin, vttering *in plaine Irishe* the
> thynges that ensewe. (p. 92; my emphasis)

But from the grafted tongue of a death's head, 'plaine Irishe' issues
as pure English.[6] From its stake-top podium, the skull warns would-
be insurgents against climbing on fortune's wheel:

> These thinges to confirme, I Rorie am he,
> Who sometyme mounted alofte in the Skie,
> And fortune castyng a fauour to me,
> Prouoked me higher, and higher to flie,
>
> . . .
>
> All men that heare this, take warnyng by me.   (pp. 95–7)

In this grotesque mimicry, 'plaine Irishe' projected through a skull's
jaw at once denies the linguistic otherness of the native language and
evacuates it of any possibility of contestation. Christopher Highley's
hearty postmodern reading of this episode – he interprets it as
introducing 'a dialogic impulse' which allows 'the enemy' to speak
(*Crisis*, pp. 56–7) – can be sustained only by ignoring the real
violence that underwrote it and policed its reception. Elizabeth
Harvey's analysis of 'transvestite ventriloquism' demonstrates that

asymmetries of power made ventriloquism 'a powerful strategy of silencing' women (*Ventriloquised Voices*, p. 142) – and the ventriloquism of Rory Óg shows that it could be used equally well to usurp the voice of dissident hibernophone males. Tadhg Dall Ó hUiginn's lament for Brian and Domhnall O'Hara, hanged by Bingham, provides a melancholy antiphon to such commandeered utterance. When the poet sees, staked on poles, heads that once nestled in women's arms, he loses his power of utterance, '*rugsad . . . mh'fhorfhuighle*' (McKenna, *O'Hara*, p. 298).

Derricke's usurpation of the native's voice is contained by its very flagrancy. When official documents used ventriloquism masquerading as translation, however, to repress the native's real utterance, the distortion had material and not just propagandistic implications. Stung into rebellion by upheavals in land-ownership and the abolition of the MacWilliamship, the Burkes engaged Bingham in a bitter struggle throughout the later 1580s (Morgan, *Tyrone's Rebellion*, p. 50). Their settled hatred of the governor, which owed much to his execution of the young sons of the principals, prompted them to present a 'Book of Complaints' to the Dublin Council in 1589 which duly appointed a Commission of investigation (*CSPI* 1588–92, p. 263). Yet, when three years before, 'ghasted' with fear, the Burkes had made a temporising submission, they had affixed their marks to 'A true discourse of the causes of the late rebellion'. Written in the first person in a language which few of them knew, the unlikely penitents abjure 'our folly', 'declare and confess . . . that the Governor did no injustice in hanging' the boy-pledges: 'in that we are well satisfied' (*CSPI* 1586–8, pp. 174, 198–203). Drawn up by Edward White, on whom Bingham relied for translation services, this is an exercise in circumscribing and scripting utterance rather than in translating the speech of the other. The twenty-one Xs scratched at the bottom testify to an impotence that is linguistic as well as political.[7]

Rendering speech as spectacle

The third and most common strategy is where the picture comes without sound, as though incomprehension rendered language inaudible; what was not understood was often not even heard. Moryson's version of the Kilultagh metrophagy illustrates the pattern (cf. p. 55 above). His telling has the eerie quality of newsreel footage panning over human wretchedness, its soundtrack mute. Without words, there is just silent spectacle. The commanders

saw a most horrible *Spectacle* of three Children . . . all eating and gnawing with their Teeth the Entrails of their dead mother, upon whose flesh they had fed 20 Days past, and having eaten all from the Feet upward to the bare Bones, roasting it continually by a slow Fire, were now come to the eating of her said Entrails in like sort roasted, yet not divided from the Body, being as yet raw. (*History* ii, p. 283; my emphasis)

Time and again, the colonial texts translate verbal exchanges into wordless tableaux. In a world where native words meant nothing, seeing compensated for hearing. It is a commonplace of postcolonial theory that the colonial/male gaze is scopic: the native, where featured at all, is seen, not heard (Bhabha, *Location*, p. 76; Parker, 'Fantasies', p. 87). Without the shared language that might enable the writer to enter the mental space of his subject, he must fall back on looking, on observation. But, asks Affergan, how does one find '*une syntaxe de la vue*'? (*Exotisme*, p. 141). The translation of what the eye beholds into words, into the colonist's language, is an unreliable manœuvre – and an especially tricky one when the language of the other is bypassed completely.

In the Tudor texts, the tussle between the senses is registered on the page as a contest between 'eye' and 'ear'. Time and again, the primacy of the eye is asserted over that of the ear: 'And it is no matter what [the Irish] professe, why should we heare their words, when wee see their deeds' (Moryson, *Shakespeare's Europe*, p. 195). Churchyard praises those who block their ears to rebel wheedlings. His hero, Gilbert,

neuer would parley with any Rebell, nor thereto permitte under his charge, saiyng alwaies that he thought his *Dogges eares* to good, to heare the speeche of the greateste noble manne emongest them, so long as he was a Rebell. (*Rehearsal*, fo. Q.ii.v; my emphasis)

Ears are not completely redundant. Little used for listening with, they serve grimmer purposes. The statute 23 Eliz.c.2 decreed that anyone who 'of his imagination, speak any false and slanderous news or tales against the queen . . . shall have both his ears cut off' (*Stats.* p. 336). Rich spitefully quibbles that the Palesmen, instructed to hang, draw and quarter one FitzSimons and to nail his ears to a pillory for irreverent and shameful speeches, let him escape with a mere hanging (*Anothomy*, p. 78). The Book of Orders of the Court of Castle Chamber records that a Kildare husbandman, John Beaghan, was condemned 'to stand three market days on the pillory in Dublin, with both ears nailed and cut off' – and worse – for 'very detestable and most disloyal speeches of her sacred Majesty, calling her Highness *Banryne done* in Irish, the which are not otherwise convenient, for the hatefulness of the words, to be published' (*Egmont*, p. 22); the offensiveness of *banríon dhonn*, 'brown(-haired) queen' – or, at worst, *banríon dána*, 'naughty queen' – evidently gained something in translation.

With English ears so resolutely shut, native organs of speech had little business talking. When Calvagh O'Donnell found no hearing for his complaints in Dublin, his speech dissolved into blubbering: he 'burst out into such a weeping as when he should speak he could not, but was fain by his interpreter to pray license to weep and so went his way' (Bagwell, *Tudors* I, pp. 77–8). The mouth is undone. After Kinsale, we are confronted in a terribly literal way with spectacle and starkly silent mouths:

no *Spectacle* was more frequent in the Ditches of Towns, and especially in wasted Countries, than to *see* Multitudes of these poor People dead with their *Mouths* all coloured green by eating Nettles, Docks, and all things they could render up above Ground. (Moryson, *History* II, p. 284; my emphasis)

In the contest between sight and sound, the eyes have it. England's superiority is asserted in terms of its power to see. Its gaze is a source of control. Hugh O'Neill's treasons are 'laid open to the peering eyes of Englands Majesty' (Gainsford, *Tyrone*, p. 16). Derricke imagines himself surveying Ireland from 'a goodly braue Piramides . . . From whence I did behold and see' (*Image*, p. 27). Its writers derive their authority from being eye-witnesses. Hypertrophied sight encroaches on hearing's patch. Patrick Cullen, one of Sir Nicholas Bagenal's 'secreat espials', conflates the two senses: 'All [O'Neill's] contrimen *speake* more spightfullie to Englishmen than anie men that ever I *sawe*' (Hogan and O'Farrell, *Walsingham Letter-book*, pp. 238, 224; my emphasis). It is a confusion common to many Elizabethan writers in Ireland: they see speech. Campion finds the wailing of the keeners 'pitifull in *apparance*' (*Two Bokes*, p. 19; my emphasis). Rich sees cries: hogs and Irish alike 'so cry and yell (as they are *seene* to doe)' (*Excuse*, fo. 5v; my emphasis).

Ireland is turned into an unvoiced spectacle. We watch the pageant through a sound-proof screen. It is a landscape of mute figures, of pictures without words. Sidney journeyed through south Munster in 1566. Hearing served only to supply a mournful backing-track to what he saw: 'there herde I such lamentable Cryes and dolefull Complayntes'. His eyes sweep across the 'waste and desolate land' and he translates turmoil and confusion into a panorama surveyed. 'Such horrible and lamentable spectacles there are to beholde': burning villages, ruined churches, deserted towns, the unborn 'seene to sturre in the Bodies of their dead Mothers' (Collins, *Letters*, p. 24).

The triumph of sight over sound in the Elizabethan writing of Ireland is well illustrated by Sir John Harington's 'Report Concerning the Earle of Essex's Journey in Ireland'. He offers a vivid, first-hand account of Essex's progress, missing no detail of the skirmishes, sieges and ambushes on the way. The colonist-poet's text is outstandingly visual: Danvers is 'shott in the face, the bullett passinge to the roote of his lefte eare' (*Nugae*, p. 283). Harington – and the actors in his text – sweep all-seeing eyes over the hostile countryside. Rebels attempting to steal army horses are 'perceaved' by Sir Christopher St Leger whose watchfulness is endorsed by the sign – 'the heade of a rebell' – which he brings back from hot pursuit (p. 270). Essex, from the vantage-point of 'the top of Croshie Juffe, veiwed the countrie rounde aboute' (p. 272). All impressions enter the text through the eye. Even at the civic reception for his lordship in Kilkenny speech is balanced against the muffling effect of the accompanying display: 'he was receaved withe as muche joye of the cittizens as coulde be expressed, either by livelie orations, or silent strewinge of the streetes withe hearbes and rushes' (p. 275).

The most striking effect of Harington's visual narrative, however, is not simply that the English see while the rebels are seen. Rather, the visual domination is so inescapable that the natives themselves are made to participate in this discourse of sight. It is not that the English 'see' the rebels, it is that 'the rebell shewed himself'. Trapped inside the colonists' perceptual field by reflexive verbs of seeing and showing, 'the rebell' is forced to make an exhibition of himself: Ony MacRory 'shewed himself by a passadge called Black-eford' (pp. 271–2). Forced by the text to turn into a spectacle, the native becomes part of the display in a *tableau vivant* of skirmishes and retreats; denied a speaking part, he must mime, his motions choreographed for comic effect. Near Adare, Desmond and Lacy appear on the south bank of the Maigue, 'in sight of' the English but 'in such disorder, that it rather seemed a morrice daunce, by theire tripping after there badge pipes, then anie soldierlike exercise'. They offer no resistance but retreat 'in a ringedaunce into the woode' (p. 279).

The transformation of the 'vnheard of hurliburlies' into *tableaux* is seen at its most extreme in Gainsford's *The History of the Earle of Tyrone* (p. 45). Gainsford is 'a spectator'; O'Neill, the object of his gaze, is 'the spectacle' – 'of humane condition . . . of mischance . . . of misery' (pp. 38, 40, 49). The climax, O'Neill's submission at Mellifont, is seen, not heard: his 'groueling to the earth', performed in 'sight of so many Captaines and Gentlemen' was 'one of the deplorablest sights that euer I saw' (pp. 40–1). But this is a particular kind of spectacle. Gainsford's intention is to 'set [O'Neill] thus on the Stage of fearefull admiration' (p. 6). The idiom of the performance is masque, not naturalism. He not only transmutes the noisy events of the Nine Years War into spectacle but, furthermore, turns speechless performances into allegorical *tableaux*. In transmogrifying O'Neill into a 'tennis ball of fortune' and in announcing that he himself has been 'a spectator of *this flourishing tree* . . . and saw his blasting and fall of Leaves', he metamorphoses actual participants into metaphors (pp. 37, 6; my emphasis). He places his readers at a double remove from events: the spectacle which screens out sound is itself transformed into masque and baroque imagery. We do not see O'Neill marching towards Kinsale but watch the allegory instead: 'Thus was all Ireland, like a turbulent sea full of billowes, even to the very shores' (p. 29). We see, not the preparation for invasion, but the metaphor that substitutes for it: 'such a Loome of mischiefe was set on worke, that at the last the cloth was wouen of his corruption, and folded together to keepe his treasons warme in his own bosome' (p. 15). Image replaces narration, explanation and analysis. The mystery of Burgh's death, 'this sonne of Mars' (p. 22), is hardly solved by Gainsford's account: 'but *hinc illæ lachrimæ*! as he was treading the measures of prosperity, an vntimely discord of Death sounding Musike deceiued him of hope, and vs of him' (p. 23). As the telling becomes more stylised, the sense of masque is heightened. Mythological characters shoulder the real actors into the wings. Although Bingham had quelled Maguire's rebellion, 'yet after a while the scattered limbs of Pelops are gathered together, and as if Anteus should recouer by touching the Earth, Mac Guier maketh a stronger party' (p. 18). We do not hear a word from the natives, and Gainsford's fetishisation of the visual ensures that we do not see them either.

Symbols, not words, do the talking. The newly arrived Lord Deputy, Burgh, summons Ony MacRory to his presence and warns him not to rebel. To this, 'Ony replied noething'. Back in his stronghold, he sends the Lord Deputy 'two bundells of dartes as a tooken'. Burgh, new to this contestatory 'rhetoric of silence' (cf. Laurence, 'Women's Silence', p. 159), has to ask his advisers to decode the 'token' (Perrott, *Chronicle*, p. 133). In the stage-play world of the Irish wars, semaphore and dumbshow replace language. FitzMaurice, a central figure in the Desmond rebellion, is seen by Hooker as the 'ringleader in this pageant' ('Historie', p. 459). Pageant can turn into puppet theatre. O'Neill's troops attack, carrying trumpets, colours and drums, 'rather for a bragging Ostentation than otherwise'. Mountjoy replies with heavy artillery, 'whereupon their Puppets Bravery suddenly vanished' (Moryson, *History* 1, p. 262). In *The Misfortunes of Arthur* (1587), Francis Bacon and his collaborators turn the wild hibernophone, quite literally, into a 'dumb shewe' figure. While in the plays of Dekker, Shakespeare and Jonson, stage-Irish anglophones might 'prate' in voluble dialect, this dart-bearing Gael with 'shagged haire' is a creature of emblem and gesture. Wordlessly, with 'threatning countenance', he 'furiously chase[s]' across stage (Hughes, p. 27). His depiction bears out Paula Blank's conclusion in *Broken English* that 'the "wild Irish" are marginalised in Renaissance English literature nearly to the point of silence'. But Blank's own exploration of how standard English gained hegemony interprets the 'triumph of English' as a process purely internal to English, achieved through marginalising *dialectal* 'differences of language'. She overlooks the fact that languages were being marginalised as well as dialects. When she turns her attention to Ireland, she restricts her analysis of 'differences of language' to Hiberno-English. In failing to acknowledge the language which lay behind the 'broken English' of Hiberno-English – Irish – she reproduces a silencing which she is disposed to condemn (pp. 149, 2).

It is hardly an exaggeration to say that the Elizabethan texts make Irish-speakers mute. But what remains when speech is denied is not necessarily silence. The mute are not noiseless and these texts are full of strange, disturbing sounds: cries, yelps, groans, strangulated shouts, whispers. The language which is refused a hearing as articulate speech is picked up instead as a chorus of forlorn and menacing sound-effects. Derricke's wood-kern, 'like to Bedlam folke', 'bewaile' and howl senselessly: 'Bohbowe now crie the knaues, / and lullalowe the karne' (*Image*, pp. 64, 67). There is nothing casual about downgrading words into cries, transforming the meanings of another language into babble. The barbarian has ever been heard to mumble: *bar, bar, bar.* A foreign language can be disquieting, its uncomprehended sounds daunting, even threatening. The Elizabethans responded to their lack of understanding by evacuating language of its semantic component. They registered only sounds divorced from sense in an ideologically charged manœuvre that transformed speech into a clatter of nonsense syllables. For there can be no doubt that what are called 'cries', with its implication of prelinguistic vocalisations, are, in fact, utterances fully shaped in language. Battle-cries, incantations, lamentations, and rumours are never wordless. English writers' fixation on native 'shriking and howling' (Rich, *New Description*, p. 13) involves not a somewhat puzzling focus on the non-linguistic supplement of Irish, but the systematic reduction of the word to the grunt. After all, cries could be discounted more effortlessly than speech could be. When Munster was quieted, the authorities were troubled by nothing beyond 'the clamorings, exclamations, and brabling of the Irish people, not woorth the remembring' (Hooker, 'Historie', p. 455). That 'cries' were often, in fact, words is confirmed by a line in Gerrard's report: everywhere he went, 'poore sterved creatures . . . whole towneshipps together, crynge out that their garrans and caples[8] were taken' ('Notes', p. 116). The two loanwords infiltrating his text preserve a snatch of the original Irish; the 'cry' houses articulate accusation.

Without speech, the Irish can enter the text only by making a racket. The ceremonies that attend festivals like Mayday and Midsummer are heard as clatter: 'what ratling, what tinkling vpon pannes and candlesticks . . . what clamors'; these are sounds known only 'amongst *Infidels, Pagans,* and *Papists*' (Rich, *New Description*, p. 42). The Irish seem congenitally noisy: 'By nature very Clamorous, vpon euery small occasion raysing the hobou[9] (that is a doleful outcrye) which they take from one anothers mouthe till they putt the whole towne in tumult.' After skirmishes, 'it is ridiculous and most true [that Irish fighters] . . . runn out to braule and scowlde like women with the next Enemyes' (Moryson, *Shakespeare's Europe*, pp. 484, 238–9). The texts are full of background noises. We catch the hum of incantations, the '*Spels* to driue away rats, & to heal diseases' (Rich, *New Description*, p. 41); the bewitching song that brings stags to bay 'by which music they fall down and lay as sleeping' (Falkiner, *Illustrations*, p. 323). Above all, rumours run riot. Moryson's text bristles with noisy whisperings: the Spanish, said to be at Sligo, 'vanished with the Rumour'. The country becomes an echo-chamber of 'Advertisements being daily multiplied' and 'fabulous Reports' (Moryson, *History* I, pp. 288, 296, 318). Even the defeat at Kinsale cannot silence the 'many thundering Rumours' presaging the Spaniards return (II, p. 255). In texts which strive to control communications, rumour is a particularly vexing commodity: the guerrilla wing of the general noise, it cannot be pinned down or scotched, subverting the univocal will of the English texts.

The consistency with which Elizabethan writers erase all but the vaguest acknowledgement of an indigenous language becomes all the more remarkable when contrasted with the attention which they pay to other European tongues. Their avoidance of Irish, seen in this wider context, cannot, therefore, be explained purely in terms of a global insensitivity to language. They turn in relief from the sounds of a language that threaten through their dissenting counter-claims and their impenetrability, and which can be responded to only by denial, to sounds for which, in contrast, their education and cultural expectations have prepared them. Gainsford laced his texts with Latin couplets. Herbert used that language to propose that Ireland be colonised along Roman lines. Sketches of leading officials often stress their language skills. Campion notes that Sussex was 'learned, and languaged' (*Two Bokes*, p. 137); Fenton praised Henry Sidney's 'deepe iudgement in the tunges' (*Ciuile Warres*, fo. A.iv.r). This broader perspective makes such men's resolute inattention to the vernacular in Ireland seem even more anomalous. Their linguistic blindspot was elective, not inevitable. The contrast is seen at its simplest textual level in Harington's dissimilar handling of Irish and Italian. He stumbles awkwardly through strange-sounding place-names: he makes little progress in his two stabs at *Inis Corthaidh*: 'Enniscorphie', 'Amias Corphis' (*Nugae*, pp. 283, 286). It is with evident relief – and a new swagger – that he escapes into the technical Italianate vocabulary of fortification. He surveys the *'strata coperta'* in Waterford, finding the defences *'a forbici* and *in barba* and . . . there correspondence hindered by the cassamates in the diche, whose piazza is narrowe' (p. 285). He writes enthusiastically to Thomas Combe about his readings in military strategy which give him a new fluency in the language of war: 'I hope at my coming home to talk of counterscarpes and cazamats, with any of our captains' (*Letters*, p. 74).

Moryson was a linguist of some accomplishment. He originally wrote his *Itinerary* in Latin and knew German, Italian, Spanish and French. His effusiveness about continental languages points up the peculiarity of his erasure of Irish. His account of his years in Ireland, from 1599 to 1603, runs to more than 700 pages. As Mountjoy's private secretary, 'at all hours (but time of sleep) admitted into his chamber', he was at the hub of the Lord Deputy's complex network of communications. Yet there is only one unambiguous reference to Irish in the whole of his *History of Ireland* and that enters almost inadvertently when he quotes O'Neill's despairing letter to Philip III, announcing his submission: 'I have in sundry Letters, both in Irish and other Languages, so signified the same' (II, p. 309). O'Neill's phrasing establishes a clear hierarchy between Irish and 'other languages', insisting on a countervailing linguistic pecking order to that constructed in the English texts. Moryson's extraordinary blank in respect of Irish contrasts with the linguistic excitement that erupts once the Spanish arrive. Suddenly, language difference is fore-grounded, translation and its hazards become part of the texture of the narrative; Spanish and Italian words are sprinkled with élan through the text. While the Irish are just 'rebels', these are 'honour-able Enemies', full-fledged foreigners, speaking 'honourable Words' (II, pp. 25, 20, 68).

In this new context, management of communications across the language divide is formal, public and ritualised. The Spanish defenders of Rincorran Castle 'beat a Drum for a Parley'; 'one of our Drums had Licence to carry their Letters' (I, p. 349). But while Moryson is fascinated by the formality of heraldic exchanges, here semaphore diplomacy is simply a supplement to words, not a substitute for them. Alongside the ritual, we are given rare access to the cut and thrust of wartime translation, including the timeless excuse of having been mistranslated. Mountjoy expostulates with Aguila through intermediaries. He complains that the Spaniards, charged with ill-treating English prisoners, did not return a straight answer 'but added scandalous Words, terming us *meschini*. To which [Aguila] answered, protesting that the Speech was ill delivered by an Harquebuzier who undertook to interpret it, but could not do it rightly' (II, p. 24). Elsewhere Mountjoy complains that when, prior to launching an artillery attack, he had offered safe passage to 'certain

Ladies and Women' of Kinsale, Aguila had 'made an uncivil Answer, that he would not be his Bawd'. To this charge of 'such ill Interpretations of Courtesy', the Spanish drum does no more than answer 'with a Spanish Shrug of the Shoulder' (II, p. 25). These enigmatic interpreters, the hapless 'harquebuzier' and the stereotypically disdainful Spanish drum, are precious sightings of intermediaries never elsewhere acknowledged in Moryson's text.

As he busies himself with translation, Moryson is in his element. The process so long occluded in his text now makes a triumphal entry. Mountjoy intercepts a letter from Aguila to O'Neill 'which he commanded me to translate out of *Spanish* into *English*'; when Aguila submits, the Lord Deputy passes the Articles of Agreement, 'in English', to his tireless secretary 'to be fair written' and translated into 'the Latin and Italian tongues' (II, pp. 42, 64). Clearly revelling in the heroic dash which translation lends to his clerical duties, Moryson jauntily sprinkles his text with Italian, Spanish and Latin. The Spanish, he reports, will defend Kinsale '*contra tanti*' (II, p. 16). He shows off his linguistic ease by offering throw-away translations. Aguila's offer to fight Mountjoy in single combat is dismissed as posturing since the Council of Trent forbade 'Romanists to fight in *Campo Steccato* (or Combat in the Field)' (II, p. 24). The secretary's innocent delight in his own linguistic dexterity gives us a rare chance to hear snatches of voices talking in another language. Disenchanted with O'Neill and O'Donnell, Aguila grumbles that he found 'no such Counts *in rerum Natura* (to use his very Words)' (II, p. 63); using the 'very words' of the enemy has not been Moryson's textual practice to this. But once the last of the Spanish sail from Ireland, the old silence settles on language. In the wake of defeat, Gaelic lords sue for pardon and submit. The process is relayed without the slightest suggestion that these negotiations, too, were conducted on the borderland between languages.

The denial of Gaelic claims to autonomy and difference which was being confirmed on the battlefield found its textual corollary in the suppression of Irish in these texts. But the same ideological imperatives which prompted its elision in the texts of conquest could require it to be foregrounded within the complementary discourse of legality which apportioned the spoils. When, between 1607 and 1609, in the calm that followed the war, the Attorney-General, Sir John Davies, investigated land-holdings and titles in Ulster to clear the way for the plantation, he displayed an attitude to Irish not found among the Elizabethans. If Irish was once too threatening to be acknowledged, Davies now crunches through it to get the job done: 'every balli-betagh, which signifieth in the Irish tongue a town able to maintain hospitality, containeth sixteen taths; every tath containeth threescore English acres' (Morley, *Ireland under Elizabeth*, p. 353). Irish words could now be turned into English title.

The identity of purpose between construing words and translating ownership was not lost on the poet Loghlainn Mac Taidhg Óig Uí Dhálaigh. In *Cáit ar ghabhadar Gaoidhil*, 'Where have the Gaels gone?', he bitterly recognises the power of such two-pronged translations to convey ownership as well as meaning. For Uí Dhálaigh, the trans-lation of Irish measurements into imperial ones is the correlative of territorial dispossession. The intrusive loanword *acraibh*, acres – here making one of its first appearances in Irish – marks the conjunction of linguistic displacement and expropriation:

> Roinnid í eatorra féin,
> an chríoch-sa chloinne saoirNéill,
> gan phoinn do mhoigh lachtmhair Fhloinn
> nach bhfoil 'na *acraibh* agoinn

('They split it among themselves, this land of crafty Niall's clan, with no screed of Flann's milk-rich plain, that's not becoming *acres*') (Gillies, 'A Poem', p. 206: 9.1–4; my emphasis).

Davies held that the 'Perfect Conquest' happened in two stages: the country would first be 'broken by a warre' and then be ready to receive the colonist's law (Davies, *Discovery*, pp. 5–6). By 1607 the sword had done its work, imposing a silence much more literal than that of the texts which charted its course. The law had to make 'a passage' among the natives: 'all their places of Fastnesse haue been discouered and laide open; all their paces cleard' (p. 270). And that imperative to achieve transparency required that language, too, be brought under the colonist's gaze and made to yield up its secrets. (Not that gazing was redundant. In a letter to Salisbury from Derry, Davies wished that the king, 'with the help of one of his farr-Seeing Glasses, could see his Commissioners': 'this Speculation' of their endeavours would make him confident of the plantation's future. Busily looking, too, were 'the Agents of London who ar sent to view'. The text is replete with 'commodities' and 'fruitfulnes' on which the eye gorges (Harris, 'Commission', pp. 53–4).)

In his report to Salisbury from Monaghan, the veil at first still seems drawn over the practical management of the exchanges between English officials and locals. There, Chichester 'propounded . . . two principal questions in writing' to the inhabitants and received, uncomplicatedly, 'their several answers' with no hint of any intervening linguistic impediment (Morley, *Ireland under Elizabeth*, p. 353). But when the Commission turned to investigate church properties, Davies reports straightforwardly that replies were made in Latin. His explanation accounts only for why Latin was the lingua franca chosen – 'because the principal jurors were vicars and clerks' (p. 361) – in a way that takes for granted the need for such mediation. His treatment of language issues in Fermanagh is even more forthright. There the reply is delivered in Irish but its content 'being translated into English, appeared to be confused', so Davies is deputed to meet the grand jury and the 'chief inhabitants'; 'by conference with them', he irons out the misunderstandings (p. 363). This process is shown to be highly linguistic. It is an exercise in construing Irish legal terminology and agreeing definitions. Davies wants to know what a *herinach* is, how much land a *ballibetagh* covers, what is meant by *termon*. He wades, unfazed, through the strange vocabulary. Far from occluding the process, he builds his narrative around it:

I had heard of the name of a corbe and of an herinach divers times since I came into this kingdom, and would gladly have learned of our clergymen at Dublin what kind of religious persons they were, but could never be satisfied by any.

He is by now 'the more curious and inquisitive' to solve the puzzle and summons 'one of the best-learned vicars in all that country', a former brehon and a practitioner of civil and common law, to guide his quest. Davies undertakes the pursuit enthusiastically and he reports his discoveries fully and with evident satisfaction: 'termon doth signify in the Irish tongue a liberty or freedom' (p. 364). 'For the name of corbe, I could not learn that it had any signification in the Irish tongue' and he extends the search to Latin (p. 365). He has 'an Irish scholar whose opinion I required' draw up 'a certificate in Latin', to authenticate the glosses (p. 366).

Davies's approach, his intellectual curiosity, his scholarly doggedness and his peculiarly non-judgemental reporting, is strikingly at odds with the conduct of his Tudor near-contemporaries. But his purpose, too, is unlike theirs. While they chronicle lulls and hurly-burlies, he is the painstaking solicitor putting the aftermath of conquest on a legal footing. In his discourse of legality, appropriation is legitimated through due process and a show of attention to small print and literal detail – and literalness must extend to language, because here language is the key to possession. There is more at stake in glossing *tearmann* and *airchinneach* than academic whimsy. If termon and erenagh lands could be shown to be independent of bishops' demesnes, they would fall forfeit to the crown under the attainder of Shane and Hugh O'Neill's lands: as a result of Davies' philological enquiries, 60,490 acres lapsed to the king (Harris, 'Commission', p. 41; Pawlisch, *Davies*, p. 79). Language is turning Crown witness: no longer able to resist appropriation, it becomes its accessory. To highlight words as part of the legal process is both to advance and sanction the undertaking: Irish definitions give, quite literally, a gloss of legality to the procedure. Davies' attentiveness to Irish is no more disinterested than is his near-contemporaries' inattention. His spotlight and their blackout ultimately serve the same ideological needs, though in a different discursive livery.

An incident in Fermanagh illustrates the wider implications of the shift. The diligent solicitor is attempting to parse the title of Maguire's ancestral lands. Word comes that an ancient brehon called O'Bristan has the required information in 'an old parchment roll'. The 'aged and decrepit' O'Bristan is summoned. The English demand 'sight of that ancient roll'; the brehon refuses, claiming that it had been burned along with his books and papers by English soldiers during the war. But when witnesses reaffirm that the roll has been seen since then, he is compelled to reveal it. 'The poor old man, fetching a deep sigh, confessed that he knew where the roll was, but that it was dearer to him than his life' and so he requests the Lord Chancellor to swear to restore it to him again. The official duly gives his word, 'smiling', and O'Bristan 'drew the roll out of his bosom, where he did continually bear it about him'. The parchment is written in 'a fair Irish character' but 'the writing was worn and defaced with time'. The English jurists 'caused it forthwith to be translated into English' and the lawyers establish just how many pigs, vessels of butter and measures of meal were traditionally due to Maguire. Afterwards, Davies tells Salisbury, he mislaid the translation but shrugs off the loss: these matters were but 'trifles'; and anyway, Maguire only 'spent them wastefully in a sordid and barbarous manner among his loose and idle followers' (Morley, *Ireland under Elizabeth*, pp. 368–9).

Davies spends a lot of time on this 'trifle' and its emblematic quality is inescapable. In the meeting of Davies and O'Bristan, the competent functionary from a new world meets the dying emissary of the old. Everything associated with the brehon is decrepit and fading, defeated by time and a changed order. That includes his language, with its message from a defunct society: 'the writing was worn and defaced with time'. The writing is on the wall for O'Bristan's Irish and, in the contrasting responses of the brehon and the English legal team, the significance of the episode is given two incommensurate interpretations. For O'Bristan, the document and what it represents is sacred; his reverence for it and his grief at the prospect of losing it is countered by the 'smiling' Lord Chancellor's levity and Davies's ultimate dismissal of it as a trifle.

In the end, Davies's engagement with Irish was disingenuous and superficial. His failure to find 'any signification in the Irish tongue' for 'corbe' is telling: the Royal Irish Academy dictionary of Old and Middle Irish requires almost a page to exhaust the nuances of *comarbbae* and its cognate *comarbus* (*DIL*, p. 352). He used key words to put a gloss on appropriation – but the inaccuracy of his glosses stored up difficulties for future generations. The bitter legacy of the Ulster Plantation is, in part, the fruit of flawed land grants: 'undertakers' given unintentionally large holdings had to retain the native inhabitants as tenants, vitiating the segregation envisaged by its planners. The fatal cohabitation that followed had, in no small measure, its roots in the linguistic inattention which has been the subject of this chapter: 'Much of the initial reason for unmanageably large grants had to do with the classic Anglo-Irish difficulty of semantic misunderstanding' (Foster, *Modern Ireland*, p. 61). Davies assumed a one-to-one correspondence between *baile biattaig* and acre (1 ballibetagh = 1,000 acres, the unit of the plantation). He failed to grasp the profound conceptual difference in the way the two languages measured land. English measured an unvarying physical space; Irish measured a fixed *value* which a variable quantity of land yielded. A *baile biattaig* represented the indeterminate quantity of land required to support 300 cows or yield an agreed number of ploughing-days (Hogan, 'Land Measures', p. 189).

The misunderstanding was reproduced in the associated survey directed by Josias Bodley, a man whose previous adventures evinced little flair for cross-cultural communication (see p. 85 below). The 1608 survey was mapped by drawing on oral testimony. Bodley explained that they 'did perambulate and view' each sector in the company of knowledgeable locals who 'could give us the name and quality of every ballibo, quarter, tate'. Plotting Bodley's against Ordinance Survey maps, J. H. Andrews found Bodley's to have a very low index of accuracy – as low as 8 per cent in one extreme instance ('Maps', pp. 145–6, 149). The maps' undermeasurement, which derived largely from errors in estimating quantity, resulted in a disparity between representation and reality.

The Ulster plantation and its outcome illustrate the hazards of presuming that different languages map reality identically. Slipshod translation served well enough to alienate land but, when meaning too went astray, the consequences could be unpredictable and tragic. In the superimposition of a quantitative definition (of space) on a qualitative one (of value) and in the shifting boundaries of interpretation which it permitted, this episode of linguistic ineptitude not only set the terms for future misunderstandings, but also symbolises the damaging incomprehension which lay at the heart of the English encounter with Irish.

CHAPTER 3

'Wilde Speech': Elizabethan evaluations of Irish

Sic ut e thymo mel apis, aranea venenum exugit, sic a linguis
bonum aut malum pro suo quisque arbitrio elicit.[1]
John Lynch, *Cambrensis Eversus*, p. 180

The Elizabethans' reluctance to train their attention on the Irish
language is part of their wider refusal to see Gaelic society in its
integrity. Their texts give no sense of native culture in its fullness and
internal coherence. Gaelic Ireland enters only as bursts of irrational
disorder: fragmentary, inexplicable and perverse. Never seen on its
own terms, the native world figures only as a series of irritants,
anomalies and departures from an English norm: 'Wee liue in Clenly
houses, they in Cabinns or smoaky Cottages. Our cheefe husbandry
is in Tillage, they dispise the Plough' (Moryson, *Shakespeare's Europe*,
p. 214). A discourse of difference opens up: native conduct and
customs, refracted through incomprehension and hostility, emerge as
deviations. The role of Irish within that discourse, however, is far
from simple. The previous two chapters have demonstrated that
whereas the Spanish highlighted language within their discourse of
difference, English writers consistently erased language difference
textually. A peculiar combination of ritually thematising selected
cultural differences while repressing the linguistic one is well illustrated in English writers' handling of one of their most assured
contrasts, that between English husbandry and Irish nomadism. But
just as that easy antithesis repeatedly comes under strain so, too,
does the occluded language difference make its presence felt.
Though ostensibly ignored, Irish was an inextricable part of native
difference; judgements about the latter inevitably implicated the
language which articulated it.

Moryson's confident *triage* between tillers and nomads was much
recycled. But, though subscribed to as an article of faith, the

distinction proved unstable. 'It seemeth incredible,' Moryson himself reports after an incursion deep into 'rebel' lands in Laois, 'that by so barbarous inhabitants, the ground should be so manured, and the fields so orderly fenced, the towns so frequently inhabited, and the high-ways and paths so well beaten as the Lord Deputy here found them.' A convoluted *non sequitur* tries to account for how marks of civility could turn up where, by definition, none could exist, until Moryson ends up conceding the opposite point to the one he wished to make: 'The reason whereof was, that the queen's forces, during these wars, never till then came among them' (*History* I, p. 178). The inadvertant concession sends his initial identification of these rebel-ploughmen as 'barbarous inhabitants' spinning. But the role reversal goes further than that. Here the English 'ploughmen' wreck what the Irish 'nomads' would reap, 'causing Famine, being the only sure Way to reduce or root out the Rebels' (p. 266). Travelling in the 'most disordered and barbarous province' of Ulster, Sidney comes on an expanse of cornfields; he camps, 'purposely to destroy the corn, whereof we found no small abundance, burning that day above 24 miles compass' (*JRHAAI*, p. 17). Unnoticed by Moryson and Sidney, their side is swapping roles with the allegedly tillage-shy natives – 'the Ground was well plowed by the Rebels. Our Men burnt Houses and Corn' – until, in the end, the English come to be characterised by behaviour that overturns their self-identity as civil ploughmen: 'we cut down great Abundance of Corn with our Swords (*according to our Fashion*)' (Moryson, *History* I, pp. 206, 268; my emphasis).

Intriguingly, this unstable *topos* sometimes coincides with evidence for the attempted suppression or inversion of native utterance. Derricke has his ventriloquist-dummy, Rory Óg O'More, denounce himself – in a 'plaine Irish' that turns out to be English – according to stereotype: 'I made from tillage the Farmors to cease' (*Image*, p. 96). Years later, Rory Óg's son, Ony MacRory, wrote to Ormond. He protested against Mountjoy's scorched-earth policy in Laois and demanded that the Lord Deputy halt 'this abominable course to cutt and reape downe grene corne, which is a most execrable course and badd example unto all the world' (Gilbert, *Facsimiles* IV.I, p. lxi). Mountjoy's recourse to the standard assurance, 'for so he termed it', when reporting the exchange to Carew obscures the fact that MacRory spoke only Irish and that the final English letter rested on a process of translation. When, some time before, MacRory had joined O'Neill during a parley with Ormond, the latter had switched to 'using long speeches in Irish to that lewd young man, because he spake not English' (*CSPI* 1598–9, p. 87). Mountjoy's telling obscures MacRory's dependence on interpreters[2] and he reduces the process of translation, simultaneously implicit and elided in his telling, to a jape. When MacRory wrote again desiring a 'conference', Mountjoy refused to read the letter and passed it on to Neale Moore, his Irish fool, instructing him to reply 'that there was none in the camp so base as to confer with him' and suggesting that he 'submit himself on his knees to him, the said Neale' (*CCM* 3, pp. 431, 439). Yet the cogency of MacRory's content survives the repression of its source language, dismantling the dichotomies set up in the English texts.

Such episodes demonstrate the anomalous place of Irish within the Elizabethans' discourse of difference. Irish is part of the cultural difference which is being anathematised but, for whatever reason, it is not one of the differences selected for attention. Yet Irish was all too apparently different – and troubling. Behind the reticence, mistrustful evaluations of Irish as yet another index of difference were being made.

ENGLISHMEN'S KNOWLEDGE OF IRISH

Informed evaluation would require a knowledge of Irish, but the Elizabethans never reproduced in Ireland the philological endeavours that underpinned Spanish judgements of Amerindian languages. Those with a good ear might pick up a smattering of Irish almost by default. Their children might learn it at the wet-nurse's breast. But there would be almost no engagement in depth with a language regarded axiomatically as a contaminant, nor any of the scholarly investigation that might permit informed assessment.

There is an almost irresistible inclination to imagine that soldiers and administrators whose whole adulthood was spent in Ireland 'must have' acquired Irish in the process. Pauline Henley's assumption that 'those who had served for any length of time would at least have understood the language, even if they could not speak it' seems reasonable (*Spenser*, p. 100). But inherent likelihood proves remarkably difficult to pin down. Henry Bagenal may have grown up in the Louth marches but his biographer's assumption that he 'must have been familiar from childhood' with Irish receives little support from the official record (Bagenal, *Vicissitudes*, p. 44). Instead, Bagenal's journal of the campaign against Maguire suggests that he depended on interpreters in his dealings with the Gaelic world. He learned from Conor Roe Maguire that Maguire had met secretly with O'Neill and O'Donnell, 'Phelim O'Hanlan being interpreter'; he relied on James McManus – one that 'speaketh English perfectly being in times past servant to Sir Lucas Dillon' – for confirmation of O'Neill's involvement (*CSPI* 1592–6, pp. 181–2). The sad little vignette that provides our only glimpse into the illicit marriage between Henry's sister, Mabel, and Hugh O'Neill is suggestive of the probable level of Irish attained by the new settlers in the marches. Mabel and Hugh are in a boat on the Bann, leaving Phelim McTurlough O'Neill astern to the fate ordained for him by O'Neill. Hugh O'Gallagher catches up with the couple to announce Phelim's dispatch. O'Gallagher later testified, through an interpreter, that 'the said Hugh said nothing, but the Countess, clapping her hands together, was sorry, as should seem of that which happened, to which the Earl in English spake with vehemency, which most of the company did not understand' (*CSPI* 1592–6, p. 109). Mabel passively comprehends the hibernophone O'Gallagher but the language actively used between the pair is English.

A generation later, Sir Thomas Browne assumed that Richard Boyle's 4-year old son, Roger, had 'Irish sufficient to be his father's interpreter' – a plausible inference in the case of a child not long weaned from the almost inevitable Irish wet-nurse. But in a climate of cultural polarisation, the language of the nursery would quickly grow rusty – even if its narrow utility in dealing with the tenantry was recognised. So, though Boyle sent a tutor, Robert Carew, capable of teaching Irish with his sons to Eton, Carew complained that they 'practise the French and Latin but they affect not the Irish' (Canny, *Upstart Earl*, p. 127).

A good linguist like Barnaby Googe could talk of 'kern galor' within six weeks of arriving in Ireland (Pinkerton, 'Googe', p. 182) and even if, as it seems, the English made no concerted effort to learn Irish, their enforced proximity to Irish-speakers must have given at least the more linguistically adept of them the rudiments mastered by Josias Bodley and his companions who spent a merry first evening in Lecale 'clamantes, Usquebathum, Usquebathum' (crying Whiskey, Whiskey) (Bodley, 'Discriptio', p. 84). To satisfy such modest requirements outside the English-speaking towns, some command of basic travellers' Irish would have been almost essential and the soldier's lexicon must have included the sort of simple contact vocabulary offered in Andrew Borde's *The First Boke of the Introduction of Knowledge*. In little more than a page, he lists the numbers from 1 to 100 and supplies twenty-six useful phrases, almost all devoted to ordering food and drink – in a somewhat peremptory pidgin: 'Man, gyue me wine! *Farate, toor fyen!* . . . Gyue me some fyshe! *Toor yeske!*' (p. 134). Such orders, gracelessly phrased and duly mispronounced, must have rung out in squalid shebeens across the country. Indeed, Bartley laconically suggests that expressions such as 'bodach bréan', 'éist do chlampar', 'stríopach' – stinking churl, shut up, whore – used in *The Famous History of Captain Thomas Stukeley* 'imply at least such knowledge of the language as might have been gained by a soldier who had seen service in Ireland' (*Teague*, p. 42).[3]

No doubt some – men like Thomas Masterson and Robert Hartpole who soldiered in the Leinster marches from mid-century and took Irish wives – gained a reasonable working knowledge of Irish (Morgan, 'Lee', p. 133). Yet Captain Tom Lee, though married to an Irish woman and long stationed in frontier society, could muster only 'broken Irishe' when questioned by one of the O'Byrnes (PRO SP 63/202, 11/88. ix). We can infer that Richard Bingham was less than fluent in Irish from a letter he wrote to his brother, George. He recounts how an informer's tip-off led him to the hide-out of 'xxx knaues' whom he then slew. His telling re-enacts his graduated entry into meaning. He tells George how 'Maguire', the informer, came upon him in the hall of Boyle Castle and how 'presentlie I demaundinge what he was; he answered that he was a poore man and had some secret busines with me wherupon I wente asyde and tooke Renolds to interpret betweene vs' (PRO SP 63/172/38ii). The sequencing indicates that neither Bingham nor Maguire had more than the rudiments of the other's language; but even if we allow that Bingham, after eleven years in Ireland, managed the preliminaries in Irish, he still needed an interpreter for the serious talking to begin. Bingham's predecessor, Sir Nicholas Malby, uniquely among his compatriots, earns a mention from the Four Masters for being 'foglamtha i mbérlaibh agus i tteangthoibh oilén iarthair eorpa' (learned in the languages and tongues of the islands of western Europe; editor's translation) (*ARÉ* 3, pp. 1814–15).

This was not the kind of knowledge (nor, probably, were these the kind of men) to provide scholarly evaluations of Irish. There was no shortage of scholarly Elizabethans in Ireland but none seems to have brought that scholarship to bear on Irish. Spenser's knowledge of

Irish has long excited speculation. But though a wordsmith's curiosity may have drawn him to pick over Irish more closely than did others – at almost forty, his borrowings of Irish words exceed those of all his contemporaries – his interest was forensic and superficial. Commentators have imagined him taking instruction from Ormond's brehon, MacClancy, or Lord Roche's bard, Teig Olyve (Smith, 'Spenser, Holinshed', p. 400, fn. 55; Henley, *Spenser*, p. 103). Yet, his handling of Irish words indicates no more than a shallow acquaintance hitched to a morbid interest. Irenæus tosses off twenty-nine loan-words (twelve of them legal terms) in the course of *A View* as tokens of his insider's command of Irish affairs (Smith, 'Irish Background'). But for all the bravura with which they are displayed, Spenser's borrowings – and borrowed errors – are drawn from the same small stock of Irish words circulating among the colonists. His glosses can be plainly wrong: he repeats Camden's error in imagining that 'Tarbert' meant 'an heigh lande'[4] and Hooker's in deriving 'galloglass'[5] from 'English yeoman' (*View*, pp. 196, 71; Smith, 'More Irish Words', p. 473; Hooker, 'Historie', p. 132). His use of the genitive or plural form 'monashul' when 'bean suibhal' was required indicates a fundamental ignorance of Irish grammar (*View*, p. 53). Nor does his handling of etymologies contradict that impression. Of 'coigny[6] and livery', the unabashed Irenæus says, 'I know not whether the words be English or Irish, but I suppose them rather to be ancient English, for the Irishmen can make no derivation or analogy of them' (p. 34). Cut off from Irish meanings, he falls back on the only option for the uncomprehending, false etymology drawn not from the source language but from his own. 'Kincogish'[7] becomes 'a word mingled of English and Irish together . . . so, *kyn*: is English and *cogish* signifieth affinity in Irish' (p. 36). A slender grasp of Welsh trips him into finding equivalence where only false similitude exists: he suggests that 'cummericke'[8] means ' "Briton, help", for the Briton is called in his own language cummeraige' (p. 46). Ní Chuilleanáin concludes that Spenser 'knew the language only sketchily'; Draper's assessment that he had 'a slight conversational and some legal vocabulary' seems about right (Hamilton, *Spenser Encyclopedia*, p. 404; Draper, 'Linguistics', p. 472).

One scholarly newcomer whose contacts with Irish and the native learned class leave a tantalising trace is Sir William Herbert. In *Croftus sive de Hibernia liber*, Irish makes a startling and suggestive entry. For Herbert, the Bible is a means of taming the natives (p. 98).

To further this purpose, he recommends the foundation of universities in Dublin and Limerick; to fund them, he proposes a levy on acreage. His calculations hold good, he reckons,

> si tritum illud et pervulgatum
> Hibernicum distichon villam recte dimetiatur:
> 'Baile chongmhas cúig céad bó
> Le toib seaght seisreagh ní gó'   (pp. 100–2)

(if the common and well-known Irish couplet measures a village correctly: 'a townland sustains 500 cows with seven ploughlands, it is no lie'). The nonchalance with which the planter reaches for the 'well-known couplet' opens up a teasing suggestion about contacts rarely even hinted at by his contemporaries.[9] The couplet breaks through the veil of so much textual silence like a visitor from another world, then disappears back into that uncanny stillness leaving only puzzlement and a resonant absence in its wake.

Several factors held the Elizabethans back from learning Irish. The most neutral of these was its perceived difficulty. Stanihurst was so convinced of its 'estraungenesse' of phrase and 'curious featnesse' of pronunciation that he imagined that 'the very Deuyll was graueyled therewith'. In evidence, he instanced the 'babbling spirite' who possessed a Roman woman but whose demonic gift of tongues came unstuck with Irish: it 'chatted any language sauing' that one (*Chronicle*, p. 18). Campion spent eight months in Ireland but explained that Irish was 'so hard that it asked contynuance in this land mo yeres than I had monethes to spare upon this busynes' (*Two Bokes*, p. 6). But in even toying with the idea of learning Irish, Campion had strayed from the consensus of his fellows. For the real impediment to learning Irish lay in the newcomers' attitude to it. Irish was a contaminant and ignorance of it was prophylactic: Sir John Bolle assured Cecil that Lieutenant Roberts, who had defected to O'Donnell, could not give much away because he had spent only six weeks among the Irish 'and wanteth the understanding of the Irish tongue' (*CSPI* 1600–1, p. 47). The newcomers' confident deprecation of all that Irish encoded absolved them from the very linguistic endeavours which would have been required to challenge their prejudices.

The disparity between the passionate advocacy of a hibernophile initiate and the implicit indifference of his imagined – imaginary – English learner shows up poignantly in Christopher Nugent's attempt to interest Queen Elizabeth in Irish. Nugent, ninth Baron

Delvin, wrote an Irish primer for the queen while he was a student at Cambridge in 1562. He modelled it on the textbook used by Elizabeth Zouch when she married the Earl of Kildare. It consists of an Irish alphabet, a little glossary – 'Tenga, Lingua, Tongue' – parallel phrases in Irish, Latin and English – 'In eol duit gealag, Possis ne hibernice loqui, Cann you speake Iryshe' – and a brief history of the language. But the era when English newcomers set about acquiring Irish had passed and, for their sovereign, Nugent's labour of love can have been little more than a curiosity. In reality, the primer reveals more about a not-untypical Anglo-Irish lord's attitude to Irish than about its recipient's. Nugent is passionate in his advocacy of the language and regretful that 'feawe or none of the Englyshe natione borne and bredd in England, ever had that gifte' [of learning Irish]. He is quick to play down the reasons: it was 'not throughe diffycultie of the speache, but onlye for want of taking the ryght manner of instruction'. Uneasily aware of the metropolitan mistrust of Irish, his own text is scrupulously loyalist, prudently offering the Irish for 'God saue the queene off Englande' (Gilbert, *Facsimiles* IV.1, pp. xxxv & Apx. xxii; Ó Mathúna, *Bathe*, p. 189). Nugent's plea for the vernacular and his confidence that it could be used to promote civility are strikingly at odds with the sentiments of the queen's new men in Ireland. In that disequilibrium lies the key to the ultimate redundancy of his offering.

To an extent, the impulse to keep aloof from Irish reflects on the newcomers' orientation to language-learning. The fearless venturing of at least a minority of Spaniards into the 'pagan' tongues of the Amerindians finds no parallel among the English. Moryson marvelled at 'the Flemings generall skill in strang languages' (*Shakespeare's Europe*, p. 378); Florio, conversely, deplored the Englishman's poor grasp of foreign tongues: in the presence of foreigners, he 'can neyther speake, nor vnderstand . . . but standes as one mute, & so is he mocked of them' (*First Fruites*, fo. 62v). Moryson commended Mountjoy's 'Skill in Tongues' but added revealingly 'so far as he could read and understand the *Italian* and *French*, though he durst not adventure to speak them' (*History* I, p. 109). He contrasts the Germans' willingness to speak Latin 'readily in discourse' with Englishmen's awkward stumblings 'when wee first goe into forayne parts'. He is mistrustful of informal approaches to language learning and he dismisses those, such as merchants, who want 'a smak of many tounges': they learn 'by roote, (I meane by practise without reading) . . . like to wemen and Children, who learning only by roate soone forgett what they haue learned' (*Shakespeare's Europe*, pp. 320–1). Such timorousness about venturing to speak foreign languages only reinforced the Elizabethans' reluctance to consort with Irish.[10]

There were more learners – and more languages – circulating in sixteenth-century Ireland than just Irish and English and the progress made by non-English newcomers points up the particularity – and ideological inflection – of Englishmen's unwillingness to engage with Irish. From Connacht in 1589 came reports of one Hypolyta, an Italian, and four Spaniards who spoke Irish 'very perfectly' (*CSPI* 1588–92: 273). But the learner with most to teach about the adventures of languages in contact in late 1580s Ireland is an Armada survivor, Captain Francisco de Cuellar. His 'Carta de uno que fué en la Armada', a caballeresque account of traversing the island, from Streedagh strand to the Antrim coast in the autumn and winter of 1588–9, charts an odyssey from gesture and incomprehension towards language and conversation.

In striking contrast to English writers' erasure of the mechanics of inter-lingual exchange, Cuellar's set-pieces are all dramas of communication, attempted at points of peril and extremity in a near-apocalyptic landscape. At first, there is only gesture: from the deck of a sinking vessel, the horrified Cuellar watches 'doscientos salvajes y otros enemigos . . . que andaban danzando y bailando de placer de nuestro mal' (two hundred natives and other enemies hopping and dancing with pleasure at our misfortune) (p. 344). Next, there is silence. Washed up on the strand, cowering in a bed of rushes above a beach strewn with bodies pillaged bare, he is joined by a young Spaniard so dazed 'que no podia hablar ni áun decirme quién era' (that he could neither speak nor tell me who he was) (p. 345). The young man dies, silently, in the night. Cuellar strikes out alone and his quest to make contact begins when he meets an old woman with two words of broken Spanish and sign language. This 'bruta salvaje' recognises his nationality and greets him in pidgin: 'tú España'. Next comes gesture. He confirms her surmise by signs, 'por señas'. The crone is an eloquent sign-maker: she conveys that they are close to her house but that there are enemies near by ready to cut off his head (p. 347). Setting off barefoot on the stony road, Cuellar is accosted by a polyglot bunch – an elderly native and a beautiful girl, an Englishman and a Frenchman. The Englishman calls him a 'poltron español' and threatens him (p. 349); the girl takes pity on him and asks the others – 'rogóles' – to leave him his clothes, indicating – *haciéndome señal* – that she would look after his gold relics in a ruse which Cuellar dismantles with sly humour, 'diciéndome que era cristiana, y éralo como Mahoma' (telling me that she was a Christian, which she was like Mahomed). He is sent off in the direction of 'un gran señor salvaje' (p. 350).

Finally, there is language. At nightfall, he reaches a group of huts where he meets a young man who speaks Latin and a greatly relieved Cuellar reports that 'nos entendimos hablando en latin' (we understood one another speaking in Latin). The 'ladino' makes him a bed of straw and, in the morning, sends him off on horseback, with a boy to guide him. Before parting from the Spaniard, the boy briefs him about the road ahead 'por señas'; but now gesture is supplemented by a stray Irish word picked up in Cuellar's transposition of the boy's message: ' "Muchos sasanas de á caballo vienen aquí y te han de hacer pedazos si no te escondes; anda acá presto." Llaman sasanas á los ingleses' ('Many *sasanas* come by here on horseback and they will make bits of you if you don't hide; off you go quickly.' They call the English *sasanas*) (p. 351). Later, stripped naked by a band of 'salvajes luteranos', Cuellar covers himself in bracken and a piece of old matting and continues alone on foot. He eventually arrives at the camp of 'el señor de Ruerge' and is given 'a bad old blanket, full of fleas' (my trans. p. 355). While waiting for Ruerge – Brian na Murrtha O'Rourke – to return, word comes of a Spanish ship anchored off the coast. Cuellar alone, limping from a leg wound, fails to make the ship before it sails – on to rocks and shipwreck, with all survivors put to the sword. Wandering once more through the countryside, lost and confused, he meets a priest disguised as a layman who greets him in Latin. Cuellar's relief at finding an interlocutor is palpable: 'Dios me dió gracia para que yo le pudiera responder á todo lo que me preguntaba, en la mesma lengua latina' (God gave me the grace to be able to reply to everything he asked me in that same Latin language) (p. 356). The priest arranges for the Spaniard to be received by McClancy – though not before the unfortunate captain has spent a picaresque interval in captivity to a smith, pumping bellows without let. Cuellar spends three months in McClancy's castle becoming, as he impishly recounts, a proper savage/native like the rest: 'hecho propio salvaje como ellos' (p. 357). The sociable Cuellar's assimilation seems to have extended to language: he is soon giving accounts of lively exchanges free, for the first time in his text, from explanations about the mechanisms of transmission. Talk flows naturally and, it appears, without mediation.

One day, for example, Cuellar is sitting in the sun with the chieftain's wife and her companions. They ask him to read their hands. This Cuellar does with ironic good grace – 'ya no me faltaba más que ser gitano entre los salvajes' (there was nothing for it but to be a gypsy among the natives) – and he spins out 'cien mil disparates' (a hundred thousand absurdities). The palmistry establishes him as a favourite 'y de noche y de dia me perseguian hombres y mujeres para que les dijese la buenaventura' (day and night they followed me, men and women, so that I'd tell their fortunes) (p. 358). Such language games cannot have been played through signs and halting translation alone. One can confidently wager that Cuellar set out after three months on Lough Melvin equipped with some smattering of Irish. There is a striking contrast, for instance, between his last conversation with his host and his lapse into gesture in his subsequent encounter with Lord Deputy FitzWilliam. McClancy reports that the English are coming to attack his castle; Cuellar and nine Spaniards undertake to remain behind to defend it. Their conference with McClancy has the rhythm of a direct exchange: 'Yo le respondí que se sosegase un poco, que pronto le dariamos respuesta' (I told him to relax a bit, that we would give him our response soon) (p. 361). There is no such fluency in Cuellar's brush with English. There is a grim return to semaphore with FitzWilliam's premonitory hanging of two Spaniards in sight of the defenders (p. 362); he sends a trumpet offering terms but the Spaniards indicate that they do not understand, 'no le entendiamos' (p. 363).

On his onward journey towards the Antrim coast, Cuellar is befriended by a group of young women and his transition from frantic sign language to amorous discourse is richly suggested by his account of the month and a half he spent with them in a mountain cabin, recovering from a leg wound – until, one day, a band of English soldiers bursts in. Suddenly, there is a return to semaphore but, this time, not in compensation for the absence of language but in deliberate substitution for it: the girls' mother 'me hizo señas que me saliese por la puerta' (made me signs to get out by the door) (p. 366).

Cuellar's long journey into language sheds fascinating if oblique light on the dominant language encounter running in parallel to his own. His fierce need to communicate, dictated by dire circumstances and, one suspects, natural inclination propelled him on an express course of language-learning, from sign language to a common second language to some command of the vernacular. That Cuellar, unlike most of his English contemporaries, seems to have advanced through all three stages was largely forced on him by events. But his narrative reveals an openness to encounter unmatched by any extant English text. No Englishman documents with such frank flirtatiousness his admiration of the women he meets. The frequency with which Cuellar breathlessly pronounces on the beauty of the native women – 'hermosísima por todo extremo' (pp. 349, 357, 359) – points to an experience of cross-cultural contact that holds one artlessly simple key to the dissimilar pattern of Spanish and English linguistic encounters. Edward Tuttle attributes the relative linguistic hybridity of Spanish America to the Spaniards' openness to *mestizaje* which he contrasts with English 'continence' in their engagement with native Americans ('Borrowing', p. 605). Victor Kiernan, too, emphasises the role of social apartheid in determining 'linguistic outcomes' in later episodes of English imperialism, in Africa and India ('Language and Conquerors', p. 193).[11]

Cuellar's text prompts unavoidable comparison with the only other romping account to emerge from the literature of encounter in sixteenth-century Ireland, Josias Bodley's 'Visit to Lecale'. In it, the young blades break the journey to Captain Richard Moryson's house to drink '*usquebathum*' with McGuinness's English-speaking wife – O'Neill's daughter, Sarah – before retreating to an oasis of English revelry in Downpatrick – and to practices that provide a potent metaphor for endogamy and a refusal of the other. In the morning, the young men greet one another in the manner of those 'bene educatos': 'erant ex nobis aliqui qui salutabant socios per viam de retro, quod non erat, meo judicio, valdè honestum, quamvis nonnulli dicunt esse bonum pro lumbis' (there were some among us who greeted their comrades by the back way which was not, in my judgement, terribly decent though others say that it is good for the member)[12] (p. 87). Nor do the following days bring them into closer communication with the natives. The only locals met, apart from servants whose presence is left to inference, are the 'Maschari quidam ex nobilibus Hibernicis', masked Gaelic lords, who visit one night. But the strangers are disguised and silent, their features concealed behind 'ivy leaves, masks of dog skin, paper noses, [and] peaked paper caps ornamented with ivy leaves' (p. 92), their voices replaced by metonymous military-band instruments: 'Nunc tympana ex illorum partibus; nunc tuba ex nostris sonabat' (now the drum from their side; now the trumpet sounded from ours). In the end, they leave 'vacui', like dogs 'cum cauda inter nates pendente', with their tails between their legs, without saying a word, 'sine dicere Valete' (p. 93).

JUDGEMENTS FROM IGNORANCE

The outcome of so little learning was inevitable: the New English sought to make sense of Ireland with 'practically no knowledge of Irish' (Maxwell, *Contemporary Sources*, p. 58). Most newcomers' brush with Irish was restricted to mastering the seventy-odd items on the colonial word-list.[13] The list was a negative supplement to English, encompassing native oddities and aberrations outside the range of the colonists' civil lexicon. The colonial mind in classificatory mode inclines to binary distinctions. What is not-English among native practices is beyond the pale. And what is not-English is, by definition, not *in* English. It is linguistically outside; if it is to be spoken of at all, recourse will have be made to the outsider's language. The Elizabethans' Irish word-list was little more than an inventory of vile customs, menacing figures, hostile terrain and despised social practices. Equipped only with this pidgin roll-call of native peculiarities, the newcomers' encounter with Irish-speakers and their language would inevitably be distorted.

The semantic fields from which the colonial word-list was borrowed are limited almost to the point of caricature. A dozen or so identify native types or occupations, generally regarded as disreputable. Another dozen cover native practices or customs codified by brehon law, all seen to be in need of eradication. A smaller cluster refers to fortifications and features of the hostile terrain. The rest cover dress, food, transport and units of non-imperial measurement. Among so many nouns, there is a clutch of adjectives – gald, garvy, roe – all nicknames (or *noms de guerre*) used by their adversaries or insults flung by them. However narrow the range of words 'borrowed', the active vocabulary was even more restricted. Twenty-four words occur only once; only ten words are used by more than five authors: bard (7), bonnought (7), brehon (9), coshering (6), galloglass (10), garran (9), glib (7), glin (6), kerne (used by all but three), tamist (7).

The Elizabethan word-list represents a very skewed relationship with Irish life and culture – and almost none at all with the Irish language. Just as English borrowings from New World languages tended to come through Spanish, French and Portuguese, so the New English borrowed, not directly from Irish but from Hiberno-English: these are all words found in the English writings of the reformers earlier in the century (Bailey, *Images*, p. 62; Irwin, 'Ireland's Contribution', p. 639). This is not a phrase-book equipping the curious traveller with the key-words for entry into another language or for initiating contact with Irish-speakers. It is more like a lexical 'wanted list' of the most dangerous suspects – most dangerous of all the kern, mentioned by all but three of the writers – and a hitlist of practices to be rooted out. The items enter a closed system of colonial classification. It is a technical vocabulary, as easily mastered by officials back home as by those living within inattentive earshot of Irish: the queen talks comfortably of 'garrons', 'kerne and gallooglasse' (*CCM* 3, p. 285; Ó Laidhín, *State Papers*, p. 35). The eponymous hero of *The Famous History of Captain Stukeley* masters it within moments of landing. He parries Gainsford's announcement that the Irish 'haue a pray of Garrans cowes and sheepe' with a simultaneous translation: 'Hang cows and sheep, but haue among theyr horse / Ile loose this head but Ile haue hobbies from them' (lines 1078, 1080–1). The very different lexicon of exchange – greetings, courtesy titles, contact questions or items from more domestic spheres – is found nowhere in these texts.

If the colonial word-list did not lead the Elizabethans into contact with Irish-speakers, neither did it lead them into any rapport, however elementary, with Irish. Its systems escape them, semantically and phonetically; as they dealt only in individual words, the articulations of grammar did not concern them. Their glosses are often inaccurate, or wrong. Moryson defines 'glins'[14] as 'low shrubby places' (Morley, *Ireland under Elizabeth*, p. 423) while Camden confidently (mis)translates 'Surley-boy' ('fair-haired Sorley') as 'Surley the Redde' (*Annales*, p. 169). The process of signification is mysterious. When Perrott explains with scrupulous pedantry that Temple More is 'in the Irish Corke-a-Henny', he seems unaware that 'Temple More', too, is 'in the Irish' and that one does not mean the other (*Chronicle*, p. 158). He remains trapped within a closed circuit of anglicisations, unable to penetrate what either name might really signify.

RECONSTRUCTING THE ELIZABETHANS' EVALUATIONS
OF IRISH

Irish, I have suggested, occupied an uncertain place within the colonists' discourse of difference. It was not one of the principal terms thematised but it was impossible to anatomise – or anathematise – those elements that *were* without recourse to an Irish lexicon. Whether textually suppressed or retained only as a negatively inflected nomenclature, Irish sparked off judgemental evaluations. The Spanish were forthright in making Amerindian languages central to their discourse of difference. They moved from linguistic analysis to sign, using philology to judge native-speakers and their culture. In Ireland, the process worked in reverse. Lacking the scholarship – or even the rudimentary knowledge – that would have allowed them to take language as their point of departure, the English projected prejudices about Irish-speakers and their customs back on to Irish speech. In short, Irish was evaluated not as a language but as a sign.

The difference in approach is illustrated by the anonymous Spaniard who spent six months in Ireland as an adviser during the Desmond rebellion. His report for the Vatican on 'The Manners and Customs of the Irish' forthrightly includes language. He hazards an opinion on the genealogy and morphology of Irish, venturing that it had an affinity with Chaldaic and Hebrew and, more perspicaciously, that 'many of the letters are aspirated, whence it happens that the words seem different when written, and when pronounced' (Moran, *Catholic Archbishops*, p. 92). The philological cast of Spanish cultural analysis found little echo among Elizabethans in Ireland. Moryson's assessment of continental languages in the *Itinerary* is hamstrung by the inadequacy of his philology: instead of moving, in the style of Acosta, from an analysis of language to inferences about its speakers, he works in the opposite direction, projecting national stereotypes back on to language. So Italian is 'most proper for making of loue'; German, 'being an Imperious short and rude kynde of speech . . . would make our Children affrayd to heare it', its 'familyer speeches and pronuntiations sounding better in the mouth of Tamberlin, then of a Ciuill man' (*Shakespeare's Europe*, pp. 437, 322).

Such projections, when made in contexts of competition or conflict, were less exercises in philology than nationalist propaganda in a linguistic idiom; the rankings so established were determined in the domains of power and contest, not of grammar and lexicon. The pattern is illustrated by 'The Excellencie of the English Tongue', written by Lord President Carew's kinsman, Richard: the superficiality of its linguistics is matched only by the ardour of its patriotism. Carew set out to demonstrate the 'excellencie' of English under four categories, 'significancie, easinesse, copiousnesse, and sweetnesse' (p. 36). His categories seem to promise evaluations of pronunciation, lexicon and grammar in the Acostan manner. But no such analysis materialises. With his investigation pulled up short by a lackadaisical methodology and exiguous comparisons, Carew switches to a highly competitive discourse that vaunts English and swipes at its rivals in an argumentation that owes little to linguistics. With its 'w', English beats Greek, Latin, French and Italian hands-down for letters and, with 'moldwarp', for words capable of expressing 'the nature of that beast' (p. 38). English is easier to learn than its rivals which are 'loden . . . with declensions, flexions, and variations' (p. 39). Spanish is caricatured as 'running too much on the O, and terrible like the divell in a play' (p. 43). Militaristic metaphors give an edge to this linguistic jockeying. Some words – like 'Hedge water', which Carew imagines to be impossible for foreigners to pronounce – serve as defensive shibboleths, 'so that a stranger though never so long conversant amongst us, carrieth evermore a watch-word upon his tong to descrie him by'. Lexical borrowings get caught up in the cut and thrust of conquest and hostilities. The 'British' words surviving in English act like 'a continuall claime to their aunctient possession'. Loanwords are spoils of war. Englishmen should confidently deploy those taken from the 'late Spanish enemie': they need 'feare as little the hurt of his tongue as the dint of his sword' (pp. 40–1). Carew mentions Irish only once. Taking up the challenge implicit in Cicero's observation that the Greeks could not translate '*ineptus*', he crows that 'our abilitie extendeth thereunto'; Irish, in contrast, fails the test (p. 42; cf. Stanihurst, *Chronicle*, p. 18). When weighed against the dominance of an aggressively competitive discourse, the insubstantiality of Carew's only reference to Irish demonstrates that the adjudication of linguistic status was shaped by discourses that had little to do with philology.

Yet, despite the absence of any formal linguistic analysis on Spanish lines, a confident metropolitan deprecation of Irish was in place by the end of the period. It is there as a throwaway one-liner in Sharpham's *The Fleire* (written before 1608). The fallen gentlewoman,

Felecia, interviewing a prospective footmen, asks 'Have you the tongues?' 'Not very well Madam', he confesses. His advocate, the maid Fromaga, intervenes: 'Madam, he has the Scottish tongue verie perfectly, and has some skill in the Irish tongue'. 'Thats a wilde speech', retorts her mistress, dismissively (fo. B.3r). Dekker airily refers to 'the vnfruitful crabbed Irish' (*Wonderful Year*, p. 187) and, by 1614, Edward Brerewood could dismiss Irish, along with Albanian, Cossack, Hungarian, Finnish, Welsh and Biscay, as a language 'of less worth and dignity' (*Enquiries*, p. 250). In all cases, judgement is pronounced with the aplomb of a commonplace.

It follows from the evidence of the newcomers' failure to learn Irish that their judgement of it would be uncluttered by scholarship or knowledge. Moryson loftily declares that he knows no Irish and then suggests that ignorance is not so much a disqualification from judgement as a value-judgement in itself: 'Irish is a peculiar language, not derived from any other radical tongue (that ever I could hear, for myself neither have nor ever sought to have any skill therein).' Since, in this case, the verdict antecedes and preempts the need for evidence, he confines himself to recycling the misconception that Irish drew heavily on Spanish before complacently wrapping up his circular argument: 'But all I have said hereof might well be spared, as if no such tongue were in the world I think it would never be missed either for pleasure or necessity' (Falkiner, *Illustrations*, p. 317).

Spenser illustrates the same unembarrassed progression from incomprehension to evaluation. Despite his abstinence from Irish, Irenæus is confident that he can glean from 'reading' chronicles which he cannot understand 'a likelihood of truth', 'a probability of things'. In declaring that 'a well-eyed man may happily discover and find out' truths 'clouded' and 'disguised' by Irish chroniclers, he presumes that a clear-sighted English hermeneutics can triumph over the local inconvenience of incomprehension (*View*, pp. 39–40). That stance is subtly at variance with Campion's. Campion, too, positions himself as a reader of superior discrimination. But, revealingly, when commenting on Irish chronicles, he holds aloof from unqualified condemnation and makes judgement conditional on engaging with Irish:

Iryshe chronicles, all be they reported to be full freight of lewde examples, idle tales, and genealogies, *et quicquid Grecia mendax audet in historia*, yet concernyng the state of that wilde people, specially before the Conquest, I am perswaded that with choise and judgement I might have sucked thence some better store of matter, and gladly wold have sought them, had I fownd an interpretour, or understode their toungue. (*Two Bokes*, pp. 5–6)

But then, Campion's attitude to Irish differs subtly from that of his fellows – as indeed his position in Ireland did. A recusant, a scholar, guest of leading Palesmen and a non-combatant during a period of relative peace, his perspective is quite unlike that of those writing at the century's turbulent end. For all the limitations of his method (the most disabling being his ignorance of the language), he approaches Irish with scholarly inquisitiveness rather than instinctive denigration. Instead of automatically condemning its poets, he defers to the opinion of those qualified to judge: native 'bardes, and rimeres are said to delight passingly theise that conceive the grace and propietie of the tonge' (p. 18). Even while subjecting the mythical origins of Irish to sceptical review, he never questions the assumptions about the elegance of the language which underwrote them: Gathelus, ancestor of the Gaels, he reports, 'greatly perfected and beautifyed the Irishe tonge' (p. 33). Campion's openness to Irish reminds us of the force of ideological orientation in shaping – positively or negatively – newcomers' linguistic evaluations.

The Elizabethan writers evaluating Irish *without* Irish were thrown back on constructing a sign. Without the knowledge that would have licensed opinions about semantic adequacy or cognitive range, the English judged Irish not as a language but as an index of difference in a context of polarised conflict. Denied access to the language in its plenitude, they judged it through proxies: the colonial word-list, proper names, the perceived burden of Irish – and keening, which served as a metonym for Irish. I structure my examination of their responses to the para-language that provided their only contact with Irish around the categories used in chapter 1 to organise my analysis of Spanish evaluations of Amerindian languages. (I omit the 'grammar' category since, revealingly, no Elizabethan grappled with it.) Drawing their seemingly haphazard observations together under that taxonomy allows us to reconstruct the nature of their negative appraisal of Irish without seeking to impose that taxonomy on – or attributing it to – them.

Phonetics
When W. R. Jones reports that 'the various Celtic languages had, of course, always sounded uncouth and barbarous to French- and

Latin-speaking Englishmen', he is both recording a judgement and, with his normalising 'of course', reenacting it ('Celtic Fringe', p. 166). In fact, there are surprisingly few direct references to what Irish sounded like to Elizabethan ears, though Davies noted that 'all the Common people haue a whyning tune or Accent in their speech as if they did still smart or suffer some oppression' (*Discovery*, p. 176).[15] With words yielding no sense, the listener relied on acoustic impressions. Moryson moves from intoning the sept-names of Westmeath to pronouncing a verdict prompted by their sound: 'the O'Maddens, the MacGeoghegans, O'Mallaghans, and MacCoghlans, which seem barbarous names' – names, he proclaims elsewhere, more fit for 'Devowring Giants then Christian Subiects' (Morley, *Ireland under Elizabeth*, p. 417; *Shakespeare's Europe*, p. 195).

Incomprehension detached sound from sense, leaving Irish to be heard as a kind of noise rather than as a language. Judgements from sound were judgements by analogy – and the analogies selected captured the prejudices of the listener rather than the phonetics of the natives' language. They delivered judgement by association. Irish was consistently equated with bestial utterance – and, more specifically, with the metaphorically beastly dialect of the ungodly: of heathens, witches, papists. Rich recounts lodging in Limerick during the Desmond wars and waking one morning to hear his landlady and 'other ould Calyolies' make 'a loud noyse, strange and hideous to hearken to'. They 'houle and . . . hollow', to mark the anniversary of his hostess's husband's death. In likening her lamentation to 'the houling of dogges, to the croaking of Rauens, and to the shrieking of Owles, fitter for Infidels and Barbarians' (*Hubbub*, p. 4), he opens up possible comparisons between Irish – or its metonym, keening – and witchcraft. Not only was it imagined that Ireland 'aboundeth with witches' but the voices of the possessed were known to issue as the 'croaking of Frogges, hissing of Snakes, crowing of Cockes, barking of Dogges, garring of Crowes' (*CSPI* 1600–1, p. ix; Jorden, *Brief Discourse*, fo. B.2r). Rich makes the comparison explicit when comparing the sound of keening women to 'a company of *Hags* or *hellish Fiendes* . . . carrying a dead body to some infernall Mansion'; they seem more like 'Devils of Hell, then Christian people' (*New Description*, p. 12). Englishmen routinely referred to Irish women as 'callyaghes' ('hags', 'witches'). That ascription, which was of a piece with their inclination to regard native women's speech as particularly dangerous, demonstrates how the colonial context intensified male anxieties about a figure around whom their fears of losing control over women and language already clustered (cf. Ní Dhonnchadha, *Caillech*; Newman, *Fashioning Femininity*).

Lexicon

If the Indian languages were often judged to be semantically inadequate, words in Ireland were over-loaded, characterised not by deficiency but by an excess of meanings, almost all of them agonistic to English semantics. 'Borrowings' from Irish were detached from their linguistic matrix. Forced to testify against the culture from which they were plucked, their referents were colonial anathemas rather than Irish realities. It was on the basis of this specialist dictionary of native abuses that implicit semantic judgements about Irish were made. Definitions were slanted and distorted. 'Thamist' is 'he that hath shewed himselfe most valiant in all barbarous creweltie'; 'Dalonyes or horsboyes . . . are the very skumme, and outcaste of the cuntrye' (Dymmok, 'Treatice', pp. 6, 8). An unfailingly negative vocabulary fixes the hostile inflection: 'cuttings'[16] are usurpations 'whereby their odious and hatefull repinings, like a menstrous cloth, haue made their disobedience loathsome' (Gainsford, *Glory*, p. 149). The poet Aonghus Mac Doighri Í Dhálaigh was alert to the reductiveness with which the newcomers transposed meanings. In *Dia libh, a laochruidh Gaoidhiol* he complained that princes of the realm – 'ríoghradh Fhódla' – were now being traduced as 'woodkerns', 'ceithearn chúthail choilleadh' (Mac Airt, *Leabhar Branach*, p. 143: 9.4).

Within a discourse of difference, Irish invariably provides the negative term. Irish meanings are seen as inversions. The lexicon leads us not into a different world with its own meanings but one where meaning is simply deformed, where sweet is sour, where the natives 'esteem for a great dainty sour curds, vulgarly called by them Bonaclabbe' (Morley, *Ireland under Elizabeth*, p. 428); where their attempt at cleaning – 'their *Nettyng* (as they call it)' – is even 'more filthie' than the rest of their unsavoury practices (Rich, *New Description*, p. 26). By defining Irish words within a system of paired oppositions, the colonists unfailingly plot Irish meanings as deviations from the benchmark English norm. Similarly, the newcomers used etymology not as a way of exploring Irish meanings but as a way of domesticating their opacity and deprecating them. Etymologies were almost invariably false: puns which played with languages other than

Irish foisted disparaging meanings on to the anglicised husks of Irish words. Pointing out that 'that fatal kingdom' was once called *Banno*, Spenser ignores its Irish meaning – '*oileán beannaithe*', 'blessed isle' – elaborately arguing instead that it 'was not called amiss *Banno* or *Sacra Insula*, taking *sacra* for *accursed*' (*View*, p. 92; cp. *FQ* vi.37.7). When Derricke sought to mock the Mac Suibhne, he used the graceless transliteration, the 'Macke Swine', to open the way for a word-play that operates within an English semiosis: 'a barbarous ofspringe, come from that Nation, whiche maie bee perceiued by their Hoggishe fashion' (*Image*, p. 11). In the early seventeenth century, when Céitinn set about unpicking the claims of the 'proim-piollâin doghníd', the dung-beetle propagandists, he relied heavily on restoring right meanings to set the record straight, tersely reiterating 'ní hionann': it does not mean; it is not the same. So with 'Macke Swine', he insists 'ní hionann "Suyn" agus Suibhne' (Swine is not the same as Suibhne) (*Foras Feasa*, p. 26). Only Stanihurst had enough bilingual contacts to derive his false etymologies from Irish. He insists, on the word of 'noble men of deepe iugement' that 'Kerne' means 'a shower of hell' (*Chronicle*, p. 114). The substitution of '*cith ifrinn*' for '*ceithearnach*' is clever, plausible and wrong (Harrison, 'Shower', p. 304). Coached by a compliant local, however, the English could bend Irish meanings to stake spurious claims. Capturing Donegal town, Sidney was pleased to avail himself of a tweaked etymology to confirm his possession linguistically: 'Donegal is to say the English town' (*JRHAAI* I, p. 22); *Dún na nGall*, 'the fort of the foreigners', is less specific in its ascription of ownership. The native poets were alert to the dangerous slippage between mistranslating and translating ownership. In *A dhúin atá it éanar*, 'O Castle that's Alone', Miles Mac An Bhaird explained that Hugh O'Donnell chose to demolish his castle in Donegal rather than have it called '*Dún na nGall ribh dáríribh*' ('Fort of the Foreigners in earnest') (De Blácam, *Gaelic Literature*, p. 144).

Cognitive range

Irish, therefore, is seen as providing a linguistic haven for customs and attitudes inimical to English values. The Elizabethans fretted about what went on in the dark corners where their 'peering eyes' could not probe. They had a horror of masks and veils; they abhorred 'glibs' and the capacious mantle which provided a 'cov-erlet' for rebels and loose women alike (Spenser, *View*, p. 53). In the same way, Irish was feared for what went on behind its screen, in the linguistic fastness never breached by the colonists. Their very incomprehension intensified Elizabethans' anxieties about the mental habits of the perplexing natives. A major strand of their evaluation, therefore, focused not on the language itself but on the communicative practices of its speakers in a manner that recalls the Spaniards' attention to the 'cognitive range' of Indian languages – though, of course, English newcomers expended no comparable philological effort in identifying the connection between the contours of Irish and the lines of thought which it promoted among its speakers. Spenser goes furthest in explicitly arguing that a language shaped specific attitudes and inclinations. Children at the breast

draw into themselves together with their suck, even the nature and disposition of their nurses, for the mind followeth much the temperature of the body; and also the words are the image of the mind, so as they proceeding from the mind, the mind must be needs effected with the words; so that the speech being Irish, the heart must needs be Irish, for out of the abundance of the heart, the tongue speaketh. (*View*, p. 68)

The Spaniards' dissection of the Indians' languages encouraged them to see the natives as simple and childlike. Working in the opposite direction, Englishmen moved from diagnosing the 'disposition' of the Irish to projecting analogous characteristics on to their language. Campion's aphorismical encapsulation of Irish, in stressing its quicksilver quality, reflected the newcomers' sense that its speakers were congenital manipulators of language: 'the tongue is sharpe and sententious, offerethe great occasion to quicke apopthegemes and proper allusions' (*Two Bokes*, pp. 17–18). Mathew de Renzy, the German-born merchant who settled in King's County under James I, set about learning Irish with a doggedness not met among the Elizabethans (Mac Cuarta, 'Mac Bruaideadha'). Judging Irish from the inside, he arrived at the same conclusions which intuitive suspicion had brought them. His letters – larded with idiomatic expressions and scraps of verse in an Irish which he handles with pedantic delicacy – testify to a scholarly mesmerism. But perhaps the very beguilement which he himself evinced alerted him to the dangerous allure of Irish. He urged that the natives be kept from learning to read or write it,

for as long as that is currant amongst them they will ever be shrewder and more suttler then the Englisch that comes out of England . . . so much [difference] there is betweene the Englisch and Irisch as onely have their mother's tongue, whereof the churles gives good testimonie.

He warned, too, against allowing the natives to study logic: it would teach them 'to make suttill and craftie questions and thereby to lerne to defend the black cro to be white, whereof their owne language teaches them ynogh' (Mac Cuarta, 'Letters', pp. 141, 147).

The Elizabethans, however, unable to defend their intuitions philologically, responded not to any intrinsic qualities or defects in the language but simply to the obdurate fact of its existence: its otherness betokened difference and an identity resistant to assimilation. It was not Irish that offended but the use of Irish; the distinction is not facetious. Stanihurst, always conscious, as his English contemporaries were not, of being in implicit dialogue – or dispute – with potential Irish readers, carefully distinguishes between the quiddity of Irish and the political implications of using it:

Now put the case that the Irishe tongue were as sacred as the Hebrewe, as learned as the Greeke, as fluent as the Latin, as amarous as the Italian, as courtious as the Hispanish, as courtelike as the French, yet truely (I know not which way it falleth out) I see not, but it may be very well spared in the Englishe pale. (*Chronicle*, p. 16)

The 'Irish' conjured up by the Elizabethans, uncomprehended, detached from philological reality, was less a language than the dissidence and contrariness which it encoded. To speak Irish – or not to speak English – is seen less as a linguistic fact than as a symbolic option, 'these outward signes being the tuchstones of the inward affection'. Irish is regarded more as a perversity than a language, another of those 'absurd thinges practised by them only because they would be contrary to vs' (Moryson, *Shakespeare's Europe*, p. 214). When deploring the earlier colonists' adoption of Irish, Moryson lines it up, alongside Irish horsewomen's incorrigible preference for riding, as Spenser had it, 'on the wrong side of the horse' (*View*, p. 61) – facing the man's right arm (the norm consecrated by English practice being left-facing) – as one more item on the negative column of a bipartite list which confirms that 'they abhorr from all thinges that agree with English Ciuility' (Moryson, *Shakespeare's Europe*, p. 214). The English were unable to argue the case linguistically that Irish was an uncivil tongue. Only Stanihurst, with his insider–outsider perspective, even hints at a philological basis for arguing that Irish lacked decorum. He contrasts Irish usage, which puts the speaker first – 'as I and Oneyle . . . I & my maister', with 'the curtesie of the English language' in placing the speaker last (*Chronicle*, p. 112). But all were agreed that Irish was both the medium of dissident Gaelic culture and the mechanism that acculturated non-Gaels to political and religious dissent.

Irish became synonymous with the political and religious dissidence to which it gave voice. It was the rebel's tongue. Rory Shihi's 'insolent letter' to Sir Thomas Norris threatening to 'Burne Spoyle kill and hang as manye of your Contryemen as I can' (PRO SP 63/195/15.i) prompted Norris to warn Cecil that 'there are verie fewe, eyther in Cytte, or Cuntrey, that can speake Ierishe, that are muche better affected' (PRO SP 63/195/15). Nicholas Dawtrey's counsel against drafting Scottish soldiers for the Irish wars rested on a conviction that linguistic and political allegiances were coextensive: 'hardly . . . can [the two peoples] be sepperated . . . because they haue all one language' ('A booke', p. 125). In similar vein, Tom Lee advised that only English-speakers be allowed to bear arms (Morgan, 'Lee', p. 155).

As well as seeing Irish as the rebels' tongue, the Elizabethans were moving towards a new sectarian identification between Irish and Catholicism. If Amerindian languages were 'pagan tongues', Irish was increasingly regarded as a papist one. While the Spanish derived their judgement philologically, the English, unable to penetrate beyond the surface of Irish, extrapolated rather from its freight. Its cargo was recusancy and the conflation of medium and message is captured in Burghley's quip to Ormond, '[s]o as now merely I must say Butlaraboo against all that cry, as I hear, *in a new language*, Papeaboo'[17] (*CCM* 4, p. xix; my emphasis). With papists refusing to 'speak, or so much as vnderstand a word of *English*', Rich warns, the old maxim will hold true 'that ten *English* wil sooner become *Irish*, then one *Irish* will be found to turne *English*' (*New Description*, p. 34). The newcomers, restricted to projecting native transgressions on to the oblique surface of an impenetrable tongue, were unconcerned with demonstrating philologically that Irish was intrinsically a 'papist' or a 'degenerate' tongue. But they knew that it was the tongue used by rebels, papists and degenerates.

The nub of English disquiet about Irish lay in this conjunction of language and identity. If Irish was suspect, it was so not for internal deficiencies of the kind imputed to American languages by the Spanish. Irish was not just an alterity that was distasteful, barbarous but safely other. Rather, its otherness was transgressive and contagious and threatened the colonial self with defilement and transformation.[18] Defection was performed through a highly charged act of translation. That is why the Elizabethans were most exercised by Irish when it was spoken, not by its natural constituency, the Gaels, but by their own *alter egos*, the 'English Irish' who, as the shifting order of the epithet registered, were turning inexorably into the 'Irish English' (Moryson, *Shakespeare's Europe*, p. 213). The attention which English commentators paid to Irish when spoken by such 'degenerates' is in marked contrast to their neglect of it otherwise. If an Irish-speaking Gael was almost too tautological to merit attention, an English hibernophone was too vexing and unnatural to escape comment. While Moryson's description of the 'meere Irish' occupies only seven pages and is largely a rehearsal of topoi undisturbed by fresh insight, he vents eleven pages on the mistrusted English Irish (*Irish Sections*, pp. 34–51). The imbalance is telling. The natives are so inexplicable – on the far side of linguistic as well as cultural barriers – that they can be reached only through clichés and formulae. The colonists *gone* native, however, are still accessible and, in reflecting a disfigured image of self, more immediately troubling. If Irish in the mouth of a Gael could be half-ignored as background noise, its insinuation into mouths putatively 'English' was altogether more alarming. It was a warning that identity was far from assured and that language was an agent of that instability. The author of 'A Discourse of Ireland' cites the 'proverb', 'English in the second generation becomes Irish but never English', to illustrate the pressure on the newcomers to be 'meere Irish with them in language apparell and manners' (Quinn, 'Discourse', p. 164).

Transformation is an Elizabethan preoccupation. In the Dedication of his 'A Treatice of Ireland', Dymmok assures his patron, Sir Edmund Carye, that he 'doe . . . reteine the power to transforme my selfe into any lykeness that you shall deuise'. Tom Lee who diced, on more than one occasion, with intimacies on the borderline between confrontation and collaboration, was alert to the ambivalence of his role. Gheeraerts's portrait depicts him barelegged below his magnificent shirt and doublet, half-Elizabethan, half – 'down from the waist' – kerne (De Breffny, 'Political Painting', p. 40). The danger, however, was that self-fashioning could tilt over into transformation – and, in a colonial context, transformation meant degeneration.

As the gulf between the Old and the New English widened,

language became caught up in the polarisation. For the newcomers, the old colonists' attachment to Irish confirmed their unreliability. Herbert condemned them for forgetting not only their ancestral institutions and their nature but even their '*loquendi modo*' (*Croftus*, p. 82). For Eudoxus, it was 'unnatural that any people should love another's language more than their own' (Spenser, *View*, p. 65). So synonymous was 'Irish' with 'degeneration' that when Gerrard complains that the 'Englishe degenerates . . . speake Irishe, use Irishe habitt, feadinge, rydinge, spendinge, *coysheringe, coyninge*', his phrasing perforce follows their degenerative drift from an English to an Irish lexicon (p. 96; my emphasis). Herein lay the administration's most immediate problem with Irish. It was the medium which had brought once 'parfet Englisshemen' to loll in various degrees of degeneration, 'waxing Irishe' or 'nowe veary Irishe' or 'nowe very wilde Irishe' (Campion, *Two Bokes*, p. 14). Campion warned that those who came too close to the Irish 'are transformed into them'. Being conversant elided into being converted: 'the veary Englishe of birthe conversant with the brutishe sorte of that people become degenerate in short space and are quite altered into the worst ranke of Irishe rooges' (p. 20). Stanihurst integrated parts of Campion's 'History' into his 'A Description of Ireland'. In reworking the passage just quoted, he added a significant comparison: 'the very English of birth, conuersant with the sauage sort of that people become degenerate, & *as though they had tasted of Circes poysoned cup*, are quite altered' (*Chronicle*, p. 115).[19]

Davies, whose *Discovery of the True Causes why Ireland was never entirely Subdued* is haunted by the spectre of 'alterage' (p. 185), amplified the Circean comparison. All previous attempts at conquest, Davies held, had been reversed as colonists 'became degenerate and meer Irish in their language, in their apparrell, in their armes and maner of fight, & all other Customes of life whatsoeuer' (p. 30). 'The game at Irish'[20] is his byword for such alterations: 'Then the estate of things, *like a Game at Irish*, was so turned about, as the English, which hoped to make a perfect conquest of the Irish, were by them perfectly and absolutely conquered' (p. 164). Transformation is indissociable from the loss of (the English) language and a consequent descent towards bestiality: 'they became degenerate and metamorphosed like Nebuchadnezzar: who although he had the face of a man, had the heart of a Beast; or like those who had drunke of *Circes* Cuppe and were turned into Beastes', so the Old English had no markes or differences left amongst them of that Noble nation, from which they were descended. For, as they did not only forget the English language, and scorne the use thereof, but grew to be ashamed of their very English Names, though they were noble and of great Antiquity; and tooke Irish *Surnames* and *Nicke-names*. (p. 82)

In evoking the Circean comparison, Stanihurst and Davies were forcing rhetorical connections between language, degeneration and the feminine. So frequently are women identified as the agents of degeneration that the language, at times, comes to be typed as feminine (Carroll, 'Representations', p. 381). As wives and wetnurses, women were seen as the agents of miscegenation. Mountjoy ascribed the decay of 'one of the goodliest provinces of the world' to the original colonists' 'matching' with the natives and adopting their language (*CSPI* 1600–1, pp. 251–2). It is hardly coincidental that the Blatant Beast, whose defining characteristic is his 'vile tongue', should share the very defects of breeding that had led the Old English to Irish: 'fowle commixture' and long fostering (*FQ* vi.i.8.3–4). Nowhere was the feminising of Irish more flagrant than in the way in which it was consistently figured as a mamillarily transmitted infection. Hybridity prompted an oral anxiety that conflated the lactic with the linguistic. In England, William Kempe had directed parents to expose their children only to 'ciuill language' and warned them against engaging 'barbarous nursses', among whom he included the Irish (*Education*, fo. E.4v–5r). Inevitably, therefore, Elyot's injunction that 'children, from their norises pappes, are to be kepte diligently from the herynge or seynge of any vice or euyl tache' (*The Gouenour*, p. 31) acquired particular cultural urgency in Ireland. The literalness with which Spenser imagined language and mental disposition to be imbibed with Irish nurses' milk placed the natives' tongue within the domain of dangerous women (*View*, pp. 67–8). The author of 'The Supplication of the Blood of the English' agreed: the Old English 'suckte theire conditions from the teats of their Irishe Nurses', changing them 'from Englishe which they sounde in name, to Irishe . . . from men to monsters' (Maley, p. 33). In Ireland, Circe turned wetnurse.

As ever, proper nouns provided the monophone's main point of contact with Irish and Gaelicised names came to symbolise the wider linguistic defection of the Old English. In representing two discrete stages in their drift from the metropolis as one – they 'cast off their English names *and* allegiances' – *A View of the Present State of Ireland* implies that the two are inseparable (p. 65; my emphasis). Translation of proper names, the linguistic guarantors of identity, was a signal treason. Moryson is appalled that 'old English Familyes degenerating into this Barbarisme, haue changed their names after the Irish tongue' (*Shakespeare's Europe*, p. 195). The emblematic quality of the traduction became focused on those nimble name-changers, the FitzUrsus, villains in a moral fable of degenerative translation end-lessly retold. Campion introduces the 'Fitzursulies, nowe degenerate and called in Irishe MacMahon ie. the beares sonne' (*Two Bokes*, p. 14). Dymmok repeats the story of how the progeny of 'Gerald Fitzursus or Bearsonne' turned mere Irish, 'calling themselves mac Mahons which signifieth the sonne of a beare, mahon[21] in Irish being a beare' ('Treatice', p. 23). Spenser, Moryson and the anony-mous author of *The Description of Ireland* who, even by the standards of his contemporaries, seems particularly oblivious to language, all reheat the old chestnut (*View*, p. 64; Moryson, *Shakespeare's Europe*, p. 195; Hogan, *Description*, p. 23). That the defection symbolised by these archetypal linguistic turncoats had never happened – a scornful Céitinn demonstrated that all the indignation had its origin in a false etymology (*Foras Feasa*, p. 26) – is incidental.

In a piece of special pleading, an anonymous – but probably Old English – author vouched for the Palesmen's continuing loyalty by claiming that they had retained their linguistic 'marks of difference'. He contended that the English of blood 'still retain all the marks of their original . . . viz. their names, surnames, language', in counter-distinction to the Irish, of whom

none, with his good-will, will be called Henry, Edward, Richard, George, Francis, or such like English names, but rather Morrogh, Moriertagh, Tirlogh, and such harsh names, both for a difference to distinguish them from the English, and as a mark of their offspring. (*CSPI* 1598–9, pp. 440–1)

But, as the newcomers knew, even English names could no longer guarantee identity. Many of those 'retayning their old names' like Tyrrell, Lacy and Burke proved rebels at heart. Such experience taught a bitter lesson about permitting colonists to father children 'of mingled race'. When Mountjoy turned to designing colonies at the end of the war, he was so anxious to protect future settlers from contamination that he took as much care to keep them from 'mixing' as 'if these newe Colonyes were to be ledd to inhabitt among the barbarous Indians' (Moryson, *Shakespeare's Europe*, pp. 203, 212, 249).

Writing

In a contest between languages played by European rules which
prized alphabetical literacy and ranked languages accordingly,
Amerindian glyphs – whose sophistication Europeans chose for
centuries to ignore (Coe, *Maya Code*) – handed the Spaniards a
walkover. Irish, with its venerable literary tradition, could not be
relegated so easily. William Daniel reminded his patron, Chichester,
that the letters used in his translation of the *Book of Common Prayer*
were the very ones that the Irish had once taught 'the neighbour
Saxons' (Dedic., 1608) – as Florence MacCarthy and Seathrún
Céitinn also enjoyed pointing out (O'Donovan, 'Letter', p. 228; *Foras
Feasa*, p. 68). The inconvenient reality that Ireland possessed a highly
regulated written language forced Hart into paradox and contra-
diction when, in *An Orthographie*, he attempted a cautious equation
between English and Latin, on the one hand, and the Celtic
languages and barbarous tongues on the other. He recalled that the
Romans had required their subject peoples to use Latin

rather than to be driuen to learne the foren and vnruled maner of speach
and writing, which they termed barbarous, as we, the French, and others,
doe account the Welsh and Irish tongues: In whose maner of writings,
peraduenture there is better order kept, than anye of vs aforesayd doe
(fo. 7r).

There was, nonetheless, a persistent downgrading of Irish as a
written language. Eudoxus articulated the metropolitan disparagement of the 'savage nation's' own records as worthless when he
dismissed 'those Irish chronicles, which are most fabulous and forged
. . . specially having been always without letters, but only bare
traditions of times and remembrances of bards' (*View*, p. 39).
Eudoxus was voicing a common metropolitan misconception.[22]
Though Irenæus might set him straight – 'it is certain that Ireland
hath had the use of letters very anciently, and long before England' –
Spenser allowed Eudoxus' retort, 'How comes it then that they are
so barbarous still and so unlearned, being so old scholars?', to close
the discussion (p. 40). An easier way of detaching Irish from true
literacy was to make a sophistical equation between writing and
printing – and between meaningful literacy and certain privileged
genres, as Rich did. Whereas once Giraldus Cambrensis had imagined an Irish illuminated manuscript to be the work of angels
(*Topography*, p. 84), Rich could argue that the Irish were trained only
'in brutish beastliness' by being 'bæreued of one of the greatest

benefites, that giueth light & vnderstanding, which is by reading of *histories*':

they haue no maner of Bookes, neither yet the vse of printing: so that for them there is no meane either to learne ciuilitie or good order: but by the example of vs that be Englishe, whome naturally they doe hate. (*Allarme*, fo. D.iii.r–v; my emphasis)

When associated with Irish, literacy became detached from the civil qualities which it was conventionally held to embody. Campion resolved the inconvenient paradox that a people systematically constructed as barbarian possessed a culturally approved index of civility by reproducing a gesture ever second nature to colonists and travellers: a readiness to concede virtue to ancestors that is withheld from the (degenerate) present generation. So he implies that the finest Irish is a thing of the past: 'But the trewe Irishe indeede differethe so muche from that they comonly speake that scarce one in five schore cane either wright, reade, or understande' the learned Irish of the poets. The venerable language is now the preserve only of certain poets 'and other studentes of antiquity' (*Two Bokes*, p. 18).

Genealogy

Little common sense – and less knowledge – was brought to the task of establishing the relationship between Irish and other languages. James Perrott's shrewd empiricism in suggesting that its vocabulary has 'much affinitie with the Walsh or British' was unusual. He pointed out that both shared the words for 'noase, hand, eie, legge and the lyke'. This, he concluded, 'makes some shew that the nations were originally the same, or else had much commixture by commerce, mariage, or mutuall ayde' (*Chronicle*, p. 19). Most speculation, however, was conducted far from real language. Stanihurst relied on a superficial similarity between 'Commestato'[23] and '*como estás*' to find something of the 'Hispanish' in the Irish greeting (*Chronicle*, p. 18). Most fanciful was Spenser's strained attempt to posit a Carthaginian root for 'MacCarthy': 'Mac, signifiethe a sonne: and Carthaye beeinge almoste verie Carthage: for y: and g: ar in moste languages changable letters' (*View*, p. 198). The obsessively genealogical bent of Gaelic scholarship had long before invented a post-Babelian lineage for Irish to demonstrate its perfection. The seventh-century grammarians whose *Auraicept na n-Éces* upheld their vernacular against the claims of Latin had daringly argued that their tongue alone had overcome the confusion of Babel: Fenius, grand-father of Gathelus, had fabricated it from the finest elements of the seventy-two languages spawned by the confusion. In consequence, no language surpassed it, '[a]r a cuibdi, ar a edruma, ar a mine 7 a forleithiu' (for its aptness, lightness, smoothness and breath) (George Calder, *Auraicept*, pp. 22, 4). This testimony to old linguistic vanities was now press-ganged by the newcomers into bearing false witness to the legitimacy of English claims.[24] The elaborate native genealogy was raided to fabricate pseudo-British antecedents who could be used to substantiate England's historical right to Ireland.

Circumventing its linguistic vaunts, the Elizabethans reinterpreted the genealogy to fix Irish with both a taint (it was barbarian . . .) and a claim (. . . but recuperably British). Genealogies were used throughout sixteenth-century Europe to legitimise '*des prétentions impérialistes*' (Dubois, *Mythe*, p. 86). Apologists of conquest were quick to pin down genealogical hints (Hadfield, 'Briton and Scythian'). Campion accepts that Gathelus introduced Irish but dismisses the 'vaine and fryvolus' chroniclers' notion that he 'and after hym Symon Brecke dyvised theire language owt of all other tongues then extant in the worlde'. Rather, he argues, a language takes shape 'not by invention of arte but by use of talke'. This leads him to surmise that – 'seeing Ireland was inhabited within one yeare after the devision of the tongues' – the language brought was 'one of 72 languages in the confusion of Babell' which drew on elements of 'the Scithians, Grecians, Aegiptians, Spaniardes, Danes . . . but specially retayning the stepes of Spanishe then spoken in Granado'. Campion, following Geoffrey of Monmouth and Gerald of Wales, is careful to slip in proof of England's 'invincible tytell' to Ireland by giving a Briton, Gurguntius, a place in the genealogy. Though Gurguntius himself had failed to conquer Ireland, he sponsored the first Irish colony when he 'seated' some Spaniards there: 'Thus had the Britaines an elder right to the realme of Ireland then by the conquest of Henrye the Seconde' (*Two Bokes*, pp. 17, 33–5). Meredith Hanmer's philology, too, is driven by colonial imperatives. He declares the 'British' words in Irish 'infinite' and ascribes their presence, in part, to the Welshmen in Henry II's conquest 'that brake the ice into this land' (Ware, *Antiquities* II, pp. 21, 19).

Camden, who draws on Campion, tries, in a syllogistic sleight of hand that plays on the shifting significance of 'British', to co-opt the genealogy of Irish to naturalise English claims to Ireland. He first represents similarities between the two Celtic languages as borrowings which cast Irish as a subsidiary derivative from an originary Welsh – 'vast numbers of British words . . . are to be met with in the Irish tongue'. Having set up the rickety proposition that Irish is 'British', it only requires a sturdy disregard for precision to arrive at the conclusion that Ireland, too, is British. Camden attempts to shuffle 'British' from a linguistic to a territorial signification by asserting that 'the ancients regarded Ireland as a British island'. That done, the path to colonisation is cleared: 'no country is more conveniently placed to transplant People into' (*Britannia*, pp. 1,314–15).

Spenser, who drew on both Campion and Camden in writing *A View*, engaged in even more daring acrobatics by attempting to establish that Irish was both barbarous – and British. Taking up Campion's hint of a Scythian element in Irish, Spenser finds its trace in native battlecries and keening, 'which savour greatly of Scythian barbarism' (pp. 55–6). There are even more Gaulish words 're-maining and yet daily used in common speach' (p. 45). But if the Gaulish connection can be used to explain enduring barbarisms like blood-drinking (p. 62), it can also establish a claim to title. Spenser grounded England's right to rule Ireland in Geoffrey of Monmouth's assertion that the island had already been conquered by ancient Britons. To find 'British' words fossilised in Irish, therefore, was to find a linguistic bedrock for that claim. So Spenser backs his contention that Gurgunt and after King Arthur 'had all that island in his allegiance and subjection' (p. 46) with the observation that 'the Gaulish speech is the very British'. Claiming that the O'Tooles, O'Byrnes and Kavanaghs are remnants of old British settlers, he relies on a combination of false etymology and incorrect Welsh glosses to advance the 'British' claim: he explains that 'O'Byrne' comes from 'the British word brin, that is woody'. Even more daringly – though equally unfoundedly – he argues that many Saxons settled in Ireland as can 'bee gathered by verie manie wordes of Irish beeinge almost mere Saxon: as for example Marh in Saxon is a horse, marrah in Iryshe is a horseman'[25] (p. 197; cf. O'Donovan, 'Errors'). Céitinn was alert to the broader colonial agenda served by such false glosses. His dismissal of Spenser's etymologies as 'breugach', deceitful, forms part of his wider refutation of England's pseudo-historical claims to Ireland (*Foras Feasa*, p. 28). Spenser would have understood that much at least: he uses that word, correctly glossed, in the *Mutability Cantos*: 'false *Bregog*' (*FQ* VI.40.4).

The House of Temperance episode in the *Faerie Queene* provides an oblique coda to Spenser's contemplation of genealogy, language change and the closely associated issue of degeneration. Alma's fleshy dwelling is constructed from matter similar to 'that *Ægyptian* slime, / Whereof King *Nine* whilome built *Babell* towre' (*FQ* II.ix.21.5–6). The vulnerable structure is assailed by Malegar – whom Jenkins argues is modelled on Shane O'Neill ('Spenser and Ireland', p. 132) – and his kerne-like 'vile caytiue wretches, ragged, rude, deformd' with their signature 'stiffe vpstanding heares' (II.ix.13.4, 9). Even more characteristic is their 'outrageous dreadfull yelling cry' (xi.17.9): these linguistic raiders on corporeal Babel are themselves degenerate and agents of degeneration. The compilers of *Auraicept na n-Éces* had imagined Fenius and his artificers fashioning the eight parts of Irish speech from '*nai n-adhbair in tuir Nemruaidh*', the nine materials of Nimrod's tower: clay, water, wool, blood, wood, lime, flax, acacia and bitumen (Calder, p. 22). The seventh-century grammarians stretched pedantry and dazzling philological inventiveness to breaking point in their quest to demonstrate the 'excellencie' of Irish. The Elizabethans, bringing to their encounter with Irish only a mouthful of negatively glossed mispronunciations, had no interest even in testing such claims. In Spenser's reworking of the allegory, Fenius's triumph over Babel, in constructing one perfect language from its ruins, is effortlessly inverted as his heirs are transformed into the agents of the tower's destruction.

When examining the paradigm shift in the way Renaissance linguists understood the link between language and thought, I suggested that comparative linguistics would challenge the traditional referential model. The Elizabethans' encounter with the recalcitrant difference of Irish and their exposure to the awkward non-alignment between its systems of meanings and theirs can only have destabilised their confidence in the anchored connection between word and thing. Writing the last books of *The Faerie Queene* in Kilcolman Castle, watching the meanings of his allegory ramify and escape his intentions, Spenser was coming to the dark realisation that language and meaning were not coextensive, that all the poet's art could not reliably indenture signifiers to a fixed signification. His own work was demonstrating that the bond which he had imagined as securing word to thing was illusory. Far from faithfully transcribing an a priori reality, language was, like Malengin, protean. That, too, was the realisation which the Elizabethans were stumbling towards from their brush with linguistic alterity in Ireland. The other's tongue did not simply translate uncontested universal verities; it conjured incommensurable meanings of its own into being. Such was the unsettling and perhaps ultimately enabling lesson that the new-comers stood to learn from their haphazard Irish experiment in comparative linguistics.

CHAPTER 4

'Translating this kingdom of the new': English linguistic nationalism and anglicisation policy in Ireland

What worthier thyng can there bee, then with a woorde to winne Cities, and whole countries.

Thomas Wilson, *The Arte of Rhetorique*, fo. A.ii.r

To judge a language in a time of conquest was an act of criticism with practical implications. Newcomers' impressions of Irish shaped their language policies. With cultural difference mapping political difference so precisely, a language regarded as housing dissent and querulous diversity could not escape the attentions of those advancing Tudor centralisation and uniformity. Irish was popish; it was the agent of an invasive otherness which had derailed the cultural integrity of the original colony; it hung as a threat over the identity of the new settlers. With the boundaries between medium and message blurred, silencing dissent shaded into silencing Irish. In the affairs of language, however, 'silence' is a purely notional state: in reality, not to speak Irish meant to speak English.

For English language policy was far from being purely defensive. Just as the newcomers' desire to gag the carping vernacular was grounded in negative evaluations of Irish, so their inclination to impose their own language rested on a chauvinistic estimation of English. This double movement, which combined an indolent deprecation of Irish with a burgeoning confidence in English, brings us close to the nub of Elizabethan cultural nationalism and the linguistic imperialism which flowed from it.

THE NEWCOMERS' ATTITUDES TO ENGLISH

Linguistic nationalism

There is an almost unspoken assumption that those setting out from Shakespeare's England on voyages of discovery and conquest travelled buoyed up with a cultural confidence that sprang, in part, from the linguistic excitement of their age (Calder, *Revolutionary Empire*, p. 21).[1] That assumption, however, is questioned by Armitage. He contends that the link between empire and literature celebrated by imperial historians and deplored by postcolonial critics came into being only in the nineteenth century 'with the rise of linguistic nationalism'. Far from Elizabethan literature gaining energy from the quickened pace of overseas expansion, he argues, 'the horizons of most Elizabethans remained firmly fixed on the Three Kingdoms' ('Literature and Empire', pp. 100–1). Armitage's argument rests on forcing a distinction between Ireland seen, in a recycling of the 'internal colonisation' hypothesis, as a domestic matter, and 'overseas' imperialism in America. Yet, it was precisely the disputed nature of Ireland's status that lay behind the Nine Years War; as the international dimension of that conflict and the radicalism of the plantations which followed it demonstrated, Ireland was not a straightforwardly 'internal' matter. Moreover, it was in Ireland, England's first colony, that linguistic nationalism gathered pace in a way in which Armitage seems keen to deny.

D. B. Quinn suggests that 'the English attitude to Welsh and Scots and Irish had in it a good measure of national pride. It is not easy to analyze its constituents. It has much to do with the ascendancy of the English language' (*Elizabethans and Irish*, p. 7). The strangely halting phrasing which leads to Quinn's dangling assertion indicates his difficulty in following up his hunch. Language certainly had something 'to do with' the Elizabethan adventure in Ireland and its long aftermath. What is surprising is how much. Newcomers' engagement with their own language is in marked contrast to their inattention to Irish. Some of the key figures in the Irish conquest combined a preoccupation with expanding England's interests overseas with an interest in expanding *English* – both linguistically, by securing its place among the leading European languages, and geographically. Moreover, ties of patronage and intellectual kinship linked such men with those promoting the language in a less hand-to-hand fashion back in England. This striking synchronism of all-too-literal military offensives with literary 'Defences' confirms that an alertness to the claims of English helped to shape the colonial mindset. In Ireland, Gosson's injunction that 'the word and the sword be knitte together' came alive (*Schoole*, fo. 34v).

The relationship between linguistic sentiment and Elizabethan nationalism is complex. Insecurity jostled with linguistic ambition in shaping the Elizabethans' edgy assertiveness. Moryson's prickly defensiveness encapsulates those conflicting sentiments:

they are confuted, who traduce the English tounge to be like a beggers patched Cloke, which they should rather compayre to a Posey of sweetest flowers, because by the sayd meanes, it hath beene in late ages excellently refyned and made perfitt for ready and breefe deliuery both in prose and verse. (*Shakespeare's Europe*, pp. 437–8)

'The ascendancy of the English language' was less an achievement than an aspiration. It was not so much, *pace* Quinn, that linguistic confidence bolstered expansionist inclinations; rather, that the tentative stirrings of both linguistic and colonial ambitions worked together to build mutually enforcing chauvinisms. Writer-colonists are not anomalous but exemplary figures: military and linguistic muscle flexed as one to a remarkable degree. Nor is the coincidence of these two distinct expressions of a burgeoning nationalist consciousness purely adventitious. The movement from one to the other simply represents a switch in idiom – from the militaristic to the linguistic – within the common 'discourse of nationhood'. There is an unmistakable unity of purpose, for instance, between Humphrey Gilbert's military and intellectual endeavours. In 1579, he quelled rebellion in Munster with calculated savagery; a year later, he completed *Queene Elizabethes Achademy* which argued for the establishment of a London variant of Oxbridge. Gilbert envisaged the 'Achademy' as a forcing-house of 'Ciuill' and 'Martiall pollicy' (p. 3), combining training in navigation, mapping, artillery, 'Skirmishinges, Imbattelinges, and sondery kindes of marchinges' (p. 5) with a new emphasis on the vernacular. He proposed that students' oratorical training be grounded in English, not Latin, and modelled on John Cheke's exercises, so that 'ornament will thereby growe to our tongue' (p. 2). His curriculum proposals privileged English – 'phisick' should be taught 'in the Englishe toung' (p. 5) – and he identified translation as a means of consolidating the vernacular: each language teacher should 'printe some Translation into the English tongue of some good worke' every three years (p. 9). While Gilbert's mentor, Cheke, stayed at home doughtily defending the vernacular against foreign incursions – keeping it 'vnmixte and vnmangled with borrowing of other tunges' (Donawerth, *Shakespeare*, p. 36) – his son pressed expansionist claims abroad, losing his life at the siege of Smerwick.

The promotion of empire and language were linked: they were not just unrelated manifestations of that notably mystificatory concept, 'Renaissance versatility'. The fact that so many of the leading translators of the age – Bryskett, Fenton, Googe, Harington – were also players in the conquest of Ireland confirms the uncanny congruity between pushing back the frontiers of English and expanding the geopolitical boundaries within which it operated. A 'nationalistic spirit' animated Tudor translation (Jones, *Triumph*, p. 43) and that spirit migrated easily between literary and political nationalisms. Geoffrey Fenton, for instance, became Principal Secretary in Ireland (1580–1608) having made his reputation as a translator (Fellheimer, 'Hellowes' and Fenton's Translations', p. 141). The slippage between the activities of colonial spymaster and gentleman translator is captured in the suppressed violence of Sir John Conway's dedicatory verse to Fenton's translation of Belleforest's *Histoires tragiques* which commends him for having 'Enforst a Frenche man tell his tale, in Englishe language plaine'; in Ireland, Fenton would force many another to 'tell his tale' more literally.[2] He conflated territorial and linguistic ambitions in dedicating *The Historie of Guicciardin* to Elizabeth as 'soueraigne Empresse ouer seuerall nations and languages' (fo. A.iv.r). Barnaby Googe, a member of the first Earl of Essex's expedition to Ulster, Provost-Marshall of Connacht, poet and translator of four works from Latin and Spanish, similarly combined privateering and colonial expansion in Ireland with a robust promotion of English (O'Sullivan, 'Googe'; Sheidley, *Googe*). The most striking confirmation of the conjunction between translation and conquest – and between conquest in Ireland and the New World – comes from George Carew, Lord President of Munster. He translated not only *Araucana*, Ercilla's epic of the Spanish conquest of Chile, but also the Hiberno-Norman metrical romance, *The Song of Dermot and the Earl*, which celebrated Strongbow's conquest of Ireland (Orpen, *Song*).

The conflation of the linked kingdoms of language and nation is made explicit in Spenser's expostulation to Gabriel Harvey: 'why a God's name may not we, as else the Greekes, haue the kingdome of oure owne Language?' (Smith, *Critical Essays*, p. 99).[3] His metaphor made it possible to think of language as a political jurisdiction whose expansion could mimic – and be enabled by – territorial expansion. Such stirrings were anticipated by Spenser's schoolmaster, Mulcaster. In the 'Peroration' of his *Elementarie*, he anticipates the reservations of readers who might question his promotion of English. They will 'saie it is vncouth' and 'of small reatch, it stretcheth no further than this Iland of ours, naie not there ouer all' (pp. 270–1). Mulcaster, in the familiar pattern, turns from the defensive – 'yet . . . it serves vs there' – to the offensive: English would 'stretch to the furthest . . . if we were conquerers' (p. 275). His equation between the esteem accorded a language and the degree to which it is backed by power and violence is incisive and prophetic: 'matters of war, whether ciuill or foren, make a tung of account' (p. 89).

The connections between the scholars extolling English at home and the adventurers who carried it westward are, as the case of Cheke *père et fils* indicated, close. Theorists were quick to recognise the link between empowering English and overpowering Ireland. In the preface to his translation, *The Ciuile Conuersation of M. Stephen Guazzo*, George Pettie castigates Englishmen 'who retourne home with such queasie stomacks, that nothing will downe with them but French, Italian, or Spanish' (Guazzo, fo. 2v). He tackles their reservations about English – 'they count it barren, they count it barbarous' – and refutes them in an extended defence of the vernacular (fo. 3r). He juxtaposes this defence of English with an endorsement of military offensives overseas by dedicating his trans-lation to Lady Norris and praising her sons, all five of whom served in the Irish wars: 'some of them like Alexander the great, seeke new Countries and new worlds to shew their valiancie in' (Dedic.).

Samuel Daniel dedicated his *Poeticall Essayes* (1599) – which include 'Musophilus' with its prophetic vision of the language's imperial destiny – to Mountjoy who was, at just that time, bringing the Elizabethan conquest of Ireland to a triumphant conclusion. 'Muso-philus' articulates with singular confidence the sense that the status of English is both secured and confirmed by its expansion. For Philocosmus, its narrow ambit is evidence of deficiency: the 'bar-barous language' lags behind 'happier tongues', 'our speech vnknown' confined to 'this little point, this scarce discerned Isle' (lines 432–3, 248–9). While Musophilus initially counters with the modest assertion that 'this spatious circuit which we tread vpon' is ample, 'a world within a world standing alone' (lines 539–41), the allurement of 'lettered armes, & armed letters' (line 882) sweeps him beyond such caution as he imagines 'this swelling tide / And streame of words that now doth rise so hie / Aboue the vsuall banks, and spreads so wide' (lines 927–9).[4] In his *Defence of Ryme*, Daniel's ambivalent phrasing comes close to conceding that it is violence and not any quality native to a language that fixes its rankings. He grants only grudging acknowledgement to the 'inuentions' of Greek and Latin,

which treasure, if it were to be found in Welch, and Irish, we should hold those languages in the same estimation, and they [the classical languages] *may thanke their sword* that made their tongues so famous and vniuersall as they are. (p. 136; my emphasis)

Such moments, where praise for English tips over into thoughts of conquest and an acknowledgement of the realities of violence, recur. Hopes for 'the triumph of English' elide with hoped-for triumphs overseas. English could secure a confident identity for itself only, it seems, outside England: language and colonisation were moving into alignment. The conviction that the status of English would be confirmed by expanding its geographical reach rested on the contemporary assumption that linguistic sovereignty was secured by empire: Camden's approval of the Anglo-Saxons who 'valiantly and wisely performed heere all the three things, which implie a full conquest, viz. the alteration of lawes, language, and attire' is more than an antiquarian footnote. His sensitivity to the equivalence between that precedent and developments in Ireland is confirmed by his approval for the efforts of the original colonists to preserve English in the towns, 'for a long time' (*Remains*, pp. 23, 30). The Roman precedent furnished even greater scope for emulation. Moryson proclaimed that 'all nations haue thought nothing more powerfull to vnite myndes then the Community of language' and he reminds his readers that 'as the wise Romans . . . inlarged theire Conquests, so they did spreade theire language', as did the Normans (*Shakespeare's Europe*, p. 213). Sir Thomas Smith was at once the author of *De Recta et Emendata Linguæ Anglicæ Scriptione Dialogus* and a pioneer of English colonial theory: his proposals for private-enterprise colonisation in Ulster provided a blueprint for later developments in Ireland and America (Morgan, 'Colonial Venture', p. 261; Quinn, 'Smith'). In eliciting Cecil's support for the Ards project, he brought together the twin strands of territorial and linguistic ambition: the plantation (where he, too, would lose a son) would

augment our tongue, our laws, and our religion . . . which three be the true bands of the commonwealth whereby the Romans conquered and kept long time a great part of the world. (Dewar, *Smith*, p. 57)

The idea that conquest should have a linguistic manifestation, that language was its *compañera*, was gaining currency. For Eudoxus, the victors' natural reflex is to sideline the native language and

scorn to acquaint their tongues thereto, for it hath been ever the use of the conquerer to despise the language of the conquered, and to force him by all means to learn his. (*View*, p. 67)

The author of 'The Supplication of the Blood of the English' concurs:

every Conquerer bringes, ever three thinges with him to establishe his Conquest: Religion, the lawe, and the language of his owne country: without which he can never have any firme footing. (Maley, p. 64)

In chapter 9 of his *New Description*, Rich asserts 'that the conquered should surrender themselves to the language of the conquerors' (p. 33). He borrowed his chapter title, 'That a conquest should draw after it Lawe, Language, and Habit', from Stanihurst (*Chronicle*, p. 15) and comparison between New and Old English interpretations is, as always, revealing. Rich's injunction was hortatory and triumphalist, Stanihurst's a wistful lament for past negligence. The Dubliner's wish that the vanquished might 'speake the same language, that the vanquisher parleth' belongs within the older, defensive discourse and Stanihurst advanced it with the ruefulness of one who knew that reality was different, that many Old English had allowed

that theyr owne auncient natiue tongue shal be shrowded in obliuion, and suffer the enemies language, as it were a tettarre, or ringwoorme, to herborow it selfe within the iawes of Englishe conquerours. (p. 16)

Stanihurst's disinterested championing of English on purely linguistic grounds, too, differs from his English contemporaries' inclination to fuse linguistic and imperial nationalisms. His enthusiasm for 'bewtifying oure English language' through translation is second to no New Englishman's. His dedication of *The First Fovre Bookes of Virgil his Aeneis* to the Old Englishman, Lord Dunsany, salutes 'so copious and fluent a language, as oure English tongue is' (fo. A.ii.v). He writes 'for thee honoure of thee English . . . too aduance thee riches of oure speeche' (fo. A.iii.r). The same ebullience infuses his poem commending Verstegan's piece of linguistic fundamentalism, *A Restitution of Decayed Intelligence*, which he praises for its '*laborem / Restituens patriae patria verba suae*' (fo. A.4r). But, as ever, Stanihurst is an anomalous figure. His is a free-standing enthusiasm for the language, unbuttressed by the dreams of expansion and conquest that propped up his English contemporaries' promotion of their tongue. His translator-colonist peers pressed on to victory in Ireland while he slipped into reluctant exile on the continent, from where he launched a philippic – written in Latin, not the vernacular – against 'that strange and florid English, currently fashionable, which plunders from foreign languages'. He contrasted English newfangledness with the speech of the Irish-English, who 'preserve among them the pure and pristine tongue' of Chaucer. What had once united English and Palesmen now separated them. While those speaking the 'New English' 'may consider their English-speaking to be excellent it is not English at all' (*De rebus*, p. 144).

Civil Conversation

The metropolitan note of linguistic imperialism sounds again in Drayton's 'Idea' where the poet chafes against the confined ambit of his language. Blocked at Calais, since 'Foraine Nations rellish not our Tongue', its only outlet is to the north and west. 'Bounded thus', its expansionist pathway would have to be 'to *Scotland*' and to 'that *Irish* Ile, / To whom my Muse with fierie Wings shall passe'. The familiar discourse of expansion melds with another as Drayton imagines English pacifying as it spreads: it would 'Call backe the stiffe-neck'd Rebels from Exile, / And mollifie the slaught'ring *Galliglasse*' (*Works* I, p. 323: lines 2, 5, 9–12). In Ireland, where suppressing the Gaelic order was presented as an exercise in reform, the newcomers imagined themselves as agents of a civilising mission. Subscription to the notion that the language of such missionaries was itself a force for civility followed with almost syllogistic inevitability: colonists' confidence that theirs was a 'civil' language underpinned the discourse of Elizabethan nationalism.

Civil conversation was central to Renaissance Europe's understanding of how civilised societies negotiated their interactions, public and private, with others. For Guazzo, admiringly invoked by Bryskett and a shadowy influence on Book VI of the *Faerie Queene* (Bryskett, *Discovrse*, p. 24; Lievsay, *Guazzo*, p. 97), it had a profound ethical resonance: 'ciuile Conuersation is an honest, commendable, and vertuous kinde of liuing in the world' (fo. 22v). The concept exercised the minds of several Elizabethans associated with Ireland. Both Fenton and Googe promoted their translations as exercises in 'vertuous conversation' (Fenton, *Tragicall Discourses*, fo. iii.v; *Actes*, Dedic.; *Golden Epistles*, fo. B.i.r; Googe, *Prouerbes*, fo. 2v). Bryskett

wrote *A Discovrse of Civill Life* 'to the end to frame a gentleman fit for
ciuill conuersation' (p. 5). Spenser explained that Courtesy, theme of
Book VI of the *Faerie Queene*, 'is the ground, / And roote of ciuill
conuersation' (VI.i.1.5–6).

The colonist-translators' interest in civil conversation was no mere
distraction from the Irish broils. It was central to their thinking
about social transformation – and it placed language at the centre of
that debate. Anna Bryson argues that Guazzo's conception of civil
conversation countenanced a separation between social and political
life and privileged the former (*Courtesy*, p. 56). I suggest, however,
that in Ireland the concept of civil conversation was more useful
politically than socially. Moreover, while in Italy civil conversation
was detachable from the specific language which encoded it, in
Ireland it became inseparable from English. Guazzo, a Lombardian,
was notably unprescriptive on the *questione della lingua*. Though
believing that '*Tuscane* is perfect, and ours imperfect', he recommended 'that euerie one speake according to the maner of his owne
countrie' (*Ciuile Conuersation*, fo. 66r, 64v). In Ireland, where language
was party to cultural conflict, there would be no such latitude. 'The
Irishe is knowen by name, speache, habitt, feadinge, order, rule and
conuersation' (Gerrard, 'Notes', p. 95) and that 'conversation' was,
according to Justice Goold, Spenser's colleague on the Munster
Council, 'savage, cruel, and barbarous' (*CSPI* 1598–9, p. 397).

'Conversation' is a key concept in Spenser's astigmatic *View of the
Present State of Ireland*. It serves as an index of the dichotomy between
native and newcomer: while the Irish delight in 'licentious barbarism',
'no nation in the world excelleth [the English] in all goodly conversation' (p. 12). Within that polarised world, the identification between
civil conversation and English, and uncivil conversation and Irish is
total. In his careful analysis of the forces of cultural metastasis which
caused the original colonists to degenerate, Spenser uses 'licentious
conversing' and 'filthy conversation' as exact synonyms for Irish
(pp. 66, 85). Conversely, 'civil conversation' and 'English' are one:
when he approvingly paraphrases 'a statute' – clearly the 1537 'Act for
English Order' – to back his preference for an English ministry, he
substitutes the formula 'whatsoever Englishman being of good conversation' for the statute's 'can speak English' (p. 88; *Stats. Irl.*, p. 123).

'Conversation' is a notably unstable signifier in sixteenth-century
Ireland, its meanings oscillating between the content – civil or
uncivil – and the medium, Irish or English, which encoded it. With

the identity of 'civil conversation' shifting between the literalness of a specific tongue and the metaphysics of a content beyond the quiddities of a particular language, it is not surprising that the Elizabethans could place little real confidence in the transformative potential of English *qua* English. English might be equated with civil conversation but could not of itself secure it. Declarations in favour of English were more useful as rituals of self-affirmation than as pragmatic interventions. However cheering Spenser found the equation between English and civil conversation, he was not beguiled into ascribing alchemical powers of transformation to the language itself. Incorrigible rebels will never be 'brought to labour or civil conversation'; they must be 'cut off' (*View,* pp. 103–4). Only when the sword had done its work and severity had cleared the way for a new order could the survivors be brought to 'an union of manners and conformity' with their chastisers,

by translating them, and scattering them in small numbers amongst the English, not only to bring them by daily conversation unto better liking of each other, but also to make both of them less able to hurt. (p. 154)

For ultimately, the efficacy of 'civil conversation' rested on its possessors' power to hurt. Far from believing that 'civil conversation' could be counted on to civilise, its imposition was seen as an outcome of coercion, not as a cajoling substitute for it. The victor would impose it afterwards, by right of conquest. Perrott spared nothing in bringing the Munster insurgents to heel: 'in the bogs he pursued them, in the thickets he followed them, in the plaines he fought with them, and in their castels and holds he beseeged them'; only then, having 'executed . . . infinit numbers', did he set about reforming their 'common conuersation' (Hooker, 'Historie', pp. 369–70).

The sequencing is revelatory. As putative agent of reform, English is ultimately parasitical on violence. No one recognised this more starkly than Spenser. His desolate valediction, 'A briefe note of Ireland', ascribed the overthrow of the Munster plantation to an inversion of that order: its planners had opted for civil conversation without having first administered 'a moste violent medecyne' (*Prose Works*, p. 238). For Spenser the sequencing was misconceived: 'till Ireland be famished it can not be subdued' (p. 244). The deluded 'devisour' of the plantation

perhapps thought that the civill example of the English being sett before

them and there daylie conuersing with them would haue brough them by
dislike of there owne savage life to the liking and imbrasing of better
civilitie, But it is farr other wise. (pp. 239–40)

Civil conversation, far from converting, is possible only between
those already converted. Spenser's insecurity about the efficacy of
civil conversation is profound. There is a troubled recognition in
Colin Clouts Come Home Againe – as well as in Book VI of the *Faerie
Queene* – that the court itself festers with *un*civil conversation: 'subtil
shifts', 'slaundring', 'leasings lewd', 'faire dissembling curtesie', 'A
filed toung furnisht with tearmes of art', 'haughtie words . . . like
bladders blowen up with wynd' (*CCCHA* lines 694–6, 700–1, 716–17;
Tonkin, *Courteous Pastoral*, p. 159). Colin, his co-ordinates adrift,
slinks back 'home' to Ireland.

Sixteenth-century Ireland concentrated the Elizabethans'
thoughts about their language. Burgeoning confidence, insecurity,
stirrings of linguistic imperialism, an unsteady identification of theirs
as a medium – if not thereby an agent – of civil conversation
informed their approaches to language policy. The final movements
of the *Faerie Queene* capture this confused amalgam of arrogance,
anxiety and aspiration. Spenser's troubled meditation on language
policy in his prose work receives a fantasy reworking in Book VI of
the *Faerie Queene*. Language is central to 'The Legend of Covrtesie',
as it was to the Elizabethan enterprise in Ireland. In both cases, it is
something of a mystificatory agent. It is a necessary supplement and,
at times, pretext to action; it enables and elevates discourses – of
violence and of a radical refusal of communication – ostensibly
inimical to its ethos. The movement of the poem confirms the
impotence of civil conversation – of English – by itself to confer
order. Civil conversation is possible only after the tumbling heads
and terrible slaughter of Book V. Calidore can set forth only when
the Lord Grey-inspired Artegall returns 'From his late conquest' (*FQ*
VI.i.4.5). For Spenser, this pattern enacts the 'ideal movement of Irish
politics' (McCabe, *Pillars of Eternity*, p. 45). Even inside Book VI, only
an undertow of violence can sustain civil conversation's unsteady
grip on the forces of disorder: 'goodly manners' are policed by the
head 'cleft . . . asunder to his chin' and 'the carkasse tumbling
downe' (i.23.5–6). Calidore makes 'gladfull speaches' to Pastorella
only after he has piled up the 'dead carcases' of plough-shy brigands
in the *crannóg*-like dwelling where he 'did hew and slay, / Till he had
strowd with bodies all the way' (xi.50.3; 47.4; 49.4–5).

If civil conversation cannot of itself tame, neither can it open up dialogue with the other. Its exemplars are abundantly endowed with eloquence: Calidore is characterised by 'gracious speach' (i.2.6), Serena by 'faire words' (v.30.6), the Hermit by his 'art of words' (vi.6.3). But outside the charmed circle of eloquence, the indigenes of Book VI are restricted to the grunt-ideolect projected on to the Irish elsewhere in the colonial record. The 'saluage nation' 'shouted all, and made a loud alarme', caused their 'bagpypes . . . to shrill' and 'made the wood to tremble at the noyce' (viii.45.9; 46.1–4). Spenser's 'Wyld Man' may share a general kinship with figures who had long inhabited the European imagination (White, *Tropics*, p. 172), but his more immediate relatives populate the State Papers, figures denied articulate speech and who like this 'bad Stuard neither plough'd nor sowed' (iv.14.7). Like the muttering stick-men analysed in chapter 2, the 'Saluage Man' is heard only to make 'great mone' (iv.12.4) and 'loudly rore' (vi.22.8). Only his gestures – 'rude tokens' and 'speaking signes' (iv.11.3; v.4.3) – survive the monophone recorder who cannot register what he does not understand. For no less than the 'saluages' whom Spenser's fellows represented as speechless in their writings from Ireland, the Wyld Man, too, has language – though one rendered senseless by the incomprehension of his hearers. It is the aphasia of Calepine, unable to make sense of these 'words', not the disphonia of the speaker, that is recorded when the narrator declares that 'other language had he none nor speach, / But a soft murmure, and confused sound / Of senselesse words' (iv.11.6–8). Meaningless-ness is in the ear of the auditor, not in the '*words*' which, on the contrary, testify that the Wyld Man is speaking some language, though one unknown to his hearers. Calepine, ironically unworthy namesake of the polyglot dictionary-maker, simply cannot gloss these 'words' – thereby bearing out Pettie's warning that soldiers who were not trained in languages would be unable to 'discourse with straun-gers . . . vnlesse it be with dumbe shewes and signes' (Guazzo, *Ciuile Conuersation*, Preface, fo. 2r).

His own language vitiated by denial, the Wyld Man neither gains – nor is taught – any other but serves instead as a fantasy embodiment of silent compliance. His only gestures are of servility and self-harm, now 'Kissing hands' (VI.iv.11.5), 'Now beating his hard head vpon a stone' (v.4.5). Biddable, indispensable, the Wyld Man strains every nerve to communicate, 'By signes, by lookes, and all his other gests' (iv.14.3). But from the courteous come no reciprocal gestures. While

Serena 'Gan teare her hayre, and all her garments rent' (v.4.8), her signing is merely solipsistic self-expression. When Arthur and Timias[5] come upon Serena and her Wyld Man rescuer, they first attack, then ignore him; Arthur reserves 'all the courteous meanes he could inuent' for his courtly friends (v.32.6). For the Saluage Man, there is neither greeting nor apology as he tags, unacknowledged, through eleven stanzas until revealed to be smitten with reverence for Arthur in stanza 41. The only gestures ever directed at him are Arthur's commands which he leaps to obey; he kills to order and stops 'at . . . commaundement' (vi.39.6; 40.9). He is studiously excluded from the conversations of the civil. While the Graces enjoin that 'Ciuility' be extended 'To friends, to foes' (x.23.9), civil conversation in the *Faerie Queene* is the exclusive currency of courtesy's initiates. The transformative power of civil conversation is, it seems, efficacious only with blanks. While the degeneration of the Wyld Man grown 'mis-shapt' (v.1.5) cannot be mended, the infant rescued by Calepine from the bear's 'bloodie iawes' can (iv.17.9). Calepine assures Matilde that 'ye may enchace / What euer formes ye list thereto apply' on his 'spotlesse spirit' (iv.35.5–6), making possible a fantasy reversal of the degenerative parable of the FitzUrsus-Bearsons (see p. 101).

Even when reworked as romance, the strains in the Elizabethan theorising of language and civility cannot be eased. 'Faire words' alone, though the cynosure of the dazzled poet, cannot order events. Unbacked by violence, they are powerless; only through violence and silencing is compliance gained. The 'vile tongue' of the Blatant Beast is temporarily 'supprest and tamed' but still at large (xii.38.2). Spenser's meditation on language and courtesy in Book vi of the *Faerie Queene* backs the dark ordering intimated in *A View*: 'anatomies of death' must stalk the land before civility has its day (104). Far from putting their faith in the civilising power of English, a significant group of articulate colonists had come, by the century's end, to recognise that their civil tongue could be imposed only in the wake of conquest. 'The Supplication' echoes Spenser's analysis in despairing of civilising the incorrigible: 'They are blacke Moores o Queene, wash them as long as you will, you shall never alter their hue' (Maley, p. 51). The natives would be curbed rather 'with correction, then with curteoisie' (p. 25). Stark implications for language policy follow: English must be imposed with punitive measures, so that 'the new springinge frye . . . may for feare of that punishment be driven to learne Englishe' (p. 65).

Ludowick Bryskett wrote *A Discovrse of Civill Life* while Clerk of the
Munster Council. Set in his 'little cottage . . . newly built neare vnto
Dublin' (p. 5), Bryskett's *Discovrse* once again juxtaposes linguistic
patriotism, civil conversation and violence in a way that confirms
their interdependency. Bryskett prefaces his work with a defence of
his vernacular. English may not have 'that copiousnesse and
sweetnes', 'that flowing eloquence' of Greek and Latin, yet 'this faire
virgin-stranger in her homely weeds' merits a welcome as warm 'as if
she had come decked in all her gorgeous ornaments' (p. 3). Moreover, Bryskett himself is 'enchacing' English with tribute brought
from Ireland: he offers 'healthfull and delicious fruites . . . to furnish
this our English soile & clime withal', to advance 'the culturation
and manuring of the same' (p. 4). Most significantly, his work is
'Written to' Lord Grey, Spenser's Artegall, here lauded as a patron of
those 'who curiously seeke to transport from farre and forraine
countries . . . strange grafts, plants and flowers . . . [to be] ingrafted
vpon the stocke of our mother English-tongue' (p. 2). Bryskett
presents as paradoxical and particularly gratifying the arrival 'of so
vnlooked for a present out of this barbarous countrie' (p. 3). Yet, I
argue, it was precisely the estranging and empowering context of a
colonial adventure that had quickened confidence in the 'stretch'
and 'reach' of English.

The alignment of linguistic confidence, violence and the effacement of competitor languages is brought out later in the *Discovrse*. As
the participants arrive for a third day of dialogue, they joke that
'their purpose was to coynie vpon me, and to eat me out of house
and home'. The pleasantry depends on the sting having already been
drawn out of the Gaelic practice to which it alludes: practice – and
word – are on their way to extinction. Though 'not yet cleane taken
away', 'coynie' is defunct among the 'ciuill' (p. 157). The violence of
its extirpation is mystified by being cloaked in the same husbandry
metaphor earlier employed to convey the 'culturation' of English.
Bryskett collapses Grey's slaughter of 'the rebellious subiects' and
his own adornment of English into one image: Grey 'hath plowed
and harrowed the rough ground to his hand'; the rebels have been
'cleane rooted out' and a good 'haruest' is assured (158–9). The
coincidence between the two harvests is not merely one of
phrasing.

The ambient context of violence frames the discussion of 'civil
conversation', delimiting its applicability to a coterie discoursing

among themselves in a foreign land. Maley argues that exercises like Spenser's discussions with Ralegh, Bryskett's dialogue and Sir Thomas Smith's, Gabriel Harvey's and Humphrey Gilbert's debate on the applicability of the Roman colonial model to Ireland all illustrate 'the way in which the humanists' pursuit of civil conversation could be both a means of securing civility against a barbarous other, and of devising ways of subduing that other' (*Salvaging Spenser*, p. 21). The gratifying dichotomy between the civil self and the savage beyond the pale which the discourse of civil conversation celebrated was interpreted as a licence to violence rather than a spur to win the other to civility through conversation. For the proponents of civil conversation were also the advocates of prophylactic conquest: 'Civility is . . . reinscribed as the necessity of military subjugation' (Jones and Stallybrass, 'Dismantling Irena', p. 161). For the assembly of lawyers and soldiers in Bryskett's planter-cottage – among them one of Pettie's dedicatees, Thomas Norris – talk of civil conversation provides only an intellectual respite from a militarised world where there is little conversation and less civility.[6] The discourse of civility conducted among the New English in Ireland parallels – and even legitimises – their preparedness to embark on what Inga Clendinnen calls 'the long and terrible conversation of war' ('"Fierce and Unnatural Cruelty"', p. 41).

ELIZABETHAN LANGUAGE POLICY IN IRELAND

Language and violence

Linguistic nationalism marched in step with the broader project of political and military expansion. The territorial extension of English rested on conquest; civil conversation, paradoxically, could be imposed only by violence. It is necessary, therefore, to preface any examination of how linguistic nationalism shaped Elizabethan language policies by acknowledging the role of the sword in advancing policies of the word. 'Words in the New World seem always to be trailing after events that pursue a terrible logic quite other than the fragile meanings that they construct' (Greenblatt, *Marvelous Possessions*, p. 63). In Ireland, words – new words, in a new language – trailed after terrible events. The implement of language policy was the sword. Only power could compel compliance and power rested on violence. '[C]an the swoord teache them to speake Englishe?', asked a sceptical Gerrard in 1578 ('Notes', p. 96). In fact, the sword would be an essential prolegomenon to language-learning.

'Word' is swallowed up inside '*s/word*' when the two elide and the drastic shift in register is mirrored in another fatal couplet caught up in the politics of language in sixteenth-century Ireland, the tongue and the head, as the 'old rhyme' prefacing John Montague's meditation on Derricke's *Image of Irelande*, in *The Rough Field*, conveys:

> And who ever heard
> such a sight unsung
> as a severed head
> with a grafted tongue.   (p. 31)

The phantasmagoric image captures the ghoulish sequencing of the transformation: heads would have to roll before the tongue would turn; literal severing cleared the way for metaphorical grafting. It would be ethically lopsided to lose sight of this macabre concatenation, to disregard the head in the intensity of one's focus on the tongue. The ubiquity of all too anatomically specific heads in texts that ignore the metonymic tongue is a salutary reminder of priorities and of the enchainment of violence and language policy.

The silencing of the native can be very literal. '*Sine me quæso*', permit me, begs Cornelius O'Deveny, bishop of Down and Connor, from the block but speech is cut off. The bishop is beheaded and, in narrating his demise, Rich's 'Patricke Plaine' replaces protest in a learned language with imputations of bestial speechlessness and silence: 'he had liued like a rauening Woolfe, and dyed like a dumbe dogge' (*Catholicke Conference*, fo. 4v). John of Desmond was wounded 'with a horssemans staffe' and, Hooker mirthlessly noted, 'he spake verie few words after' ('Historie', p. 446). The slaughter is relentless. The slash of its blade echoes like a refrain through these texts: in the suppression of the Desmond rebellion, there was 'pitifull murther, for man, woman, and child were put to the sworde' (Churchyard, *Rehearsal*, fo. E.iv.v; cf. fo. F.i.r.). Heads roll: 'some days two heads and some days four heads, and other some days ten heads' (*CSPI* 1574–85, p. xciv). 'Two lustie kernes' were rounded up by one of Pelham's men. The soldier slew one, 'the other he compelled to carrie his fellows head with him to the campe: which when he had doone, his head also was cut off and laid by his fellows' (Hooker, 'Historie', p. 430). Captain Willis, Docwra's interpreter during meetings with Niall Garbh, cut off the head of Edmund Mac Hugh

Maguire and with his company 'hurled it from place to place as a football' (*CCM* 3, p. 156).

Stakes rise out of the landscape, topped with impaled head. When James of Desmond was hanged, drawn and quartered on Ralegh's orders, his head was 'set on the towne gates of the citie of Corke, and made the preie of the foules' (Hooker, 'Historie', p. 433). So many heads of 'beggarly rogues' were daily staked that Burgh could wryly boast to Cecil that 'the air about Dublin is . . . corrupted' (*CSPI* 1596–7, p. 315). Talk follows after slaughter. Humphrey Gilbert relegated speech to a formality of submission coaxed from the defeated by admonitory decaputees when, during his Munster campaign, he lined 'eche side of the waie leadyng into his owne Tente' with 'the heddes of all those . . . whiche were killed in the daie'. The vanquished, coming to surrender, passed through this 'lane of heddes' where 'thei sawe the heddes of their dedde fathers, brothers, children, kinffolke, and freendes, lye on the grounde before their faces, as thei came to speake with the saied Collonell' (Church-yard, *Rehearsal*, fo. Q.iii.v). Speech is circumscribed by violence. When Carew captures the Súgán Earl, he finds him 'muche reserved in his speache' but adds menacingly that 'after a few dayes I doubt not but to make him speake more freelye' (MacCarthy, *Life*, p. 324). The power imbalance infests translation. Having translated the tip-off that propelled Richard Bingham into slaughtering 'xxx knaues' (see above p. 78), Reynolds, the interpreter, was dispatched to Bingham's brother, George, with the fruit of his linguistic mediation: 'a horse loade of heads' (PRO SP 63/172/38.ii).

But control of speech was never assured. The Hydra's heads rolled (Hooker, 'Historie', pp. 412, 433, 446) but insolent tongues wagged on. Sorley Boy, compelled to behold the staked head of his slain son, Alexander Óg, was reported to say – with all trace of translation suppressed – ' "It is noe matter . . . my sonne hath many heades" ' (Perrott, *Chronicle*, pp. 46–7). But a silence would fall. '[G]reat companies' of rebels were slaughtered, 'whose blouds the earth dranke vp, and whose carcases the foules of the aire and the rauening beastes of the feeld did consume and deuoure', so that a man could travel from Waterford to Smerwick and 'not meet anie man, woman or child' nor 'see anie beast, but the verie wooluates, the foxes, and other like rauening beastes; manie of them laie dead being famished, and the residue gone elsewhere' (Hooker, 'Historie', pp. 459–60).

Dudley Bagenal, who paid for his unprovoked murder of the

elderly chieftain, Mortagh Óg Kavanagh, with his life, was left with 'his tongue drawn out of his mouth, and slit, as some of the women confessed who put him in his winding sheet' (*CSPI* 1586–8, p. 289). When Munster rose again in rebellion, in 1598, native servants performed 'many execrable murders and cruelties' on their planter-masters, leaving 'some with their tongues cut out of their heads' (*CSPI* 1598–9, p. 300). But even as they wreaked vengeance on the anatomical tongue, the graft of the metonymic one was starting to take.

ANGLICANISM AND ANGLICISATION

Commenting on Samuel Daniel's bold evocation of English's imperial destiny at the end of *Musophilus*, Greenblatt remarks that

It is as if in place of the evangelical spirit, which in the early English voyages is but a small flame compared to the blazing mission of the Spanish friars, Daniel would substitute a linguistic mission, the propagation of English speech. ('Learning to Curse', p. 562)

The conduct of the Reformation in Ireland provides an opportunity to test Greenblatt's hunch. Religion and language occupied mirror-image positions within England and Spain's colonial ventures. Spain's was a religiously sanctioned nationalism; the Counter-Reformation imperative to evangelise over-ruled – though it never ruled out – linguistic nationalism. Events in Ireland suggest that the reverse was true for the English: language was too central to their religious and national identity to be compromised in the interest of evangelising others.

Theological differences only partly explain the contrast between the feverish evangelising of the Spanish and the half-hearted gestures of the English. Expansionist Elizabethans were, Lestringant argues, the spiritual inheritors of the Huguenot pioneers in the New World whose Calvinist '*pessimisme missiologique*' sapped their evangelising impulse (*Huguenot*, pp. 126, 237, 273); Pagden, similarly, attributes Englishmen's indifference to converting native Americans to the 'profoundly isolationist pull' of the Calvinism to which so many of them inclined (*Lords*, p. 45). For Englishmen, religion was less a stimulus to praxis and conversion than an internally directed experience and a *locus* of cultural confidence. That confidence was bound up with the iconic status of English. In its advocacy of the vernacular and translation, its promotion of popular education and literacy and its indebtedness to printing, the Reformation was everywhere a linguistic as well as a theological event. In Ireland, where vernaculars were part of a wider contest, we see with particular clarity the centrality of language to the making of English identity. For Englishmen, '[t]he real triumph of the language first occurred in the domain not of words but of the Word' (Waswo, *Language and Meaning*, p. 199): the decisive contribution of vernacular translation to the Tudor Reformation meant that Englishmen's burgeoning linguistic confidence was bound up with Protestantism (Delisle and Woodsworth, *Translators*, p. 33). Assmann shows that certain religions, like Judaism, insist on the untranslatability of their sacred mysteries ('Translating Gods', p. 30). In its own way, Anglicanism, too, was language-specific: far from being simply a medium amenable to translation, English was part of its message, a *verum nomen* that could not be translated without loss. The Church of Ireland would not willingly go native linguistically or uncouple language from doctrine as proselytising required.

The additional status of the Reformation as a political movement which advanced the centralising impulse of the Tudor state ensured that, in Ireland, 'Anglicanism' meant 'anglicisation'. The 'Act for the English Order, Habite, and Language' (1537) decreed that the Church of Ireland ministry should be English-speaking. It stipulated that when no 'Englishman' could be found for a living, 'proclamation should be made on four successive market days' to find an English-speaker; only if none emerged could an Irish-speaker be appointed (*Stats. Irl.*, p. 124). Ordinands had to vow to learn English, to 'bid the beades . . . and preach the word of God in English' and keep 'a schole for to learne English' (pp. 125–6). While, in 1537, the Act was almost purely aspirational, it later 'assumed considerable practical and symbolic significance in the eyes of some civil and ecclesiastical leaders . . . as the original and definitive statement of the necessary link between anglicization and Reformation' (Ford, *Reformation*, p. 13).

The choices made when anglicisation and evangelisation pulled in different directions confirm the priority given to linguistic over spiritual colonisation. Moryson captures the tilt in the balance: 'Some then wished the Bible to be translated into Irish, because many of the people vnderstoode not English, but others thought better by education to make the English tounge vulgarly practised, because the vnity of language is of great power to breede vnity of affections' (*Irish Sections*, p. 99). The persuasiveness of the anglicising argument is confirmed by the reformers' dilatoriness in having the key Protestant texts translated into Irish. Ó Cearnaigh's translation of the catechism, *Aibidil Gaoidheilge 7 Caiticiosma*, was published in 1571; the New Testament took a further thirty-six years to appear and the Book of Common Prayer, forty-one – a gestation that hardly indicates urgency (Ó Glaisne, *Gaeilge*, p. 7; Williams, *I bPrionta*, pp. 22, 31). When, at last, James I's Lord Deputy, Chichester, took steps to have the prime texts 'printed and taught in the Irish tongue', Sir John Davies imagined that they would 'incredibly allure the common country people' (*CSPI* 1603–6, pp. 241, 467; cf. Ó Buachalla, 'Na Stíobhartaigh', p. 89). But the moment for allurement had passed. The Nine Years War had confirmed the religious communities in their opposed identities. William Daniel's preface to his translation of the New Testament acknowledges its belatedness: the long delay had caused 'the heauy losse of many thousand soules' (fo. 1r).

The linguistic squeamishness which held the reformers aloof from the vernacular pushed them towards embracing a paradoxical surrogate. Elizabeth's 1560 'Act for the Uniformitie of Common Prayer' teasingly recognised the wisdom of making the service available to the people 'in such language as they mought best understand'. Yet it balked at the obvious solution, arguing implausibly 'that the same may not be in their native language, as well for difficultie to get it printed, as that few in the whole realm can read the Irish letters'. Instead, it plumped for what McAdoo calls the 'fantastic expedient' of sanctioning Latin versions of the reformed services where 'there cannot be found English ministers to serve' (*Stats. Irl.*, p. 296; McAdoo, 'Irish Translations', p. 252). Education policy confirmed the bias towards English. The ethos of Trinity College, Dublin, modelled on Emmanuel College, Cambridge, was English and Puritan. It lost its early flush of interest in Irish as a vehicle for proselytising when William Daniel left: 'the fundamentally anglicizing assumptions behind the Reformation sought to eliminate the use of the Irish language, and made it difficult to attract native ordinands' (Ford, *Reformation*, p. 107).

The conflict between Reformation *pure et dure* and Reformation as handmaiden to anglicisation showed up most clearly in the clash between appointing incumbents capable of communicating with their parishioners and promoting 'English ministers' as the 1560 Act required. The paucity of Irish-speakers in the Church of Ireland at the end of the century suggests that the dilemma was almost invariably resolved in favour of the latter. The transformation in the linguistic profile of the Meath ministry illustrates the trend. Surveying its 224 parishes in 1576, Bishop Brady found that only eighteen curates knew English; by 1604, only three of its thirty rectors were listed as knowing Irish (Collins, *Letters*, p. 112; *CSPI* 1603–6, p. 172). Bishop Lyon of Cork complained in 1596 that there was no Irish-speaking preacher in all Munster (*CSPI* 1596–7, p. 14).[7]

The instinctive preference for appointing Englishmen chafed against an awareness that Irish-speakers were indispensable if congregations were to be won beyond the Pale. Sidney advised the queen that, in the 'heathennish' parts 'where the English Tounge is not understood, it is most necessarie, that soche be chosen, as can speake Irishe' and recommended that 'Searche' be made accordingly in the universities and among Gaelic-speaking Scots. When the see of Ossory fell vacant, he advised the queen to appoint 'soche a Person, as is acquainted withe the Language and Manners of this Countrey People' (Collins, *Letters*, pp. 113, 127); an Irish-speaker, Gaffney, was duly appointed. The queen was receptive to such arguments and cited fluency in Irish as a reason for appointing Brady to Meath, Daly to Kildare, O'Connor to Killala and John Crosby, brother of the interpreter Patrick, to Kerry (Williams, *I bPrionta*, p. 10; *CSPI* 1588–92, p. 436; 1601–3, p. 622).

That 'Searche' had to be made to find suitable hibernophones suggests that part of the difficulty lay on the supply side. Once-tractable Palesmen were withdrawing into recusancy and alienation. Leverous, whom Croft had commended for being 'best able to preache both in the Englishe and the Iryshe tonge', was deprived of his see in Kildare in 1560 for refusing to take the Oath of Supremacy (Shirley, *Original Letters*, pp. 62–3). The performance of Gaelic appointees was even more discouraging. James MacCaughwell was translated to Cashel in 1569 but was quickly dispatched by the titular incumbent, MacGibbon, who attacked him with an 'Irish skaine'[8] (Hooker, 'Historie', p. 339). His replacement, Miler McGrath, packed his diocese with Irish-speakers – men who could 'speak neither English or Latin but more like a kernagh than a prelate'; far from being the vanguard of a hibernophone Reformation, however, most were the rascally McGrath's Donegal relatives (Marron, 'McGrath', pp. 167–8).

Yet, the pattern of appointments shows that Irish-speakers, even when available, were repeatedly passed over. Fenton proposed a Palesman, Nicholas Stafford, for Ferns, arguing that the Oxford graduate was 'able to teach in Irish . . . whereby he may sway them' but an Englishman, Graves, was preferred (*CSPI* 1600, p. 440; 1600–1, p. 36). The consistency with which this bias operated meant that countless English churchmen found themselves linguistically marooned among uncomprehending parishioners. Craik, who succeeded Leverous in Kildare, craved recall from a see 'where neyther I can preach unto the people nor the people understande me' (Shirley, *Original Letters*, p. 95). Two years on, Craik's renewed appeal to the queen shows that he had made little progress in remedying either deficiency: 'I cannot fructify nor profit the people for as much as they understand not me nor I them' (Ronan, *Reformation*, p. 55).

Incoming ecclesiastics almost uniformly failed to equip themselves with the language of their putative parishioners (Ellis, *Tudor Ireland*, p. 219). Offered the primacy of Armagh by Cranmer, Revd. Turner passed up the promotion, reasoning that he would have no listeners there, 'but must preach to the walls and stalls: for the people understood no English'. Cranmer blithely reposted that he could learn the language and 'with diligence' master it in a year or two (Mant, *Church of Ireland*, p. 215). Few newcomers rose to Cranmer's challenge. Those who knew by bitter experience the disadvantage of not speaking Irish learned neither the language nor the lesson implied for future appointments. Craik followed the letter bemoaning his isolation among hibernophones with one appealing for additional preachers – from England (Shirley, *Original Letters*, p. 108). The career of Loftus, the Englishman who became Archbishop of Dublin in 1567, illustrates how experience of linguistic isolation failed to translate into an option for the vernacular. Left behind among the natives when Craik retreated to an oasis of English in St Patrick's, he was soon being touted by Sussex for preferment to Armagh for his 'goodly gift of utterance in the pulpit'. That this 'gift' worked only in English is confirmed by his subsequent plea to Cecil to release him from Armagh: not alone was the see not lucrative but he was unable 'to do any good in it, for that altogether it lieth among the Irish' (Ronan, *Reformation*, pp. 72, 201). Backing his translation to Dublin, Sidney focused on the benefit of releasing him to 'a greater flock to understand hym than he had before' rather than on the needs of his linguistically excluded northern flock. Nor were they to the fore when it came to selecting his replacement. Terence Daniel, an able bilingual, was interested; Brady favoured Garvey, 'a sharp preacher in the Irish tonge' but Loftus himself seemed to have forgotten the inconvenience of incomprehension when urging the appointment of Cartwright, a Cambridge-educated English Puritan (Shirley, *Original Letters*, pp. 229, 315, 321). Sidney, unconcerned in this instance with making 'Searche', ensured that his man, Lancaster from Salisbury, was elevated (Ronan, *Reformation*, p. 245).

The overwhelming impression is that a candidate's command of Irish was paraded when it suited but that lack of the vernacular was, of itself, no disqualification. When Sidney made the case for appointing the Englishman, Dixon, to Cork and Cloyne, he played down the vernacular, arguing that it was 'fit to be bestowed on an Englishman by reason of the places there frequented with our nation and speech'. But when, a year later, the adulterous Dixon was deprived, Loftus opportunistically marketed his ally, the enthusiastic iconoclast Matthew Sheyne, as 'fittest for the place, as he is acquainted with the country's language' (Ronan, *Reformation*, pp. 325, 358). There is a sense that native clergymen could expect advancement only *faute de mieux*. Loftus mentioned MacCaghwell's fluency in Irish when suggesting him for Cashel but added revealingly 'the lyvinge [is] verie small, and not mete for any but of that contrey birthe' (Shirley, *Original Letters*, p. 263).

The usefulness of natives linguistically was more than offset by other considerations. The Commissioners for Ecclesiastical Causes reported with distaste in 1564 that 'the rest of the Bisshops . . . be all Irishe, we nede say no more' (Shirley, *Original Letters*, p. 140). With so little attention paid to the vernacular, uncomprehending natives were left to parrot English as best they could. Archbishop Long told Walsingham that, in Breifne, he found 'such harkenynge to the woorde preatched, by them that could understand, and by the others imitating them, thoughe they understod nothinge' (*CSPI* 1574–85, p. cxxxv). The failure to hitch language to evangelisation when, at mid-century, all was still to be played for ensured that the Reformation in Ireland would be sacrificed to 'the anglicising assumptions' that shaped it (Ford, 'Reformation', p. 67). Ford concludes that the administration sought to build a reformed church *de novo*, importing English clergy as 'the vanguard of an anglicizing movement' and willingly shedding its Irish-speaking rump (*Reformation*, p. 14). The very measures which disabled the diffusion of Anglicanism were, in important ways, the real point of the exercise.

The Gaelic intelligentsia certainly saw Protestantism and English as synonymous. When Eoghan Ó Dubhthaigh satirised the native Anglicans, Mathew Sheyne, William Cassidy and Miler MacGrath, in his poem 'An Chliar Ghliogair' (The Prating Clergy), he fixed his invective in English loanwords, the linguistic correlatives of their apostasy: '*ní mó leo Muire ná* dog, / *dar* by God, *ní rachaidh leo*'; '*Drong do* sheduction *lán* / *do chuir* corruption *sa chóir*' ('they care for Mary no more than for a *dog* / *by God*, they won't get away with it', 'a crew full of *seduction* / that put *corruption* in the choir') (Mhag Craith, *Dán na mBráthar*, p. 133: 25.3–4; p. 138: 42.1–2; my emphases). Ó Dubhthaigh mocks their new status by mimicking the words that give them spurious title, '*cairt 's dinntiúir*' (charter and indenture); he scoffingly rigs them out in lexical borrowings, '*bútuis*', '*spuir*' (boots and spurs) (p. 144: 69.4; p. 145: 71a.1,4). For the poet, linguistic and confessional defections were one.

How much weight, therefore, does Bradshaw's argument that a 'strategy of the word', comparable to the Spanish option for vernacular evangelisation, challenged the dominant 'strategy of the sword' carry? In reality, any attempt to document the existence of a persuasive strategy not only demonstrates its minority status and inefficacy but exposes its subscription to an ultimately anglicising agenda. William Herbert, on whom much of Bradshaw's case hangs, could equally well be used to exemplify the shortcomings and contradictions of the persuasive strategy. Recognising that prayers 'in a strange tongue could be to [his Kerry tenants] but altogether unprofitable', Herbert had Nicholas Kennan prepare translations of the Ten Commandments, the Articles and the Lord's Prayer; similarly, he had the Dean of Ardfert 'preach the truth to his country people in the Irish tongue' (*CSPI* 1586–8, p. 533; Bradshaw, 'Sword', p. 487). But his need to commission translations sixteen years after the appearance of Ó Cearnaigh's *Aibidil* only highlights the failure of the administration to make available the essentials of a vernacular evangelisation. Equally, the conduct of his fellow-planter, Edward Denny, who stripped the dean of his living, confirms that the prevailing attitude of the new settlers worked against the promotion of an Irish-speaking ministry (*CSPI* 1588–92, p. 192).

But beyond the shortcomings of the 'strategy of the word' in practice is the crucial fact that vernacular evangelisation no more challenged the anglicising assumptions of the Reformation than its Spanish equivalent questioned the ultimate primacy of hispanicisation. Both strategies accepted unquestioningly the colonists' right to assimilate the other to metropolitan systems of belief: '*seule la technique d'évangélisation est différente; pas le fait*' (only the method of evangelisation is different; not the fact) (Affergan, *Exotisme*, p. 119). 'Persuasion' in a time of conquest is hardly dialogic. Its asymmetry (it flows in one direction only) precludes the reciprocity of real communication or of authentic engagement with the other's language. Far from being at odds with anglicisation, the 'strategy of the word' enlisted Irish against itself. It viewed Irish instrumentally as a linguistic collaborator, sundered from its own cultural inheritance and complicit in its own eventual dissolution. Herbert, who advocated extirpating the 'leprosy' of Gaelic law and overthrowing the native poetic order (*Croftus*, pp. 85–6) saw little place for Irish in the larger scheme of things. In so far as the language would survive such deracination, it would serve as a zombie tongue humming sacred hymns to reclaim the natives for virtue (p. 114). Ultimately, his perspective chimes with Spenser's, who also imagined reducing the vanquished tongue to an empty vessel making songs. Irenæus cites the lesson of Cyrus who had changed the tunes of the defeated Lydians to 'certain lascivious lays and loose gigs, by which in short space their minds were so mollified and abated that they forgot their former fierceness and became most tender and effeminate' (*View*, p. 70).

The Anglican church's recourse to the vernacular was never intended to be other than short-term and provisional. The Edwardian reformers envisaged the use of Irish as a stop-gap: Divine Service could be 'translated truly into the Irishe tongue, *unto* suche tyme as the people maye be broughte to understand the Englishe', just as FitzWilliam conceded that where a priest did not know the Lord's Prayer in English, he could 'learn it to them in Irish . . . *till* it may please God to bestow upon them greater blessings' (Collier, *Egerton Papers*, p. 14; Brady, *State Papers*, p. 117; my emphasis). The ideological inflection of this chronology is shown up when it is set against the proposals of the waspish native Protestant, Sir Turlough O'Brien of Ennistimon, who wrote to Burghley in 1591 condemning the slow pace of reform in Connacht. His sequencing of language usage reverses the metropolitan one. The handful of lords capable of understanding English should have daily prayers 'in thenglish tonge *untill* by the providence of God the same may be used in the Irish tonge to thedifyenge of the more nomber' (Cunningham, 'Native Culture', p. 21; my emphasis).

Comparison with English-language policy in other Celtic areas confirms that vernaculars other than English would be tolerated as media of evangelisation in proportion to the conformity of their speakers. Reformation-inclined Welsh passed muster; recusant-inflected Cornish did not. In Wales, cultural distinctiveness was not at odds with political assimilation: the Tudors were hailed as Welsh, the gentry backed the union and Welsh-language enthusiasts like William Salesbury were also Anglican partisans. If Irish seemed 'clean contrary' to English, Welsh – which Salesbury and Lhuyd insisted on calling 'British' – could be co-opted as a supplement to it and as a precedent which, paradoxically, legitimised expansion (Bradshaw, 'Tudor Reformation', pp. 47–53; Jones, *British Tongue*, p. 60; Lhuyd, *Breuiary*, fo. 50r; Roberts, 'Welsh Language'; Salesbury, *Dictionary*, Dedic.). This comfortable arrangement allowed English scholars to evaluate Welsh in purely linguistic terms. Sir Thomas Smith surveyed it with such complacent observations as 'our Welsh countrymen aspirate "r"' (*Works*, p. 127). In the West Country, however, the 'Act of Uniformity' (1549) provoked resistance; the 'Supplication of the Commons of Devon and Cornwall' petitioned that Latin be retained as the liturgical language. As dissent was as much confessional as linguistic, no such latitude was granted. 'The English liturgy became an effective instrument in anglicising the region' and the pattern was repeated in the Isle of Man (Bailey, 'Conquests', pp. 14, 18, fn 5). But even with Welsh, an implicit term was fixed on its operation. The final clause of the 'Act for the Translating of the Bible and Divine Service into the Welsh Tongue' (1562) required that an English-language Bible, too, be placed in 'every Church' so that Welsh monophones 'may by conferring both Tongues together, *the sooner* attain to the knowledge of the English Tongue' (*Stats.*, p. 568; my emphasis). In Scotland, the emergence of an indigenous Gaelic-speaking Calvinism in the Gaidhealtachd makes the situation there distinct from that in Ireland. The Scots-speaking establishment in the lowlands, however, was as contemptuous of Gaelic as their southern neighbours were of Irish and equally loath to countenance vernacular evangelisation (Dawson, 'Calvinism'; Withers, *Gaelic*).

Sixteenth-century Ireland brings home the distinction between the Spanish/Counter-Reformation strategy of the Word and the

English strategy of the *word* – their English words – quite literally. For not only were Irish Catholics acted upon, however ineffectually, in one conversion enterprise but, as agents of the Counter-Reformation at home and overseas, they were actors in another. It is unsurprising that in Ireland, Counter-Reformation propagandists, Gaelic and Old English alike, mobilised the vernacular (Cunningham, 'Native Culture', p. 166). The linguistic endeavours of Irish counter-reformers overseas, however, shows up even more sharply the particularity of Englishmen's exclusive privileging of their vernacular. Irishmen whose own lives were caught up in a drama of translation, in exile among continental languages, engaged energetically with questions of philology. Flaithrí Ó Maolchonaire's labours abroad – as founder of the Irish College in Louvain, as Hugh O'Donnell's interpreter in Spain, as the author of *Discursus de gentibus et linguae origine* – were inseparable from his command of languages (Walsh, *O'Neill*, pp. 29, 54, 69; Ó Cianáin, *Flight*, p. 48; Ó Maolchonaire, *Desiderius*, p. xiv). William Bathe, a Palesman and founder of the Irish College in Salamanca, pioneered the direct method of language-teaching: his *Ianua Linguarum*, with its focus on drilling and vocabulary-building, promised fluency in three months (Proem). It influenced Commenius' *Janua Linguarum Reserata* and was taken up by Jesuits in the New World as a model for equipping evangelists with the language of their mission (Ó Mathúna, *Bathe*, p. 87; Hogan, *Distinguished Irishmen*, p. 393). Another Jesuit, Thomas Filde, exchanged English colonisation in Ireland for its Counter-Reformation equivalent in America. His trajectory took him on a language-learning itinerary which has no parallel among Englishmen crossing the Irish Sea and confirms the contrasting roles assigned to language in both enterprises. He mastered Tupi – in which he would later write a catechism – before joining Anchieta in the Brazilian mission in 1557; in Paraguay, he preached in Guarani. He ended his days teaching indigenous languages to Jesuit novices (Techo, *Historia* I, pp. 139–55; III, p. 181).

The price paid, willingly, for the Anglicans' abstinence from the vernacular was becoming clear by the early seventeenth century in the silence that settled on the ruins of the official church, captured in the refrain of the 1615 Munster visitation: 'No curate, no people. Church and chancell ruyned' (Murphy, 'Visitation', p. 179). Religiously, there was no contest. Linguistically, where English was the language of power, the silence fell the other way.

Enacting linguistic colonisation

The scale of the Elizabethans' ambitions for English are best appreciated by measuring them against the tentative gestures of the Pale reformers. An embattled linguistic minority, the Palesmen concentrated on buttressing their language. The 1515 'State of Ireland and Plan for its Reformation' has an edge of siege mentality about its appeal for more English settlers, 'for hyt is necessary that . . . [the Pale] be inhabyt with Englyshe men, not onely to noryshe our Englyshe langage, but also to encrese archery' (*SPH8* II, p. 24). Justice Luttrell's 1537 proposals convey both the extremity in which English found itself and the modest aspirations of the reformers: the children of the Pale should be taught English 'thoughe the fader cann none, it were necessarye to have a curat, that can speke Englyshe, in every parishe . . . to lerne dayly the said chyldren Englyshe, and ther Beleve'. Luttrell, too, links bolstering English to strengthening the colony's defences more generally: English lessons should be followed by archery practice (*SPH8* II, p. 508).

The gentle metaphors which James Stanihurst, speaker of the Irish Parliament and father of the writer, Richard, employed when, in 1570, he called for the foundation of grammar schools, evince an altogether uninvasive promotion of English. His ambition extends only to local reform of the colony, trusting to the rippling effect of education to carry the language beyond that. He imagines schools in the Pale where

babes from their cradells should be enured under learned schoolemasters with a pure Englishe tonge, habite, fasshion, discipline, and in time utterlie forgett the affinitie of their unbroken borderers, whoe possiblie might be woon by this example, or at the leaste wise loose the opportunitye which nowe they have to infecte other.

Any broader expansion of English is envisaged as a kind of communion: if adjacent Gaels could but sip 'this liquor . . . owre unquiett neighbores woulde finde such swetnes in the taste therof as it should be a readie waye to reclaime them' (Campion, *Two Bokes*, p. 144). The newcomers, however, were geared to expansion rather than containment. Davies approved of the Normans' use of French 'as a marke and badge of conquest' (*Discovery*, p. 127); as the metaphors shift from bulwarks to banners, linguistic defensiveness gives way to linguistic imperialism.

Tudor policy towards Irish was grounded on a refusal to countenance 'difference or distinction' (Davies, *Discovery*, p. 272). Claire McEachern defines the 'founding paradox' of sixteenth-century 'English nationhood' as 'a state seeking to secure a universal compliance with its hierarchical imperatives through the medium of a common language diversely disseminated' (*Poetics*, p. 32). But if it was feared that 'the newly deregulated Word' would escape social control and unleash deviant political and theological expression in England (p. 92), how much more threatening still were the unregulated words of a tongue imagined to be the linguistic incarnation of dissent. Linguistic diversity hung as a threat over the centralist state, even in Wales, where language was more easily co-opted to the Tudor project, as the language clause in the Welsh Act of Union, 1536, acknowledged:

Because that the people of the same Dominion have and do daily use a Speech nothing like, nor consonant to the natural Mother Tongue used within this Realm, some rude and ignorant people have made Distinction and Diversity between the kings Subjects of this Realm and his Subjects . . . of Wales, whereby great Discord, Variance, Debate, Division, Murmur and Sedition hath grown between his said subjects. (Durkacz, *Decline*, p. 4)

When John Alen, the Norfolk-born Master of the Rolls in Ireland, argued, in 1538, that townspeople should be 'compellid to teche ther chyldren, or cause them to be tought, to speake Englyshe', he did so precisely on the grounds that linguistic conformity promoted political compliance: 'bycause that lyke langage and lyke habyt by great occasions to induce lyke obedyence' (*SPH8* ii, p. 483). This, too, was the premise of the 1537 'Act for the English Order, Habite, and Language' which brought the linguistic firmly within the ambit of the political. 'Conformitie, concordance, and familiarity in language, tongue, in manners, order, and apparel, with them that be civil people', it contended, were singularly conducive to bringing 'rude and ignorant people' to a knowledge of God and, no doubt more pertinently, to 'the good and vertuous obedience . . . they owe to their princes and superiors'. It recognised the persuasiveness of cultural difference in encouraging a sense of separate identity:

there is againe nothing which doth more conteyne and keep many of his subjects . . . in a certaine savage and wilde kind and maner of living, then the diversitie that is betwixt them in tongue, language, order, and habite, which by the eye deceiveth the multitude, and perswadeth unto them, that they should be as it were of sundry sorts, or rather of sundry countries.

It blusteringly attempted to minimise the salience of such tokens with the feisty assertion that, appearances notwithstanding, 'indeed they be wholly together one bodie'. As the 'deceptions' of diversity seemed more compelling than assertions of corporal unity, however, the Act sought to repress the sundry and enunciated measures that might bring its proleptic declaration of unity to pass. Accordingly, it decreed

that the said English tongue, habite and order, may be from henceforth continually (and without ceasing or returning at any time to Irish habite or language) used by all men that will knowledge themselves according to their duties of allegeance to be his Highness true and faithfull subjects.

Those who used Irish would be known 'of another sort and inclination' to loyal subjects (*Stats. Irl.*, pp. 120–1).

In the context of 1537, the Act was, at most, a declaration of intent and, in reality, an ineffectual defensive measure (Bradshaw, *Constitutional Revolution*, p. 42). As the century progressed, however, aspirations were steeled by conquest. In 1594, Beacon used the precise phrasing of the Henrician Act when denouncing Irish as one of the elements 'that doth more containe, and holde the subjects of *Salamina* [Ireland], in their disobedience and savage life'. By then, the state was better placed to enforce 'one vniformity' with the severity he advocated (*Solon His Follie*, p. 94). Measures which had been conceived defensively were reinterpreted to justify militant offensives. The 'Book of Instructions' issued to Bingham for reducing the inhabitants of Connacht 'to obedience, and to the ymbracing of Iustice and Englishe Ciuill conuersation' recommended that the long-revoked Statute of Kilkenny's language provisions be applied 'with all seueritie' (PRO SP 63/135/80); the 'Short notes to be considered upon the reducing and settling of Munster' urged that the statute for English habit and language be 'severely enforced' (*CCM* 2, p. 285).

In defensive mode, colonial language policy aimed to protect the colonists from mutating into Irish-speakers. On the offensive, it sought to set in motion a transformative project of its own, anglicisation. For Beacon, the 'mutability' which had long foiled the 'Reformation' of Salamis could be challenged, paradoxically, only by a counter-mutation (*Solon*, p. 4). Reform called for 'a thorough and absolute mutation and change, of auncient lawes, customes, and manners of the people' (p. 20), a cultural overthrow so absolute that no 'shadow and resemblance' of the old order would survive (p. 47). Davies, too, is preoccupied with reversing the vector of transformation. Hitherto, the run of play in the 'Game at Irish' had seen Englishmen mutate into Irish-speakers. But, with the 'barbarous Country . . . broken by a warre' (*Discovery*, p. 5), translation in the opposite direction could begin. The time was ripe to replace Brehon Law with common law, to 'conuert their Mantles into Cloaks' and to turn Irish into English. Indeed, the alteration was already afoot. Parents, impatient with the 'great inconuenience in mouing their suites by an Interpreter', were ensuring that their children acquired English. Davies endorsed the shift, clearly articulating the state's equation between linguistic transformation and control:

so we may conceiue an hope, that the next generation, will in tongue & heart, and euery way else, becom *English*; so as there will bee no difference or distinction, but the Irish Sea betwixt vs. And thus we see a good conuersion, & the *Irish Game turned againe.* (pp. 271–2)

Strictly speaking, anglicisation and de-gaelicising were distinct. Irish did not have to be silenced for English to prosper but a project of transformation left little space for a 'meane course' (Beacon, *Solon His Follie*, p. 49) of bilingualism. Cultural amnesia, the erasure of names and associations, required a blanking out of Irish. For the author of 'The Supplication', the failure of the first colonists to impose English represented a lost opportunity to excise native memory: had it been done, the natives would have 'utterly forgotten them ever to have ben Irishe' (Maley, p. 65). Herbert recognised that a successful colony would only be built on a razed cultural landscape (*Croftus*, p. 80). Invoking Machiavelli, he argues that native laws and customs must be shredded, '*distractis et dissipatis*' (p. 86). Only then would the imitative natives embrace English ways, initially with hollow compliance but eventually by internalising them, '*primo moribus, postea mentibus*' (p. 80). In urging that bards and brehons, 'the keepers of remembrances of the auntient state', be cut off, Dawtrey, too, was arguing for a blow against memory ('A booke', p. 87). The statutes proscribing poets and storytellers, the professional memorialists of the Gaelic world, sought to do just that (*SPH8* II, p. 215; *CCM* I, pp. 214–15; Jackson, 'Irish Language', p. 22).

Irish had no place in the Elizabethans' long-term plans. Perrott's 'Opinions of suppressing rebellion', addressed to Elizabeth during the Desmond rebellion, recommended 'that Orders be set downe for enlarging the *English* tongue, and extinguishing the *Irish* in as short a time as conueniently may be' (E. C. S., *Government*, fo. c.4v).[9] The 'extinguishing' of Irish is prepared for in their dreams of quiet. For

Spenser, noise epitomised Ireland. Colin Clout defined England's tranquillity, through litotes, as the absence of Irish noise: 'No wayling there nor wretchednesse is heard, . . . / No nightly bodrags,[10] nor no hue and cries' (*CCCHA* lines 312, 315). In the *Faerie Queene*, the episode where Artegall and Talus[11] silence the smooth-tongued rebel, Malengin, is followed immediately by the triumphant party's entry to Mercilla's court where 'clamors ceasse' (*FQ* v.ix.23.9). The idealised silence of Mercilla's court rests on the graphically literal suppression of the dissident tongue: marking the entrance is a 'Poet bad' 'whose tongue was for his trespasse vyle / Nayld to a post, adiudged so by law' (25.2–3). This figure, identified by 'cyphers strange' and whose tongue had once reeled off 'bold speaches' and 'rayling rymes' against her majesty, unmistakably echoes the Irish bards in the *View* (25.6–9; 26.3). But where the prose text could only denounce, the poetic one can act out its fantasies of silencing.

Silencing would not be restricted to literary tropes. In the wake of the Nine Years War, 'Ireland was left as a payre of cleane tables, wherein the state might write lawes at pleasure' (Moryson, *Shakespeare's Europe*, p. 227). Ireland is imagined as ready for translation; it offers a *tabula rasa* on which to write a new English lexicon. New names are settled on the wasted countryside. Mountjoy builds a fort in what had been O'Neill's country 'which of his own Christian name was called Charlemont'; another near Dungannon is given his title (Moryson, *History* II, pp. 150–1). 'Translation as a colonist phenomenon . . . took the tangible and physical forms of transposition, transportation, transmission and . . . the transference of land from Irish landholders to English ones' (Tymoczko, *Translation*, p. 19). Davies conflates the figurative and physical senses of 'translation-as-transference' when he contentedly remarks that the inhabitants of Cavan 'have learned to talk of a freehold and of estates of inheritance, which the poor natives of Fermanagh and Tyrconnel could not speak of' (Morley, *Ireland under Elizabeth*, p. 384).

The project of wholesale translation is suggestively captured in the one area where monophone Englishmen were capable of venturing linguistically, that of proper names. To change a man's name, as Spenser coolly recognised, was to uncouple the individual from collective memory. Irenæus urged that each man should be compelled to abandon his sept name in favour of a personal surname and that the 'Oes' and 'Macs' should be 'utterly forbidden and extinguished'. Tagged by a name without memory, each man with his 'several surname' would 'learn quite to forget his Irish nation' (*View*, pp. 155–6). The loyal Palesman, Nicholas White, had correctly identified the connection between the newcomers' wider transformative project and literal translation when he warned Burghley that they 'spare no cost to translate this kingdom of the new' (Canny, 'Edmund Spenser', p. 14).

Anglicising the elite

A language shift was under way well before the seventeenth century. Stanihurst's question – 'Why is English-speaking so much despised in Irish areas? What Irish lords can you name who share our vernacular?' (*De rebus*, p. 145) – was as disingenuous as it was rhetorical: the answer to its second part, even when he asked it in 1584, was far from the ringing negative he implied. Two parliamentary sessions, held a generation apart, testify to the shift taking place. For many of the lords attending the Parliament of 1541, where Henry VIII was proclaimed King of Ireland, English was little more than an uncomprehended ceremonial language. The bilingual Thomas Cusack opened the session in English, the Lord Chancellor replied 'and after, bothe the effecte of the preposicion and answer was briefly and prudentlie declared, in the Irysshe tong, to the said Lordes, by the mouthe of [James] the [tenth] Erle of Ormonde, greately to their contentation' (*SPH8* III, p. 304). A generation later, Irish was still to be heard in the chamber, but English was no longer confined to loyalist Anglo-Irishmen. In 1571, the Earl of Clancare came 'from the uttermost part of Munster' to ask Sidney's pardon for his late rebellion. Sidney seems impressed as much by the bilingual delivery as by the submission itself:

And when he had uttered his mynd on this matter in English in farre other and better termes than I thought he could, for that he sawe many in the chamber in Irish mantells, whereof indeed there were some of right good accompt, he desired that he might reiterate there his former speeches in the Irish tongue, which he did with so good words and gesture, that they that understood him and were of judgement wondered at it. (Sidney, 'Memoir' v, p. 307)

The change is premonitory: this time, it is a Gaelic lord who moves with ease between Irish and English; nor was he alone.

That some command of English was useful, or even imperative, for those confronting an expansionist English administration is easily imagined. The real question is whether such a development represented an option – a pragmatic response to a changing reality – or an imposition. The evidence suggests that it represented the outcome of a sustained policy which made embracing English a condition of entry into the emerging anglicised state. Conquest was a slow campaign of attrition. As individual lords were brought to heel, indentures linked their passage into the new order to a rite of language-learning. There was an integral 'scheme of cultural anglicisation' (*Revolution*, p. 199). The relentlessness with which such terms were imposed over the succeeding half century – in 1599, Elizabeth was still instructing Essex to bind submitting rebels 'to use English habit and language' (*CCM* 3, p. 295) – amounts to little less than a policy of social and linguistic engineering.

Henry VIII wrote to the citizens of Galway, in 1536, requiring them to

indevor theym selfe to speke Englyshe, and to use theym selffe after the Englyshe facion; and specyally that you, and every of you, do put forth your childe to scole, to lerne to speke Englyshe. (*SPH8* II, p. 310)

Here was the key to extending English usage: to promote it among the coming generation. The policy would soon be extended to Gaelic Ireland, with measurable effect. The (re)grant of Powerscourt to Turlough O'Toole, in 1542, required that he and the other beneficiaries use 'to the best of their knowledge, the English language [and that] they shall bring up their children . . . in the use of the English tongue' (*CPR* I, p. 81). As O'Toole himself relied on one FitzWilliam 'who came as his interpreter', the real focus was on the future, on anglicising the next generation. With minor variations, the formula requiring submitting lords to 'bringe uppe their childern after thEnglishe maner, and thuse of thEnglishe tonge', echoes through agreements made with Manus O'Donnell, Con O'Neill, the O'Mores and O'Connors and hosts of lesser lords (*CCM* I, pp. 184, 198; *SPH8* III, p. 291; cf. *CSPI* 1509–73, p. 134; MacCurtain, 'Women', p. 58; *CBC*, p. 175; O'Flaherty, *Chorographical Description*, p. 321). The administration showed little inclination to treat such undertakings as perfunctory rituals of compliance. When Brian MacGillapatrick, Lord of Ossory, submitted in 1537, he undertook to use English and have it taught to his children (*SPH8* III, p. 321). Four years later, when St Leger applied for Ossory's letters patent, he was able to inform Elizabeth that his son (probably Brian Óg/Barnaby) 'hath bene this yere and more in your Inglisshe Paale, and is well brought up, and speketh good Inglisshe' (Gilbert, *Facsimiles* iv.1, p. xxii).

Moreover, there was a concerted attempt to draw scions of the principal familes inside the ambit of English influence through an ironic exercise in counter-fosterage. In his 'Discourse of Ireland', Humphrey Gilbert suggested that one way to bring the country to 'cyvill governaunce' was 'to have allwaies the nobilities children of Ireland to be pages of honour to the kinge of England' (Quinn, *Gilbert*, p. 126). Charles, son of Sir Cormac MacTeig MacCarthy, Lord of Muskerry, was Sir Walter Ralegh's page; Florence Mac-Carthy spent part of his youth under the guardianship of Sir William Drury (*CSPI* 1588–92, p. 417; MacCarthy, *Life*, p. 13). Edmund Butler, Ormond's younger brother was, Sidney reminded Walsingham, 'a page of my own bringing up' (*CCM* 2, p. 346). The best known of all Sidney's protégés was Hugh O'Neill, whom he 'bred in my house from a little boy' (Morgan, *Tyrone's Rebellion*, pp. 92–3). A new pattern of wardship, too, sought to overturn that exercised by Irish lords whose charges, Irenæus opined, were 'brought up lewdly and Irish like' (*View*, p. 29). When Sir John O'Dogherty died, Docwra took charge of his son, Cahir, making him 'conversant with English statecraft and literature' (Meehan, *Fate and Fortunes*, p. 292). Brian Óg MacDiarmada, whose father was patron of the *Annals of Loch Cé*, became a ward of Theobald Dillon who sent him to Trinity to learn 'the English language and habits' (Walsh, *Men of Learning*, p. 20).[12]

Elizabethan policy-makers anticipated the author of *The Irish Hudibras* in recognising that the education of the native élite 'at the English court . . . something Refin'd their Gibberish' (Farwell, Dedic.). Brian Óg MacGillapatrick graduated from school in the Pale to the household of Prince Edward, where he was educated alongside Henry Sidney and Thomas Butler, the future earl of Ormond. Gaelic panegyrists struggled to assimilate the new trend to the older pattern of fosterhood. Flann Mac Craith imagined young Butler as the 'bedfellow' – 'aoin-leapthadh' – of the Prince. Domhnall Mac Dáire represented Patrick FitzMaurice, the future Baron Kerry who was educated at the courts of Mary and Elizabeth, as a 'dalta na láoch ó Lonnainn' (a pupil of the London warriors) (O'Daly, 'Panegyric', p. 474; Bergin, *Bardic Poetry*, p. 58: 37.4).

While, at mid-century, Chancellor Alen could complain that 'veray feawe of the Irishry woll put thaire childern to lerne the Englishe tonge' (*SPH8* iii, p. 526), the sons of Gaelic gentlemen attended English-speaking institutions in increasing numbers as the century advanced. When forty barrels of powder exploded in Wine-tavern Street in Dublin, the casualties included youngsters who had come from all parts of Ireland to be educated (*ARÉ* iii, p. 2,013). O'Neill brushed off the administration's demands that he educate his sons 'out of this barbarous country . . . in good manner and civility in England' (*CSPI* 1596–7, p. 483). But his refusal was political: linguistically, his sons were being schooled for their encounter with an English-speaking world. When Sir John Harington visited 'the arch-rebel himself', he found O'Neill's two sons wearing 'English clothes like a nobleman's sons' and 'both of them [learning] the English tongue'. When he presented O'Neill with a copy of *Orlando Furioso*, the earl 'solemnly swore his boys should read all the book over to him' (*Letters*, p. 77). The number of young men from the principal Irish families outside the Pale studying at the English universities and Inns of Court is a measure of their assimilation into the English-speaking world. Seán Mac Oliver Burke who, Sidney reported, spoke no English, sent his son, David, to Oxford and the Inns of Court (Collins, *Letters*, p. 104; *CSPI* 1596–7, p. 155). In 1602, the son of Cormac MacCarthy, Lord of Muskerry, was at Oxford, his identity split between two names, Cormac/Charles (*Salis.* xii, pp. 337–8). Naughtan O'Donnell's anglicisation followed a more equivocal progress: he was removed from Oxford to share a cell with his father, Niall Garbh, in the Tower (Meehan, *Rise and Fall*, p. 15). This reminds us that there were darker paths of entry to the English-speaking world. When Donal Spáinneach submitted in 1600, he was required to send one son 'to be brought up at school' in Dublin – and to surrender a second to the Castle (*CSPI* 1600–1, p. 56). The indenture marking Aodh Conallach O'Reilly's submission to Sidney is typical of dozens of others in requiring him to hand over his son, Seán, as a pledge (*CCM* i, p. 377; cf. pp. 184, 190, 211). Conn Mac Calvagh O'Donnell, who had been a hostage in the Pale, needed 'no interpreter by reason of his good bringing up with that worthy knight Sir Thomas Cusake' (Morgan, *Tyrone's Rebellion*, p. 125).

Knowledge of English became a yardstick of compliance. English-speakers were rewarded; hibernophones who were passed over learned to read the writing on the wall. The Commissioners adjudicating among the three competitors to the chieftaincy of Clandeboy awarded it to Sir Brian McFelim's son, Felim, because he was 'a modest man . . . that speaks English' (*CSPI* 1574–85, p. 464).

Linguistic considerations proved persuasive for the administration when backing Sidney's erstwhile hostage as Aodh Conallach O'Reilly's successor. Whereas the other claimant, Edmund, 'speaketh no Englysh' (PRO SP 63/102/64), Seán – now metamorphosised into Sir John – 'mayntayned himselfe very cyvyllye . . . [and] spekyth the Inglyshe tonge' (*CSPI* 1574–85, p. cvii).

This massive state intervention in the formation of two generations of Irishmen was, of course, conceived as rather more than a programme of state-sponsored language-learning. It was an experiment in acculturation that put its faith in the power of a shared upbringing to solder political bonds. But if teaching English was not the end in itself, it was clearly a vital part of the undertaking and, in the event, probably its principal legacy. Complete transformation was only rarely achieved. St Leger's ward, Richard Burke, later the second Earl of Clanricard, became sufficiently anglicised to attract the epithet *Saxanach* – though his English had become so rusty by 1579 that he had to confess that it 'would not serve him to use any large discourse of his dutiful meaning towards Her Majesty' (*CSPI* 1574–85, p. 163). Donough O'Brien, tutored at the court of Elizabeth, proved an ideal protegé: Carew found him 'as trewly Englishe as yf he had beene borne in Myddlesex', a transformation vouched for by the fact that he 'hathe drawne more blood of his owne people than is to be beleeved' (Gilbert, *Facsimiles* IV.1, p. 108).

But, as O'Neill's subsequent career as, in the queen's words, 'the most ungrateful viper to us that raised him' demonstrated (Moryson, *History* II, p. 225), the outcome of this elaborate educational experiment was far from assured. Even if 'in Courte trainde up', the woodkern reverted to kind once back on his 'shaking boggs' (Derricke, *Image*, p. 42). Edmund Butler, the Lord Deputy's erstwhile page, turned rebel. Even when Sidney sent 'some servants of mine, his old and familiar fellows' to win him back, Edmund held to his rebellious purpose and never thereafter would Sidney's 'pretty and foregrown page' come to him (*CCM* 2, pp. 346, 349). We learn that Grace O'Malley's son, Tibbot Burke, had 'been brought up civilly' by John Bingham 'and can speak English' only from the letter in which Elizabeth endorsed his continuing detention for insurgency (Chambers, *Granuaile*, p. 113). At times, the policy served only to allow the neophytes to make a plaintive swansong. Bingham took three young Burkes as pledges. All, in the words of the Burke's 'Book of Complaint', 'most devilish and Turkishly were executed'. Ulick, the 14-year-old son of the Blind Abbot, 'having learned the English tongue, and somewhat could write and read', knew that literates were entitled to be shriven and so, as he was led to his death, cried out 'I can read, why doth not Sir Richard permit me to have the benefit thereof' (*CSPI* 1588–92, pp. 265–6). Yet if its protégés' subsequent conduct repeatedly disproved the colonists' wistful equation between shared language and shared loyalty, the policy was still bearing fruit linguistically. The rebellious alumni were, at least, coming to articulate their dissent in the language of their adversaries.

Some Irish lords were starting to internalise the equation between English and civility – or at any rate, to subscribe to such formulae when arguing in an English forum. Donal O'Sullivan Beare went before the Privy Council in 1587 to refute the charge made by Owen, his uncle and challenger, that Beara was 'barbarous and uncivil'. He claimed, rather, that 'the country was not so barbarous, but that the heirs thereof were always brought up in learning and civility, and could speak the English and Latin tongues.' Donal turned the tables on his uncle, suggesting that he had imputed ignorance to all 'to excuse his own ignorance and want of bringing up, being not able to speak the English language' (*CSPI* 1586–8, p. 342).

A generational shift was under way. Tibbot/Theobald Burke who slew – and was slain by – James FitzMaurice was 'learned in the English language and law'. But when his father, the chieftain of Castleconnell, was made a baron in a gesture of consolation, the old man 'made many grateful speeches in his language' before swooning from the 'unwonted straitness' of his new English robes (Bagwell, *Tudors* 3, p. 45). Calbhagh O'Molloy's want of English disqualified him from taking his seat in James I's Irish parliament; his submission in 1599, however, had indicated that his son, Cahir – who re-emerged as 'Charles' – was at school in Dublin (Walsh, *Chiefs and Leaders*, p. 284). While the administration was principally concerned with grooming sons in English civility, it is evident that daughters, too, were picking up English. O'Connor Faly's daughter, Margaret, secured the release of her father, long imprisoned in England, 'a hucht a bérla' (on account of her [English] language) (*ARÉ* 2, p. 1531).

At the end of the period, Bishop Montgomery took an inventory of his dioceses, Derry, Raphoe and Clogher. In recording the languages spoken by his clergymen, he left a precious census of language use among a key sector of the population in one of the remoter parts of the island – a record that captures the delicate shift in language learning. Of twenty-three ministers, nine spoke Irish and Latin, eight Irish, Latin and English, four Irish, Latin and Scots, one Irish and Scots and only one, the gluttonous vicar of Taughboyne, is dismissed as 'minime doctus' (Alexander, 'O'Kane Papers', p. 89). Nor does Montgomery suggest that their knowledge is perfunctory. The erenach of Dunboe is 'very learned in the manner of his people' – 'perdoctus more suorum' – in Irish, Latin and civil law (p. 88). Montgomery captures a moment of transition. Those schooled in the old patterns of learning – '*bene dicit hibernie et latine*' – are being joined by men trained '*more anglorum*'. Four of the Scots-speakers had studied in Glasgow and the schooling of the coming generation pointed to English. John McCardull of Clogher spoke only Irish and Latin but his son was studying in Drogheda and two other young men were training for the ministry in Dublin (p. 91). The rector of Cumber's two brothers spoke English and Neal O'Donnell, school-master and brother of the melancholy rector of Donaghmore, knew Irish, Latin and English (p. 88).

Payne's description of Limerick schoolboys learning 'to conster the Latin into English' (*Briefe Description*, p. 3) suggests to Corcoran that they were acquiring both languages together in a manner that would survive into the eighteenth century, producing an English that was 'formal, bookish, and Latinised' (*State Policy*, p. 33). Evidence of the new language seasons the textual record with hibernicisms as the century draws to a close. A curious macaronic item written by Thady Dowling, Chancellor of Leighlin, at the turn of the century seems to play out in its own performance the language-learning adventure contemporaneously taking place across the country. Jumbled in its language(s) and intentions, it begins in Latin before drifting into English with a proposal to

translate into Irish carractors & idioms, a pious kalender and an almanack for certyn yers The Irish A.b.c. with the vowels and consonants and other parts of introduction into the knowledge and redyng of the language, with some prayers & lytle treatisse, with a short vocabularie begyning with the irish words & with all an Antydall contayning the properties, operations & qualities of . . . herbes & beastes and make them as litle Incheridien as I may. (PRO SP 63/210/62)

Dowling's text both exemplifies and explains the process that had brought him to a plateau of imperfect mastery and unstoppable fluency. He explains that he gathered 'some croomes of learning in the country, some whers in one scoole & some quarters in another', before going to Dublin 'to learne the institutions of both the lawes' with Patrick Cusack, a 'fre scoolmaster'. The extravagance with which he handles his new vocabulary, relishing it more for its excess than its precision – telling us that, as a student, he 'laye nightly in one bed with Mr byrne, a Civilian of comendation & had the vse and revolving of his boks with his confrances & resolutions' – bears the hallmark not only of the precocious learner but of Hiberno-English-speakers for generations to come for whom the surprise and possibility of this other tongue seemed never to become entirely neutralised or natural.

The desire to be heard by an administration becoming increasingly monophone as the bilingual Old English were sidelined pushed many towards venturing into an English to which the sounds and structures of Irish still clung. A letter to Docwra written on behalf of Niall Garbh hits on approximations to English words only through bold improvisation: 'Please send the sauger madger' (sergeant major) (*CSPI* 1601–3, p. 47). And is it just fancy that allows us to hear a snatch of Hugh O'Neill's Hiberno-English accent when he writes to the Earl of Salisbury as his humble 'shuter'? (*CSPI* 1603–6, p. 359). A campaign of conquest keenly attentive to the cultural was causing the Irish-speaker – Gaelic lord and ambitious upstart alike – 'to turne the other ende of his tongue, and speake Englishe' (Stanihurst, *Chronicle*, p. 14).

CHAPTER 5

New world, new incomprehension: patterns of change and continuity in the English encounter with native languages from Munster to Manoa

> She complimented me
> in a language I didn't know;
> but when she blew cigar smoke
> into my ears and nostrils
> I understood, like a dog,
> although I can't speak it yet.
> Elizabeth Bishop, 'The Riverman', *Works*, p. 106

When Ralegh, in his *History of the World*, reflected on the incomprehension that lay behind the haphazard naming of the New World, he did so with the weary knowingness of a new historicist. In seeking to disentangle geographical fact from 'fantastical opinion', he turned to linguistics, sceptically unpicking false etymologies as part of his empirical method. He dismissed the 'fancy' that identified Ophir/Parvaim with Peru. The latter was less a placename than a misunderstanding:

the *Spaniards* vtterly ignorant of that language, demaunding by signes (as they could) the name of the Countrie, and pointing with their hand athwart a riuer . . . the *Indians* answered *Peru* which was either the name of that brooke, or of water in generall.

He rejected Montanus' claim that Yucatan was biblical Joctan with the same philological incisiveness: '*Iucatan*, is nothing else in the language of that Countrie, but [*What is that?*] or [*What do you say?*] For when the *Spaniards* asked the name of that place (no man conceiuing their meaning) one of the Saluages answered *Iucatan* (which is) *What ask you*, or *What say you?*' (p. 175). In such moments, Ralegh's perspective seems closer to critics like Greenblatt and Todorov, who both fix on that very episode as a 'symbole des malentendus', than to his linguistically inept contemporaries (Todorov, *Conquête*, p. 129; cf. Greenblatt, *Marvelous Possessions*, p. 104). He distances himself from his men's toponymic bunglings:

'The same hapned among the *English*, which I sent vnder Sir *Richard Greeneuile* to inhabite *Virginia*. For when some of my people asked the name of that Countrie, one of the Saluages answered *Wingandacon*, which is as much to say, as, *you weare good clothes*, or gay clothes' (pp. 175–6). In his alertness to mistranslation, Ralegh's mindset seems a new world away from the linguistic heedlessness of the New English in Ireland. The piquancy of the apparent disjunction is that it is illusory. For Ralegh was both the conjurer of language who represented his two voyages to Guiana as dramas of translation and 'conference' *and* the Munster planter who accumulated places and rendered placenames senseless, whose encounters with non-anglophones – the 'churl' near Rathkeale, the defenders at Smerwick – silenced talk with withies and 'the swoord'.[1] But it nonetheless suggests that there were revealing differences in the colonists' approach to language in Ireland and the New World.

For a remarkable number of Ralegh's closest associates in the New World, Ireland had been 'their earlier America' (Rowse, *Grenvill*, p. 64; cf. Sheehan, *Savagism*, p. 54). Humphrey Gilbert, Ralegh's half-brother and the pioneer who nudged the Elizabethans towards thoughts of planting in the western hemisphere, left behind his own *legenda negra* in Ireland, immortalised in 'songes and Rimes' as 'an enchaunter . . . ridyng on a Deuill' (Churchyard, *Rehearsal*, fo. R.i.r). Sir Richard Grenville, leader of the 1585 and 1586 voyages to Virginia, had the largest estate of any 'undertaker' in Munster (Rowse, *Grenvill*, p. 276). William Pelham, who crushed the Desmond rebellion, and Richard Bingham, who enforced martial law in Connacht, pooled their slender poetic gifts to cobble together commendatory verses for George Peckham's *Trve Reporte* of Gilbert's voyage.[2] William St Leger, who was aboard the Destiny on the last voyage to Guiana, like Ralegh too feverish to venture up the Orinoco, was the son of Sir Warham, an important Munster planter and Ralegh's comrade-in-arms there. Ralph Lane, leader of the first settlement in Roanoke, came to America battle-hardened from Ireland where he had overseen the extirpation of the O'Mores from Laois to Clanmorris. By 1592, he was back in Ireland's 'raw and waterish climate', serving as muster-master until his death in 1603 (*CSPI* 1596–7, p. 148). In 1602, he wrote 'A discouery' urging the 'plantacion of an *English Collonie*' in Ulster (PRO SP 63/210/524). Thomas Harriot, Ralegh's scientific adviser and Southern Algonkian specialist, spent ten years as Ralegh's tenant in Molana Abbey on his

return from Virginia, while John White, illustrator and Governor of
Roanoke, wrote his account of the fifth voyage 'from my house at
Newtowne in Kylmore', from where he surveyed Ralegh's Munster
estate (Hakluyt, *Principal Navigations* VIII, p. 406; cf. Quinn, 'Munster
Plantation'; Wallace, *White*, p. 6).

This coincidence in line-up allows us to observe how the same cast
responded to the language sub-plot in the two dramas of encounter
and colonisation, acted out an ocean apart. At first viewing, the
differences appear far more striking than any similarities. The utter
unfamiliarity of the New World and the intense sensation of stepping
into the marvellous excited expectations and attitudes altogether
unlike those prompted by what Lane, back in Ireland once again,
called 'the tediousness of the brokenness of this lost kingdom, in the
daily confusions of it' (*CSPI* 1598–9, p. 482). The wonder of the new
contrasted with a weary familiarity bred of old enmities and
prejudice. The texts of the first English voyagers to America convey
a sense of primal encounter, of fresh beginnings. These differences
are picked up in the different approache to language on both sides of
the Atlantic. At the most pedestrian level, the obdurate otherness of
the Amerindian languages was inescapable and could not but be
thematised in the first narratives. There were no Old English
intermediaries, as yet no bilingual natives, to ease interlingual
exchanges to the point where the very existence of the other
language could be repressed in the text.

At the same time, the exoticism of this new environment extended
Englishmen's experiences beyond any European lexicon: to recount
the wonders of tapirs and manati meant to learn new names. In
Ireland, the New English had dangerously confused similarity with
sameness. Ireland was in many ways so like England – so *almost*
England – that all its little disparities seemed like deliberate vexa-
tions, wrinkles of difference that needed to be ironed out. In the
Americas, however, where a discourse of difference, rather than one
of similarity-mistaken-for-sameness, held sway, linguistic difference
was at first seen as just another strand in the rich weave of exotic and
unthreatening otherness. Whereas the recalcitrance of the Irish
tainted their language by association, the Indians, in the first phase
of encounter, were regarded as potential allies against the Spanish.
This pattern of triangulation shielded them, initially, from being
caught up in a polarisation between European self and American
other (Montrose, 'Work of Gender', p. 194). Manipulation of the

local language to mobilise alliances could be strategically useful rather than compromising.

For all these reasons, the Amerindian languages could be treated with a tolerance impossible in Ireland. For these reasons, too, engagement with them could be trumpeted rather than suppressed. The superficial amity of relations, where recourse to the native tongue paid dividends, encouraged writers to parade such exchanges in a way unthinkable in Ireland. In 'The discoverie of the rich, large and beautifull Empire of Guiana', Ralegh represents a band of Indians as paddling anxiously away from his party until they 'came within call, and by our interpreter [we] tolde them what wee were, wherewith they came backe willingly abord us: and of such fish and Tortugas egges as they had gathered, they gave us'. Another group plies Ralegh's 'Captains' – the rank-pulling was, no doubt, interpolated in translation – with the local brew 'till they were reasonable pleasant' (Hakluyt x, pp. 392–3). If language was necessary for food, it was even more essential if the newcomers were to talk their way to goldmines. And when, as happened, there was no gold, native words would have to serve in the exhortatory – or exculpatory – texts of the prospectors as gages for treasures whose only manifestation was lexical.

The relatively high profile given the Amerindian languages in the texts of, especially, Ralegh and Harriot should not be taken as marking a sea-change in the colonists' handling of indigenous languages in their passage westwards from Ireland. Whether placed in the spotlight or shunted off-stage, the native's tongue was, in both cases, made to serve the colonists' ends. For all the parading of interpreters, glossaries and set-pieces of translation, incomprehension lay at the heart of English engagement with the Indians' languages. In Ireland, incomprehension – subversive mutterings and beastly howls – intensified mistrust and hostility. In the New World, it permitted a latitude of interpretation that erred, initially, towards the optimistic and positive: whatever they were really saying, the Indians were imagined to be welcoming and supportive of English acquisitive projects. But incomprehension, whether positively or negatively inflected, in refusing to hear the others' story while making incursions into their way of life, is not only in itself a kind of violence but an almost certain precursor to it. For all the shifts in plot and characterisation that happened as the action moved west, Ralegh, Lane, Grenville and the rest of the Munster touring company would effectively replay in the Americas the old, power-distorted language encounter which they had rehearsed in Ireland.

The narratives of Englishmen's first encounters with the inhabitants of the New World seem like encapsulations of a mythic moment, where the awkward emissaries of the Old Continent glimpse a pre-lapsarian world which they are destined to destroy. Barlow, leader of the first expedition dispatched to Virginia by Ralegh, anchors off Roanoke, surveying the 'goodly woodes full of Deere'. Then, on 'the third day we espied one small boate rowing towardes us having in it three persons'. One comes aboard and is given a shirt, a hat and a 'taste of our wine'. He takes to his canoe again, fishes 'and in lesse then halfe an houre, he had laden his boate as deepe, as it could swimme' and returns to the ships, dividing his gift between the two barks (Hakluyt VIII, pp. 299–300). This is a moment unlike any we have met in Ireland. A sensation of wonder shimmers over the newcomer's perception of the native, who stands apart, resistant to reductive appropriation (cf. Affergan, *Exotisme*, p. 83). The direction of the encounter hangs in the balance. The Englishman is poised between moving into a creative encounter with otherness or falling back on a taxonomy of difference. Language – and the newcomer's assumptions about what language did – held the key to the possibility of reciprocity. Relational semantics implicitly offered some chance of entering into the 'marvelous dispossession' (Green-blatt, *Marvelous Possessions*, p. 149) of another's language and its subtly distinct universe. Referential semantics offered only the illusion of encountering a foreign – and, therefore, presumed inferior – version of one's own. Even Montaigne, who could imagine that '[t]he very words that import lying, falshood, treason, dissim-ulation, covetousnes, envie, detraction, and pardon, were never heard of' among the Indians (*Essayes*, p. 102), was still indentured to a discourse of comparison rather than alterity. An emerging sense that the relationship between language and reality might be rela-tional rather than referential could, for the moment, prompt little more than disquieting intimations of native difference; linguistics had a long way to travel before it could give insights into the integrity of cultural difference. For the moment, the limits of the colonist's sympathy for the other were set not just by the imperatives of acquisition but by the limits of the linguistic theories which guided his encounters.

In his first voyage to Guiana, Ralegh's noisy text, full as it is of jockeying with Spaniards and a show of cross-cultural communication with Indians, quietens as he catches a vision of paradise:

here we beheld plaines of twenty miles in length, the grasse short and greene, and in divers parts groves of trees by themselves, as if they had beene by all the arte and labour in the world so made of purpose: and still as we rowed, the deere came downe feeding by the waters side, as if they had beene used to a keepers call.

But Eden, as ever, has its serpents. The river has 'divers sorts of strange fishes, and of marvellous bignes: but for lagartos it exceeded, for there were thousands of those ugly serpents' (Hakluyt x, p. 388). If the New World is not as idyllic as it first seems, neither is it wordless. But words are often unheard and rarely understood. When the Indian fish-giver came aboard Barlow's ship, without 'shewe of feare or doubt . . . he had spoken of many things not understood by us' (Hakluyt viii, p. 300). The insouciance of Barlow's phrasing at once understates the extent of the Englishmen's incomprehension and dismisses the value of what is lost thereby. With the peculiar assurance of the monophone, the colonist sees incomprehension as a disability affecting only the native. As anglophones' representations of Irish showed, ignorance of the other's language induced not humility but disparagement. The gloss to John White's drawing of 'The arriual of the Englishemen in Virginia' represents the Indians as making 'a great an horrible crye . . . like wild beasts or men out of their wyts'. The inclination to regard speakers of an unknown tongue as bestial – albeit amenable to domestication – continues as White imagines that, once the natives perceived the Englishmen's 'courtesie', they – like Ralegh's 'deere . . . to a keepers call' – 'came fawninge vppon vs, and bade us welcome' (Quinn, *Roanoke Voyages*, p. 414).

In the absence of understanding, the colonist projects his own comforting gloss on to sounds and gestures whose conventions escape him. The day after meeting the fisher-canoeist, Barlow is visited by Granganimeo. In his up-beat interpretation of the parley, the captain is as oblivious to the conventional nature of gestures as he is to the cultural specificity of kinship and caste designations when he identifies his visitor as 'the kings brother'. Recognising no impediment to transparent communication, Barlow runs together description and a naively optimistic interpretation: Granganimeo made all signes of joy and welcome, striking on his head and his breast and afterwardes on ours, to shewe wee were all one, smiling and making shewe the best he could of all love, and familiaritie. (Hakluyt VIII, pp. 300–1)

That the colonists' confidence in their ability to decode 'signes and tokens' (p. 301) was misplaced is repeatedly confirmed. Ralph Lane exchanged belligerently gesticulating hibernophones for what seemed, initially, like more biddable natives in Virginia. When he set out in search of 'Minerall Countrey', the Indians, warned of his advance by their fellows on the coast, withdrew from his path. In the midst of a deserted landscape, 'wee heard certaine Savages call as we thought, Manteo[3] . . . whereof we all being very glad, hoping of some friendly conference with them, and making him to answere them, they presently began a song, as we thought, in token of our welcome to them: but Manteo presently betooke him to his piece, and tolde mee that they meant to fight with us'. The accuracy of Manteo's translation is vouched for by a sign which Lane was less likely to misread: 'a vollie of their arrowes' hits his boat (p. 330). Lane was learning that songs and dances have their own grammars.[4]

Gilbert's conduct in Ireland had evinced little flair for cross-cultural communication; he showed no amendment of approach when he crossed the Atlantic. While his crew included Stephen Parmenius, 'to record in the Latine tongue, the gests and things worthy of remembrance', there was no interpreter on board (Hakluyt VIII, p. 67). Unconscious of the possible dissonance between the transmission of a West Country-originated sign and its reception by Micmacs, Gilbert,

for solace of our people, and allurement of the Savages . . . provided of Musike in good variety: not omiting the least toyes, as Morris dancers, Hobby horsse, and Maylike conceits to delight the Savage people. (p. 47)

In the event, his principal speech act in Newfoundland excluded the natives in an exercise that would be risible were its implications not so far-reaching. On 5 August 1583, in the harbour known to the English as 'St John's', before a motley assembly of European fishermen, Gilbert formally took possession of the territory for the queen and her Church. The proclamation was duly interpreted for the other Europeans. There is no mention of native witnesses to the performance. The indigenous 'Newfoundlanders' are acknowledged – and dismissed – in just one reference: 'savages altogether harmlesse' (p. 58). There is a sense of *déjà vu* as well as of arrogant absurdity in Gilbert's act. It recalls the *Requieremiento* delivered in Spanish to bewildered natives who were thereby being divested of their patrimony. The parallel is chilling: when speech acts overlooked their real interlocutors so completely, the existence of the other would be registered only through conflict. And Gilbert, who in Ireland considered 'his Dogges eares to good' to listen to anyone defying his edicts (Churchyard, *Rehearsal*, fo. Q.ii.v), made no secret of the threat backing his words: 'if any person should utter words sounding to the dishonour of her Majestie, he should loose his eares' (Hakluyt VIII, p. 54).

The disregard for the other implicit in marginalising communications prepares the way for violence. The pernicious drift from casually sidelining understanding to embracing aggression is acted out by Peckham, Gilbert's 'chiefe adventurer and furtherer', in his 'A true report of the late discoveries . . . of the Newfound Lands'. Starting from the convenient but unsustainable proposition that English emulation of the Spanish in the Americas would be both 'profitable to the adventurers' and 'beneficiall to the Savages' he envisages winning the 'willing assent of the Savages' to the Englishmen's 'quiet possession' of Micmac ancestral lands through 'peaceable conversation'. The Indians would sooner be won 'by courtesie and mildnesse, then by crueltie or roughnesse'. Spurred on by his own pacific vision to contemplate how this might be achieved, however, Peckham jibs at the effort required, covering his retreat with disingenuousness and euphemism: although the English

are not so throughly furnished with the perfectnesse of their language, eyther to expresse their mindes to them, or againe to conceive the Savages intent: Yet for the present opportunitie, such policie may be used by friendly signes, and courteous tokens towards them. (Hakluyt VIII, p. 99)

The collapse from an ideal, 'perfectnesse of their language', to the bathetic is complete when it transpires that the only communication envisaged is 'some kindes of our pettie marchandizes and trifles', bells, beads and 'collers of Bewgle'. The absolute abdication of linguistic effort is confirmed by his blustering proposal to make known to the Indians that they would be safe, provided they offered the 'Christians' friendship, 'eyther by speeche, if it be possible, either by some other certaine meanes'. From that point in his discourse, the slippage is ineluctable. If, after all 'fayre meanes', the Indians continue 'in withstanding them [the English] afterwards to enjoy the rights for which both painfully and lawfully they have adventured themselves thither', the English will be entitled 'to use the Lawe of Armes' and, if they do, 'shall no whit at all transgresse the bonds of equitie or civilitie' (pp. 97–101). In his descent into countenancing force, Peckham is fortified by the Irish precedent: since Strongbow triumphed over the 'populous and strong' kingdom of Leinster, the English can hardly now fail against 'these Savages, being a naked kinde of people' (p. 123).

The Virginian Indians, decimated by diseases to which their European carriers were largely immune, imagined that airy English spirits killed them 'by shooting invisible bullets into them' (Hakluyt VIII, p. 382). Less invisible were the bullets and arquebusses hanging over the fragile dialogue between Ralegh's agents and their increasingly unwilling hosts. The firing-range of English guns fixed the co-ordinates of the encounter: in Barlow's 'Conference with a Savage', the canoe with 'three persons' came within 'foure harquebuz-shot from our shippes'; the fisher-visitor set his lines 'two bow shoot into the water' (pp. 299–300). Exchanges were framed by violence. Relying, no doubt, on Manteo to interpret, Lane gained invaluable 'understanding and light of the Countrey' from the *werowance*, Menatonon, whom he found 'of a very singular good discourse in matters concerning the state'. But Lane also lets slip the inequality of a 'conference' conducted '[w]hen I had him prisoner with me' (p. 322).

J. W. Shirley concludes that Lane and Grenville 'were too close to their violent battles with the Irish and too intense in their hatred of the Spanish and Portuguese to approach the natives with . . . understanding' ('American Colonization', p. 109; cf. Kuppermann, *Settling*, p. 171). In Ireland, Lane enthusiastically backed Bingham's draconian rule, regarding the Irish as an enemy amenable only to violence: 'the end must needs be a sharp war' (*CSPI* 1592–9, p. 191; 1596–7, p. 151). He spoke of them as 'beggars', 'rascals', 'wild rogue[s]' and, at times, as when contemplating 'unkennelling the wolf [Fiach Mac Hugh] out of his den', as animals (*CSPI* 1592–6, pp. 189, 190, 292). None of his many letters addresses Irishmen and the only Irish loanwords in them are correlatives of acquisitiveness: he has taken a 'prey of 2,500 creights'[5] and has a 'want of garrons' (p. 373). Grenville's only recorded brush with Irish came when, making an inventory of his Munster acquisitions in 1589, he admitted a stray loanword: 'vii Irish caples' (Rowse, *Grenvill*, p. 271). Nothing in the record of his American exploits suggests a change of conduct.

When Indians went to the bad, they began to seem Irish. White's account of the Indians' – suspected – murder of the fifteen men whom Grenville had left behind on Roanoke visualised an Indian pulling a knife from that most stereotypically Irish of garments, a 'mantell' (Hakluyt VIII, p. 394). By the end of Lane's one-year stewardship in Virginia, relations between the Indians and the Europeans had broken down. But the iron that had entered the soul in Ireland was not confined to Lane's. Lane ordered the *werowance*, Pemisapan, to meet him on Croatan; when the *werowance* tried to escape, he was 'shot thwart the buttocks by mine Irish boy with my petronnell'. Still running, he was pursued by 'an Irishman serving me, one Nugent'; Lane, following, met Nugent 'returning out of the wood with Pemisapans head in his hand' (pp. 341–2). In its replay of incomprehension and violence, there is little difference between the way Ralegh's captains related to native languages in Virginia and in Ireland.

Yet, overall, the Elizabethans' engagement with Amerindian languages was far from being an exact rerun of their behaviour in Ireland. The priority that Ralegh and his agent, Harriot, attached to gaining a command of local languages which could ease their passage to wealth and control marks the point where the management of language in the two colonial ventures diverged. Ralegh's accounts of his voyages to Guiana in 1595 and 1617 show his own explorations to have been intensely – even *essentially* – linguistic. Like so much about Ralegh's 'large, rich, and beautifull Empire of Guiana', his 'discoverie' of it was a fiction. Everywhere he went, the Spanish had already been. Above all Berreo, Governor of Trinidad, had beaten him to exploring the Orinoco; when Ralegh captured him, he 'gathered from him as much of Guiana as hee knew' (Hakluyt X, p. 354). He arrived in a landscape already inscribed by the marks of others; he came belatedly, as a supplement, not an originator – as a critic; and as a critic, his focus is on language. Berreo might have penetrated regions where Ralegh, no whit abashed to acknowledge himself 'a very ill footeman', would never go (p. 404). Still, Ralegh stresses, Berreo might have been a fine walker – but he lacked language: he had 'neither friendship among the people, nor any interpreter to perswade or treat' with natives. True, he had counted the one hundred rivers flowing into the Orinoco, 'but he knew not the names of any of these'. In the Americas, Ralegh knows the usefulness of commandeering the local languages and the price of incomprehension; in condemning Berreo, he is also passing judgement on his fellows in Ireland – and on himself. Berreo 'had no meanes to discourse with the inhabitants at any time: neither was he curious in these things, being utterly unlearned, and not knowing the East from the West'. But Ralegh, as least now that he had gone west, recognises the importance of language. Of those from whom Berreo had learned nothing, 'I got some knowledge, and of many more, partly by mine owne travell, and the rest by conference: of some one I learned one, of others the rest, having with me an Indian that spake many languages, and that of Guiana naturally' (pp. 370–1).

Ralegh's is a journey into language. He conceives of the encounter in terms of talk. Arriving in the West Indies in March 1595, he spent five days anchored off Trinidad and, as he recorded restively, 'in all that time we came not to the speach of any Indian or Spaniard' (p. 349). For Ralegh, the 1617 voyage was an almost entirely linguistic event. While his doomed son, Wat, and Keymis, his lieutenant, sought out the elusive goldmine, Ralegh, too ill to venture upriver, stayed aboard the 'Destiny' where the only activity, besides burying the dead and refitting the storm-damaged barks, was linguistic. Seven Indians are brought aboard, accused of spying. They affect to speak no Spanish and communicate only 'by signs' (Edwards, *Last Voyages*, p. 215). An Indian captured on shore reveals that one of the captives held on the ship *does* speak Spanish and the latter, unmasked, is interrogated. Ralegh learns of the sacking of San Thomé – the off-stage climax of the expedition and his effective death-warrant – through this convoluted drama of translation. He responds with another translation blitz, ordering Spanish-speaking villagers to be rounded up; from their interrogation, he gets confirmation of the story.

Interpreters were airbrushed from English accounts of their encounters with Irish-speakers. Lane's account of how he quizzed Menatonon – largely to discover the whereabouts of a 'great store of Pearle that were white, great, and round' – imported that mode of reportage to Virginia. He carefully varied the formulae whereby he attributed his information to his reliable source – 'he tolde me', 'hee described unto mee', 'hee signified unto mee'; 'Menatonon confessed unto me' (Hakluyt VIII, pp. 323, 327) – and in doing so, he snuffs out all trace of the intermediary. In contrast, interpreters are highly visible in Ralegh's New World narrative. Their prominence calls attention to one of the most notable features of his text and its break with practice in Ireland: its systematic disclosure of the mechanics of cross-cultural communications. Ralegh's network of language-workers is scarcely less extensive than the entourage which he gathered about him in the heady first days of his favour at court. He arrives in Trinidad poised for talk. With him comes his 'Indian interpreter, which I caried out of England' and, along the way, he adds to his store (Hakluyt x, p. 353). Returning downriver, with the onset of the rainy season arguing against delay, he detours to arrange with Topiawari, a sympathetic *cacique*, to bring one of his people to England, 'as well to learne the language, as to conferre withall by the way' (p. 409). When he returned in 1617, his network was even more extensive. While 'my old servant Leonard the Indian' had moved away, he could call upon 'Harry', *cacique* of Cayenne, who 'was also my servant and had lived with me in the Tower two years' (Edwards, *Last Voyages*, pp. 210–11).

Ralegh does not just identify his interpreters: he lets us see them at work. For once, there is no mystifying how speeches flow between the mutually uncomprehending. When Topiawari comes to confer in Ralegh's tent, the interpreter is squeezed in, too: 'I shut out all but our selves, and my interpreter' (Hakluyt x, p. 410). At an earlier meeting between the two men, the interpreter had also been to the fore: 'I beganne by my interpreter to discourse with him [Topiawari] of the death of Morequito.' On that occasion, Ralegh even showed how they got around the tricky problem of translating colour words: Topiawari sought to convey that his people had been invaded by warriors wearing 'hattes of crimson colour, which colour hee expressed, by shewing a piece of red wood, wherewith my tent was supported' (pp. 399–400). A similar sense of straining to be understood clings to Ralegh's account of meeting five Trinidadian *caciques* whom he had 'rescued' from Berreo and interviewed through an interpreter.

I made them understand that I was the servant of a Queene, who was the great Casique of the North, and a virgine, and had more Casiqui under her then there were trees in that yland: that shee was an enemie to the Castellani. (pp. 353–4)

The elements of Arawac and Spanish carried over into Ralegh's paraphrase convey a lively impression of a macaronic pooling of all available words in the interest of making sense.

Ralegh and his agents are explicit to the point of pedantry about the linguistic routes along which meaning travelled. Ralegh's detailing of the circuitous path by which he learnt of the assault on San Thomé has already been mentioned. Later, as a last throw of the dice, he relates how his men, retreating from San Thomé, had been approached by a *cacique* 'and by one of his men which spake Spanish (having as it seemed been long in their hands) he offered them a rich gold mine in his own country' (Edwards, *Last Voyages*, p. 243). Keymis conscientiously appended 'A Table' to his account of the voyage which he made on Ralegh's behalf to Guiana in 1596: it noted, where known, the languages of the tribes surveyed: some 'speake the Tivitivas language'; others, known to 'eate them whome they kill', 'speake the language of the Indians of Dominica' (Hakluyt x, pp. 491–3). Not only that: he tells Ralegh that 'John your Interpreter' speaks the Caribs' tongue – a potentially useful qualification given that the monsters with 'eminent heads like dogs . . . speake the Charibes language' too (p. 465).

Yet, to say that Ralegh and his associates foregrounded in the narratives of their American conquests what they had repressed in Ireland is not to suggest that the Indian languages or their speakers enjoyed any favours thereby. While the mode of representation changed, the power relations between the colonial and the indigenous language was just the same, and just as damaging.[6] The highlighting of New World languages in Harriot's and Ralegh's texts served the colonising intent of their writers just as surely as the sidelining of Irish served textually to deny a difference which contested the pretensions of Tudor uniformity. The guidelines for the aborted 1582 voyage to Virginia had required the ship's geographer to note 'the dyversitie of their languages and in what places their speache beginnethe to alter' and Salmon suggests that Harriot was acting on similar instructions during his year in the colony (*Harriot*, p. 3). Mapping linguistic demography was not a disinterested pursuit. Harriot comments on the linguistic diversity of the Virginians in his last section, 'Of the nature and maners of the people' in which, he scrupulously acknowledges, he is interested 'onely so farre foorth' as it confirms how far the natives are from 'troubling our inhabiting and planting'. His observation that 'the language of every government is different from any other, and the further they are distant, the greater is the difference', is unqualified. But coming alongside his estimate that any one 'government' was 'able to make not above seven or eight hundreth fighting men at the most'

(Hakluyt VIII, pp. 374–5), it is clearly intended as an assurance that such a fragmented polity could not mount a united challenge to the English. The divisiveness of language difference, so alarming to commentators in Ireland, was here running in the colonists' favour. Keymis predicted that the fissiparousness it promoted would, in the Americas, be the Spaniards' problem: they would find it exceedingly difficult to hold together an empire with 'those huge countreys of the Indies having no common linke of affinitie, lawe, language, or religion' (Hakluyt x, p. 485).

If the diversity of the Indian languages seemed to give assurance that their speakers could not mount an effective challenge to English claims, the genealogy of those languages, suitably counterfeited, could be used to substantiate those claims. Just as the alleged 'British' origin of Irish had been trotted out to establish England's ancient right to occupy the island, so imagined traces of Welsh found in Amerindian languages were used to stake claims in America. In his attempt to prove England's 'lawfull title' to Newfoundland, Peckham revived the old legend that a Welsh prince, Madock ap Owen Gwyneth, had discovered the New World in 1170 and 'planted colonies' there and 'then gave to certaine Ilands, beastes, and foules sundry Welsh names, as the Iland of Pengwin'. Furthermore, 'there is a fruit called Gwynethes which is likewise a Welsh word' and 'divers other Welsh wordes at this day in use' so that, strictly speaking, the queen is simply being restored to her 'ancient right and interest in those Countries' (Hakluyt VIII, p. 108).

There is nothing academic about Ralegh's engagement with the languages of the Orinoco delta. Keymis bluntly identifies the utility of harnessing local languages to English advantage. Telling Ralegh that he proposes to bring another guide who 'speaketh all their languages' back to London, he promises that he will 'find him many wayes able to steed your Lordship in your designes and purposes' (Hakluyt x, p. 458). Far from recording a reciprocal encounter, Ralegh's texts reveal his profoundly solipsistic engagement with the language of the other. For him, native words would not, in the end, lead to mutuality or real communication. They would be used instrumentally, to scoop up strategic information on location and, more imperatively, when American reality failed to deliver his dreams, to conjure up the recalcitrant marvels of the New World rhetorically.

For, in truth, Ralegh had little to show for his adventures except words. He returned from the 1596 voyage, as he acknowledged to Howard and Cecil in the dedication of 'The discoverie of the large, rich, and beautifull Empire of Guiana', 'a beggar, and withered'. His venture was regarded as a 'journey of picory'. His claims to have found gold were scorned. There were whispers that if he *had* specimens, he had bought them in Barbary on the voyage home. He even had to counter insinuations that he had travelled no further than Cornwall (Hakluyt x, pp. 339–40). With no gold ore to smelt, he turned wordsmith, to make the mythical realm of the Inga of Manoa glister on the page. Discoverer of nothing, Ralegh shaped his 'discoverie' into a work of rhetorical substitution. Once, when weighing up the question of whether Mandeville's headless monsters really did inhabit the upper reaches of the Orinoco, Ralegh reasoned that 'whether it be true or no, the matter is not great, neither can there bee any profit in the imagination' (p. 406). It is a curious comment for one whose only hope of profit now lay in feeding the imagination of his readers.

'The discoverie' is extraordinarily discursive. Ralegh is forty pages into his text before he starts to paddle up the Orinoco. Up to that point, he concentrates on proving the *textual* existence of the riches that he had not been able to find in reality. He quotes López de Gómara – first in Spanish and then, for good measure, in English – to attest to the existence of unimaginable wealth in Guiana (p. 357) and uses Thevet to the same end.[7] Travellers with tales to tell are called as witnesses. If, as Greenblatt argues, Ralegh's writings are 'surrogate actions' (*Ralegh*, p. ix), then the lexical items that he brings home and the speech acts which he performed in Guiana must also be seen as substitutes for tangible achievements. Failing to uncover riches, he mines the native languages to bring back a word-trove.

The rhetorical challenge confronting Ralegh in writing 'The discoverie' was to confirm two claims that could not be substantiated any other way: that 'most of the kings of the borders are already become her Majesties vassals' and that Guiana 'hath more quantity of gold by manifolde, then the best partes of the Indies, or Peru' (Hakluyt x, p. 341). His only proof was verbal. To uphold his claim to have won Indian vassals for Elizabeth, Ralegh highlighted his 'conferences' with *caciques* where he had sought to uncover local patterns of allegiance and to draw the Guianans into alliances against the Spaniards. He sends 'our Orenoquepone' to the tribe bordering on Topiawari's people, 'making them know that we were enemies to the Spaniards'; a pact of sorts is entered into at a subsequent meeting (p. 402). Ralegh boasts of 'dilating at large . . . her Majesties greatnesse' to Topiawari: if he cannot expand Elizabeth's empire territorially, he can at least stretch her sway oratorically – and lexically (p. 399). He underlines the 'large discourse' he made in praise of her everywhere he went,

so as in that part of the world her Majestie is very famous and admirable, whom they now call Ezrabeta Cassipuna Aquerewana, which is as much as Elizabeth, the great princesse or greatest commander. (p. 354)

By showing as fully as he can how negotiations were conducted and language difficulties surmounted, Ralegh conveys an impression of informal treaties freely entered into, where well-briefed *caciques* solemnly pledged allegiance to the queen and thus, symbolically at least, became her vassals. Where obfuscation served in Ireland, on the Orinoco only the illusion of full disclosure could sustain the fiction of assent voluntarily given to English claims, sanctioning the colonists' self-deception that theirs was a guiltless cupidity. Chapman forged a link between blameless acquisition and eloquence in his dedicatory verse to Keymis, *De Guiana Carmen Epicum*, where he imagined that

(as if ech man were an *Orpheus*)
A world of Savadges fall tame before them,
Storing their theft-free treasuries with golde.
(*Plays and Poems*, p. 281: lines 165–7)

Greenblatt suggests that in the Europeans' narratives of the New World, 'the marvelous stands for the missing caravels laden with gold' (*Ralegh*, p. 73). In Ralegh's writings, it is native words that must deputise in the awkward absence of minerals, answering to the second rhetorical challenge which he set himself: to prove the existence of gold. Mere mention of the local language seemed to trigger thoughts of treasure, as when Ralegh, in what only *seems* like a *non sequitur*, moves directly from recording that he left his boy, Hugh Goodwin, with Topiawari 'to learne the language' to 'I after asked the maner how the Epuremei wrought those plates of golde' (Hakluyt x, p. 414). When, as always, questions about the location of gold elicited only tantalising deferrals – over the mountain, beyond the impassable cataract – the *words* for gold – *les mots pour le dire* – had to stand in instead. Though native hostility stymied Lane's expedition into 'Minerall Countrey', his dreams of gold encouraged him to work semantic alchemy on its unstable Algonkian signifier. He mused that the 'Minerall they say is Wassador, which is copper, but they call by the name of Wassador every mettall whatsoever' (Hakluyt VIII, pp. 328–9). The inconclusive gloss allowed him to dream on.

The early voyages to Virginia had been scarcely more successful than the Guianan episode in freighting caravels or in firing the popular imagination. The Oxford-educated mathematician Thomas Harriot, one of the *cadre* of intellectuals whom Ralegh assembled to advance his ventures, sailed on the second voyage to Virginia under Grenville and spent ten months there, garnering all the information he could about native resources, polity and customs. He brought an impressive linguistic flair to his task. He may have learned Algonkian from Manteo and Wanchese, whom Barlow had delivered to Durham House on his return from the 1584 voyage; Quinn speculates that he may even have gone on the first voyage and he certainly acquired considerable fluency in Virginia (Salmon, *Harriot*, p. 5; Quinn, *Harriot*, p. 6). His 'A briefe and true report' sought to refute 'slanderous and shamefull speeches bruted abroad by many that returned from thence' and to assure sceptical investors and adventurers that it 'may returne you profit and gaine' (Hakluyt VIII, pp. 349–50). He recognised that Virginia offered not instant riches but the less marketable prospect of reward for toil. Early travel-writers used inventories to evoke 'a cornucopia beyond the American actuality' (Fuller, *Voyages in Print*, p. 50). Harriot sought to authenticate *his* list by drafting in native words to body forth abundance lexically. His tract, freighted with seventy-six Algonkian words, is an extended glossary 'of Merchantable commodities' (Hakluyt VIII, p. 353). Native names – 'Sassafras, called by the inhabitants Winauk', 'an herbe called Wasebur, little small roots called Chappacor, and the barke of the tree called by the inhabitants Tangomockonomindge' – are used both to vouch for the existence of raw materials guaranteed to 'yeeld good profit' (pp. 355, 357) and to give an exotic allure to the medicinal extracts and dyes identified.

The 'Report' is the record of a consuming quest for knowledge and for words: 'through inquiry', 'I learned', 'I after understood', 'they tolde me two stories', 'through conversing'; he painstakingly investigated native belief 'by having speciall familiaritie with some of their priests' (pp. 357, 377–8). But Algonkian words are valid only in so far as they can be cashed in for English terms. The surplus is expendable but useful in the interim, alluded to but not recorded, to evoke excess. So plentiful are fowl that Harriot has 'the names in the countrey language of forescore and sixe'. The variety of fish – speared by 'shooting . . . into the fish after the maner as Irish men cast darts' – is such that it surpasses an English lexicon: there are many 'whose names I know not but in the countrey language' (pp. 369–70). Harriot reproduces some native tree-names like 'Rakiock' which he reckons 'to be fit . . . for masts of ships'. But he logs only those words that can be translated into timber: there are many others

whose names I know not but in the Virginian language, of which I am not now able, neither is it so convenient for the present to trouble you with particular relation: seeing that for timber and other necessary uses, I have named sufficient. (pp. 372–3)

Those not immediately exploitable are a kind of extravagant supplement whose names, known but not patented in the text, serve as shadowy promises for the future. Meanwhile, what cannot be translated into European utility is consigned to the flickering immateriality of existing '*but* in the countrey language'.

It may be that 'Right names were the first foundation / For telling truth' (Heaney, 'Open Letter', p. 29) but even the most industrious collectors of Indian words had no qualms about replacing them with English ones once they had served their turn. Harriot identifies the 'right name', then replaces it with one from the class of English neologisms that were springing up and which domesticated the new by simply classifying it as an alien variant of the home-grown norm. So 'Pagator' is 'a kinde of graine so called by the inhabitants . . . English men call it Guiny-wheat or Turkey-wheat'. At other times, an English term is uprooted and its semantic field defiantly extended to a native American species – even when the native name is to hand. 'Okindgier' are 'called by us Beanes' though they are, in fact, 'much different'. By the same logic, 'Wickonzowr' are 'called by us Peaze, in respect of the Beanes, for distinction sake' (Hakluyt VIII, pp. 359–60). Similarly, Ralegh's insistent pairing of the native name with its makeshift colonial neologism consistently sidelines the original: 'Hamaca, which wee call brasill beds' (Hakluyt x, p. 393).[8]

This pattern of learning and then setting aside imposed rigid limits on exchanges between the two sides. Harriot found out what he needed to about the native religion, then pronounced that it was 'farre from *the* trueth': the definiteness of that article confirms the status of all Indian meanings – supplementary, or wrong. That the natives had 'no letters nor other such meanes as we to keepe Records' only further marginalised their beliefs in his eyes (Hakluyt VIII, p. 376; my emphasis). A year after completing his 'Report', he was surveying Ralegh's lands near Lismore, signing his map of Molana 'Tomas Haryots of Yohal' in the phonetic script which he had devised for recording Algonkian (Wallace, *White*, p. 11; Salmon, *Harriot*, p. 1). No Englishman in Ireland replicated the linguistic feats that Harriot had performed in America. That he spent years in Ireland studiously ignoring the vernacular, as far as the record goes, only sharpens the paradox.

A readiness to replace Indian words with European ones boded ill for the longer-term direction of language acquisition.[9] Ralegh, for one, seemed to assume that once the languages of the Old Continent had arrived, they would be readily taken up by the natives in an act of self-translation – as with the five *caciques* on Trinidad who 'are called in their owne language Acarewana, and now of late since English, French and Spanish are come among them, they call themselves Capitaines' (Hakluyt X, p. 353). Native names in these accounts have a strange insubstantiality and are lightly erased. Gilbert sailed to 'the newfound land' through a seascape already overlaid with European names, 'Penguin Island', 'Baccalaos' (Hakluyt VIII, pp. 49–50). Barlow performs the eclipse effortlessly: 'the king is called Wingina, the countrey Wingandacoa, and now by her Majestie Virginia' (p. 300). Lane shows no greater inclination to accept local names: 'there is a Towne which we called The blinde Towne, but the Savages called it Ohanoak' (p. 322). Ralegh and Keymis compulsively intoned the local toponomia – 'Cunanamma, Uracco, Mawara, Mawarparo, Amonna' – but once places were possessed through such litanies of acquisition, names were expendable. As well as bagging the above-named rivers, Keymis was busily Englishing the delta 'from Cape Cecyl [via "Port Howard"] to Raleana' – 'which the Naturals call Orenoque' – because, while the landscape was not without names, they were not European names. The Spanish had not yet described that coast in any 'sea-card' and so Keymis 'thought the libertie of imposing English names to certaine places of note, of right to belong unto our labours' and to flatter their 'favourers' (Hakluyt X, pp. 454, 459, 480). Weighed against names validated by European cartography, native names seemed lightweight and disposable. Ralegh, Spenser's Timias,[10] extends the quest of the *Faerie Queene* to the Americas when he comes upon a river 'which because it had no [mapped] name, wee called the river of the Red crosse, our selves being the first Christians that ever came therein' (p. 381).

'Christening' was an irresistible reflex but a profoundly secular one – almost idolatrously so when Ralegh speaks of the Spaniard Martinez as having 'Christened' Manoa 'by the name of El Dorado'. Guides and interpreters had their identity anglicised by being given 'christian' names: Leonard, Martin, John, Gilbert. Topiawari's son became known, presumably as a gesture to Sir Walter, as 'Gualtero' (Hakluyt x, pp. 361, 467). Of 'Christening' in any religious sense, there is no evidence. Even the comparatively fluent Harriot balked at a task that demanded 'more then wee had meanes for want of perfect utterance in their language to expresse' (Hakluyt VIII, p. 378). White complacently remarked that the Virginians were

verye Desirous to know the truthe. For whenas wee kneeled downe on our knees to make our prayers vnto god, they went abowt to imitate vs, and when they saw we moued our lipps, they also dyd the like. Wherfore that is verye like that they might easelye be bro[u]gt to the knowledge of the gospel. (Hulton and Quinn, *American Drawings* II, p. 425)

His unconscious echo of Archbishop Long's abandonment of the natives of Breifne to parroting what they could not understand (see p. 130 above) points to a similar laxness in approaches to evangelisation in Ireland and America: if the natives could not be brought 'easelye' to reform, they would not be brought at all. As in Ireland, English indifference to evangelisation contrasts with the proselytising zeal of the Counter-Reformations' agents. The scholarship which French Jesuits were contemporaneously bringing to bear on the language of the Hurons replayed, with more tolerance, the philological endeavours of the Spanish and was in marked contrast to Harriot's faint-heartedness about preaching in Algonkian (Jennings, *Invasion of America*, pp. 45–57; Hanzeli, *Missionary Linguistics*; Healy, 'French Jesuits').

During the 1595 expedition, Ralegh sent a group of captains on the trail of 'a great silver mine'. A *cacique*, Wanuretona, had told Ralegh through an interpreter that over the mountain the English could 'satisfie our selves with gold and all other good things'. Ralegh himself set off with a smaller party 'to viewe the strange overfals of the river of Caroli', and detailed Captain Whiddon's men 'to see if they coulde finde any Minerall stone alongst the river side' (Hakluyt x, p. 403). Ralegh's description of the sequence of falls is one of those moments in 'The discoverie' where his prose strains to rise to the marvellous. But his vision is too earthed by his own preoccupations and the strong current of his habitual perceptions to meet the new in anything other than on his own terms, bearing out Greenblatt's judgement that his 'vision could never accommodate more than a single consciousness – his own' (*Ralegh*, p. 167). English townscapes shimmer, mirage-like, in the spray of the cataracts,

every one as high over the other as a Church-tower, which fell with that fury, that the rebound of water made it seeme, as if it had bene all covered over with a great shower of raine: and in some places wee tooke it at the first for a smoke that had risen over some great towne.

The covetous gaze sees not the unfamiliar in its otherness but only the gratification of its own desires:

I never saw a more beautifull countrey, nor more lively *prospects* . . . the deere crossing in every path, the birdes towards the evening singing on every tree with a thousand severall tunes, cranes and herons of white, crimson, and carnation pearching in the rivers side, the aire fresh with a gentle Easterly winde, and every stone that we stouped to take up, promised either golde or silver by his complexion. (Hakluyt x, p. 404; my emphasis)

In just the same way, the encounter with indigenous languages was strictly instrumental. There was no venturing beyond English certainties on to the liminal space opened up through contact with the other's language. Edwards contrasts Ralegh's 'capacity for sympathy and tolerance' for the Indians with his anathematising of all things Irish (*Threshold*, p. 79). But the supposed dichotomy between Ralegh's attitude to the Irish and the Indians is less real than Edwards suggests. The Indians' usefulness and their provisional abstinence from violence, it is true, encouraged him to condescend to them rather than execrate – or execute – them. But, as his cooption of their language for his own ends indicates, there was no greater inclination among Elizabethans in America to see the world through another's eyes than there had been in Ireland. The indigenous languages were mastered by a European agenda, as meanings were lost or reinvented in translation. As Indian signifieds were shoehorned into rough English approximations, the opacity and cultural particularity of the other was being overridden or ignored. Only an unthinking extension of European chronometric conventions to Algonkian allowed Barlow to imagine that his native informants were telling him that a certain city was 'above one houres journey' away (Hakluyt viii, p. 306).

More sophisticated observers trampled no less clumsily over native meanings. Concepts that had no European equivalent were obliterated through paraphrases that foisted on to them categories of kinship and politics alien to the New World. Ralegh plays up the role of the interpreter when reporting his conference with Topiawari. He makes a great show of the literalness of the translation, noting the Indian's turn of phrase – the invaders came 'from so farre off as the Sunne slept, (for such were his owne wordes)'; he 'was every day called for by death, which was also his own phrase' (Hakluyt x, pp. 400–1). But the distortion worked on the *cacique*'s concepts is nonetheless breathtaking as he is made to speak of 'nephew', 'king', 'ransome', 'owner of that province', 'borderers', 'frontiers' (pp. 413–14). An anthropologist conversant with kinship and property-relations among modern-day equatorial Indians points out 'the violence done when we force their words to work as our words do' (Campbell, *Waiwai*, p. 129). The obliviousness to conceptual asymmetry which had poisoned the Tudors' attempt to force an equivalence between 'acres' and *baile biattaig* had arrived in the Americas.

The textual attention which Ralegh lavished on his management of language difference in the Orinoco was strategic. It assembled native specialist witnesses to testify to claims which he had otherwise failed to substantiate and it gave a veneer of due process and plausibility to his alleged acquisition of rainforest vassals for the queen. But a rhetorical trope could not guarantee understanding. The difficulties go beyond the inadequacy of interpreters and translations – but those problems should not be underestimated. When Ralegh returned to Guiana, he found that his 'servant Harry' who had spent two years in the Tower with him, 'had almost forgotten his English' (Edwards, *Last Voyages*, p. 212). Robert Harcourt, perhaps the most engaging of the explorer-linguists of the age, sailed to Guiana in 1613 and sought out Leonard Ragapo, then a *cacique*. Ralegh had brought him to England in 1595 but Harcourt is no more than polite about his residual command of English: 'he can a little understand and speak our language' and elsewhere he hints at the deficiency of the interpreters whom he had brought from England (Harcourt, 'Relation', pp. 497, 494). But the incomprehension went deeper than purely technical impediments. So oblivious is Ralegh to the difficulties of cross-cultural communications that he inadvertently admits into his text evidence of the misunderstandings besetting exchanges which he buoyantly imagines to be successful.

What the five Trinidadian *caciques* made of the concept of 'north' or of a 'virgine' queen ruling it is best left to conjecture. But when, to reinforce the point, Ralegh showed them a picture of Elizabeth, even he seems aware that the image excites an interpretation that is slipping beyond his control: 'they so admired and honoured [it], as it had bene easie to have brought them idolatrous thereof' (Hakluyt x, p. 354). Harriot, too, fought off his uneasiness about the mismatch between his attempt to convey that the Bible did not 'materially and of it selfe' contain virtue and the Indians' desire

to touch it, to embrace it, to kisse it, to holde it to their breastes and heads, and stroke all over their body with it, to shew their hungry desire of that knowledge which was spoken of. (Hakluyt VIII, p. 379)[11]

There was no equality in the exchanges between European and Indian. The newcomers' approach to indigenous languages was self-interested and almost invariably distorted by the threat of violence. Ralegh's 'Journal' of his 1617 voyage is a bleak, skeletal record of feverishness and collapsing illusions. It has no room for the rhetorical inventions of 'The discoverie'. In its terse recital, the violence infesting the encounter shows closer to the surface. The Spanish-speaking Indian who reveals that one of the three Indians held prisoner by Ralegh *does* know Spanish confesses only 'after many threats'; the villagers who are brought in to confirm the story wrung from the Spanish-speaking prisoner are rounded up by sixteen English musketeers (Edwards, *Last Voyages*, pp. 215–16).

There would be no fertile exchange or hybridity in the encounter between Englishmen and the people of the New World. The stand-off was enforced at the most literal level. 'The great sea-captains of the age . . . do not appear to have wasted much time or thought upon sex; they were men of action' (Rowse, *Grenvill*, p. 59). Be that as it may, the memorialists of the first voyages were at pains to stress the continence of their men. Harriot recorded with satisfaction that the Indians 'noted . . . that we had no women amongst us, neither that we did care for any of theirs'; baffled, they surmised that Englishmen were not of woman born (Hakluyt VIII, p. 381). Lane recorded that when the Indians withdrew cooperation, they 'abandoned their Townes . . . and retired themselves with their Crenepos', which is glossed in the margin as 'their women' (p. 327). Lane's rare resort to a loan word recalls the parallel New English usage of *cailleach*: both words insisted on the otherness of native women and fenced them off behind a linguistic *cordon sanitaire*. Ralegh pointedly contrasts the chaste conduct of his men with the concupiscence of the Spanish, who took local women 'for the satisfying of their owne lusts'. While the English had many 'excellently favoured' and 'starke naked' native women 'in our power', he is convinced that none of his men 'by violence or otherwise, ever knew any of their women' (Hakluyt x, p. 391). In Ireland, the degenerative drift of Old English was invariably accounted for in gendered terms. The rules of engagement in America would see to it that there would be no replay there.

The uncoupling of language from the feminine is seen at its most striking in Ralegh's declaration that the Tivitivas 'have the most manly speech and most deliberate that ever I heard, of what nation soever' (p. 383). (Clearly more manly than Irish, which as a language that Ralegh had heard often enough is an implied term in that comparison.) Indian women were safe from the attentions of Englishmen, because the latters' fantasies of rape were focused elsewhere – on the feminised land. Keymis imagined that in Guiana 'whole shires of fruitfull rich grounds, lying now waste for want of people, do prostitute themselves unto us, like a faire and beautifull woman, in the pride and floure of desired yeeres' (p. 487).[12] Ralegh opens 'The discoverie' by fulminating that Carlos V 'had the maidenhead of Peru' (p. 346). He closes it with a terrible fantasy of despoilation:

Guiana is a countrey that hath yet her maydenhead, never sackt, turned, nor wrought, the face of the earth hath not bene torne, nor the vertue and salt of the soyle spent by manurance, the graves have not bene opened for golde, the mines not broken with sledges, nor their Images puld downe out of their temples. It hath never bene entered by any armie of strength, and never conquered or possessed by any christian Prince. (p. 428)

Guiana is conceived of as a fragile membrane, sheathing Ralegh from consummating his treasure-lust. His verbal ejaculation of desire evokes the land's vulnerable perfection negatively by conjuring up the destructive forces poised to annihilate what they covet. But in rushing priapically on to anticipate how, once taken, Guiana can be held by defending a channel so narrow 'that no ship can passe up but within a Pikes length of the artillerie', he is imaginatively contemplating the rape of Guiana and giving it his assent.

The difference in the prominence given to representations of the indigenous languages so marked in Elizabethan texts emanating from Ireland and the Americas should not obscure the fact that whether in the spotlight or the shadows, language is always only a tool in the hands of the colonists. 'Conversation' would be no more 'peaceable' in the New World than it would be 'civil' in Ireland. Ralegh's 'Discoverie' may have begun by seeking 'speech', but when it gazed on the gold-complexioned 'face' of Guiana at the end, it envisaged loosing not the tongue – but an orgy of male violence. The 'manly language' of the natives featured in that fantasy as little more than an accessory to rape.

CHAPTER 6

The clamorous silence

One hand to an ear for the vibration,
The far wires, the reverberation
Down light-years of the imagination.
Derek Mahon, 'Aran'

Fínghin Mac Carthaigh Reagh/Florence MacCarthy, the Lord of Carbery whose duality stung Carew into styling him 'the Machiavellian ambodexter' (Stafford, *Pacata Hibernia* I, p. 118), spent the last thirty years of his life detained in London. He passed his long years of confinement seeking the redress of English law and shoring fragments against the ruin of the culture which he had tried, unsuccessfully, to reconcile with the new order. He sought to interest the new men, focused only on an anglicised future, in the Gaelic past.[1] MacCarthy wrote to the poet, Fear Feasa Ó an Cháinte, in about 1602. Curiously, the letter, found among Cecil's papers, is written first in Irish and then, with the transition 'Which in English is. . .', in translation, like a specimen parallel-text. He tells Ó an Cháinte – who spoke no English – that, to solace 'thouermuch melancholie' of his confinement, he has resolved

to write somewhat in Ireish for the queenes Majestie, which I do purpose, to the end she may understand it, to cause the whole somm of the matter . . . to be put in English, by the help of my frends here, that are skillful and learned in their owne languadge (De Brún, 'Litir', p. 52)

and he summons the *file* to assist him.

Thirty years later, MacCarthy was still in captivity – and still writing his monumental 'Chronicle of Ireland' in a gesture of defiant salvage. Among the old manuscripts which he assembled as source material was a copy of the late fifteenth-century Annals compiled for Fínghin Ó Mathgamhna by his *ollamh*, O'Fihely. These Annals – pored over by the captive in the Tower to produce a work that has not survived, for an intended readership that was entirely indifferent – themselves intimate lost possibilities of creative interaction between the two languages: O'Fihily was Oxford-educated; his patron translated Mandeville into Irish, in 1475 (Ó hInnse, *Annals*, pp. viii-ix; Stokes, 'Gaelic Maundeville').[2]

Fear Feasa Ó an Cháinte replied to his patron's summons in *Gluais a litir go Lunndain*, 'Go, letter, to London'. The *file* begged to be excused from journeying, arguing *'Cách thoir ní tuigfidhe liom'* – that in the east, no one would understand him (Bergin, *Bardic Poetry*, p. 153: 18.1). But in the west, too, there was increasingly little security for the learned classes or their language.

The great fascination of the Elizabethan writing of Ireland is that it records not only the origins of a silence – that of Irish – but of a new volubility and linguistic adroitness. 'The Great Silence' might entail a psychic loss that would be literally unspeakable (De Fréine) – but it would not be quiet.

In the New World, conquest brought silence. Carlos Fuentes speaks of the 'ruidosos conquistadores, cuyas voces ásperas y resonantes contrastaban con las voces de pájaro de los indios' (the noisy conquistadors, whose harsh and resounding voices contrasted with the bird-voices of the Indians) (*Valiente mundo nuevo*, p. 64). Cortés' advance rendered the Mexica 'incapable de réagir, de parler' (Le Clézio, *Rêve mexicain*, p. 20). Words were frozen, inadequate to the new situation; and the native Americans have never fully repossessed them.[3] Octavio Paz's 'Los hijos de la Malinche', Malinche's Children, is a meditation on the continuing, defeated silence of Mexico's taciturn ('parcos') campesinos; Paz interprets their reserve, dissimulation and 'malas palabras' (bad language) as the markers of a 'gente dominada' (*Laberinto*, pp. 78–89). Le Clézio contrasts the noise of the Aztec world with the silence that followed its collapse: 'ce silence, c'est celui de la mort d'un peuple' (this silence is that of the death of a people). Such a silence, Le Clézio argues, was a necessary condition of the Spanish victory: Spain's New World would be founded on the silence that effaced the native world-view (*Rêve mexicain*, pp. 58, 231). Alvar, too, evokes that silence: 'Lo que los Españoles no llegaron a interpretar quedó en el mundo del silencio' (What the Spanish didn't succeed in interpreting remained in the world of silence) ('La lengua', p. 253). We close the circle on our comparison of Spanish and English linguistic colonisation by acknowledging the very different outcomes for native-speakers on the opposite sides of the Atlantic and recognising that the reasons for the Indian silence – disease, genocide and centuries of exploitation – go far beyond issues of linguistic colonisation (Crosby, *Ecological Imperialism*; Pereña, *Genocidio*).

The outcome of linguistic colonisation in Ireland was more paradoxical. The English imagined that to silence Irish was to silence dissent and excise memory; they envisaged English as an instrument of control and its imposition a way of instilling attitudes felt to be native to their civil tongue. They dreamed of a univocal Ireland; the reality, however, was more complex and equivocal. In some ways anglicisation had less to do with language than with silence: it sought to induce quietness rather than speech. As a strategy for silencing, however, the translation of the native into English would fail; Irish speech was, to an extent, silenced but Irish-speakers were not. Bardic poetry picked up intimations of the silence that would, in time, overtake the Gaelic world. But Irish was vigorously resistant, discomfiting the state and raiding its texts with incursions. Moreover, it was part of a polyphonic pattern of native contestation. And as Irish-speakers started to commandeer and subvert English, detaching it from the civility and allegiance imagined to be natural to it, linguistically ambidextrous natives could confound the Englishman, isolated on the narrow springboard of his expansionist language. The incorrigible natives would sooner co-opt the colonist's tongue to express their dissent than, *pace* Drayton, be 'mollified' by it. By translating their dissent into English, they turned it into a polyvocal site of contending meanings and conflicting styles of communication.

INTIMATIONS OF SILENCE

How far was the cultural rupture, symbolically inscribed on the palimpsest of Ó Mathgamhna's Annals, in their translation from Munster to the Tower, apparent to the Gaelic learned classes of the day? Their response is recorded in annals, like those of Loch Cé and the Four Masters, and in the bardic poems. Ostensibly, neither was a format poised for flexible response. Working within conventions consecrated by tradition, annalists and bards can appear transfixed by the scale of change assailing Gaelic society. Programmed to praise the dead and extol the warlike, *The Annals of Loch Cé*, for instance, seem propelled into accommodating the death of Sir Nicholas Malby within a formula that pitches gnomic impartiality towards self-parody: 'duine uasal bud ferr ina re, ocus do cuir se cuicced Connacht uili fo doeirsi' (he was the noblest man of his time and he put the whole province of Connacht in bondage) (*ALC*, p. 458).

Some commentators interpret formal constraints as confirmation that the learned classes failed to respond to the crisis overtaking their world. Dunne characterises their reaction as 'highly pragmatic, deeply fatalistic, increasingly escapist and essentially apolitical' ('Gaelic Response', p. 11). Michelle O Riordan attempts to deny bardic poetry any political relevance by insisting that motifs like uniting against the foreigner were merely fossilised conventions abstracted from contemporary reference (*Gaelic Mind*, p. 64). Her insistence that 'expression . . . in the bardic poetry cannot be interpreted as figurative in one period and literal in another' (p. 128) sees poetic expression as static and dehistoricised, and poetic formulae as inert, undynamic and incapable of being reworked to reflect new realities. But expression, however tradition-bound, is more protean than O Riordan's bleak ordinance allows. Breandán Ó Buachalla overturns her assertion that continuity and change are mutually exclusive by demonstrating that 'change within continuity has been the central pattern of the Irish cultural tradition' ('Poetry and Politics', p. 152).[4] A motif hollowed out by time can also, in time, become invested with new meanings when literal events infuse the literary with a new resonance – and trope and history rhyme.

Far from being static, Ó Buachalla argues, the poetry written after the flight of the earls is characterised by 'thematic mutations' which articulate new perceptions about language, religion and ethnicity ('Poetry and Politics', p. 160). As counsellors, as negotiators, as the targets of oppressive legislation, poets occupied a front-line position in sixteenth-century Ireland (O'Rahilly, 'Irish Poets'; Breathnach, 'Chief's Poet', pp. 55–9). It is unsurprising, therefore, that they were alert to the threats hanging over their language. The *filí* felt the insult of linguistic intrusion keenly and articulated their indignation through a withering recourse to loanwords. Tadhg Dall Ó hUiginn urged Richard Óg Burke not to accept 'an t-ainm iasachta' (the foreign name) of sheriff (Knott, *Poems* 1, p. 161: 8.2). But when the young man took 'an t-ainm allmhardha'[5] (21.2), the barbarous name, Tadhg Dall bemoaned that he had exchanged a venerable title for a foreign borrowing, 'ainm síor ar ainm n-iasachta' (48.2). The amiable arrangement suggested by the terms 'loanword' and 'borrowing', which construct the receiver as the beneficiary of a reciprocal transaction, is altogether inappropriate for the power-backed dynamics of lexical incursions in a colonial context (cf. Mazzio, 'Staging the Vernacular', p. 209). The learned classes' conviction about the excellency of their tongue drew on a confident assumption of lexical self-sufficiency, encapsulated in Céitinn's assured judgement:

> Milis an teanga an Ghaedhealg,
> Guth gan chabhair choigcríche

('Sweet is the Irish tongue, / A voice without foreign aid') (Leerssen, *Mere Irish*, p. 232). With steely pride, Céitinn added that while Hebrew was older and Latin most learned, Irish was indebted to neither for sound or word, 'fuam nó focal'.

For a *file* to admit 'loanwords' to his verse was, therefore, an almost self-mutilating act of protest, a mockery curdled by the very lexical defilement it railed against. English words were metonyms for English incursions. Aonghus Ó Dálaigh's lament in *Ar Éirinn*, 'On Ireland', that the land is 'ag breith *basdardadh*', 'generating *bastards*', replicates the intrusion lexically (McKenna, *Dánta*, p. 74: 8.4; my emphasis). Laoisioch Mac an Bhaird execrates a youth who took to English ways, 'A fhir ghlacas a ghalldacht', by scathingly enunciating the English words which symbolised his defection: brísdi, clóca, cóta, sbuir, buataisi, locaidhe, ráipér, sgarfa (Bergin, *Bardic Poetry*, pp. 49–50). There were strong class overtones to such censure (Ó Tuama, 'Gaelic Culture', p. 30). If English was seen as uncouth – *allmhardha* – then the resort of the lower orders to it could be seen as both galling and grimly appropriate: the 'uncouth tongue' came well stocked with base words fitted to satirising their defection. Ó an Cháinte's 'Mór doghníd daoine dhíob féin', 'Some people fancy themselves', mocks anglicised parvenus as 'trú bhíos na *bhastord*', 'blackguards who're *bastards*' (O'Grady, *Catalogue*, p. 555; my emphasis).

The paradigm of 'change within continuity' which Ó Buachalla identifies means that the poets' response to linguistic incursion should be sought less in overt statements than in oblique reworkings of the topoi associated with voice, sounds and language. Praise of sweet, soft voices – *bogglór* – was a staple of praise poetry. When

Tadhg Dall used the figure of enchanting fairy music – 'ceól sírreachta sídhe' – echoing through the lordship of the hibernicised Seán Mac Oliver Burke as an emblem of his harmonious rule, he was reaching back to one of the oldest figures in Irish literature (Knott, *Poems* I, p. 131: 68.1; II, p. 259). The irruption of alien voices which threatened precious sounds with silence was managed inside the tradition, as in Fcar Flatha Ó Gnímh's elegy for the soul of Ireland, 'Beannacht ar anmain Éireann', written in the wake of the flight of the earls:

> atá Treabh Briain na mbogglór
> dom dhóigh ar dhobrón torrach

(The soft-voiced race of Brian is, / I think, pregnant with sorrow) (Bergin, *Bardic Poems*, p. 115: lines 3–4). Motifs that had routinely eulogised the sounds of the Gaelic world were now reworked to elegise its dislocation. This was performed both through a dialectic that contrasted the varied signifiers of *bogglór* with the uncouth sounds which menaced it and, as a certain silence fell, through a melancholy, inverted roll-call where the old formulae summoned up sounds and voices heard no longer.

In 'Mithigh sin, a ráith na ríogh', 'It is time, o fort of kings', which celebrates Maguire's recovery of Enniskillen Castle from the English, Eochaidh Ó hEóghusa has a rare opportunity to set enumeration of the consecrated sounds triumphantly against the invasive noises, ritually restoring, one by one, the acoustics of the Gaelic world. For more than a year, the castle had been 'at uaimh fhaolchon allmhardha', (the den of foreign wolves), whose usurpation is represented as an invasion of alien speech: 'Gá ttám ní tuigthí an fadsa / comhrádh aithnidh umadsa' (all that while, no recognisable speech was understood around you) (Bergin, *Bardic Poetry*, p. 130: 3.4; 4.1–2). The poem is structured as a celebration of the sights of the Gaelic world, all evoked with the formula *do-chífe*: 'you shall see'. What is remarkable is how so much of what is seen is the trace of language. The pivotal sound in Ó hEóghusa's representation of the castle's fortunes is *congháir*, 'clamour'. Under occupation, it was *gan* (without) *congháir* (6.3); restored to the Irish, the *lios* echoes to the poets of Ireland *ag congháir* (16.3). Ó hEóghusa's poem addresses the castle, inviting it to imagine the delights (*aoibhnius*) it will once more see in its 'parkland bright with bending boughs': 'san fhaithche ghégórthais ghil' (10.3). The castle will see harps and story-tellers

(17.2–3) – and see the swelling breasts of the hillside reddened with the footprints of a band of poets:

> Ó shliocht bonn mbuidhne fileadh
> . . .
> do-chífe ceinndearg a ccruth,
> cíche do gheillearg ngrianach. (12.1, 3–4)

Sound infuses sight in a synaesthetic enactment of the erotics of language.

But the sequence of restoration celebrated by Ó hEóghusa ran against the tide of history. Aonghus Fionn Ó Dálaigh's elegy for Clancarty (*d.* 1596), 'Soraidh léd chéile a Chaisil', 'Farewell to your spouse, Caisil', laments that the haunts of the Gael are 'lán don fhoirinn iasachta', 'full of the foreign band' (McKenna, *Dánta*, p. 71: 31.4) where native voices are heard no longer, 'Gan ghuth aoinfhir d'fhuil Gaoidheal' (6.2). So it is that two of the great laments written out of the desolation which followed 1607 convey intense bereavement through inversion, tolling out the silenced sounds. Loghlainn mac Taidhg Óig Uí Dhálaigh's 'Cáit ar ghabhadar Gaoidhil?', 'Where have the Gaels gone?', powerfully evokes the emptiness in the wake of the military collapse by bleakly scanning a landscape where halls and mansions, churches and assembly-places stand void, the voices of their one-time companies stilled, 'a ccongháir ní claisdear leam' (their clamour I cannot hear) (Gillies, 'A Poem', p. 204: 2.3). In their stead, a 'dírim uaibhreach eisiodhan', an arrogant, bellicose batch, holds sway (8.2), like 'clár óir fá fhoirinn tacoir', fake chessmen on a golden board (10.2). He hears 'no more voices that seem full-sweet': 'ní chluin guth as láinbhinn leis' (16.3). The silence of the lost, the exiled and 'the living-dead', 'cuirp bheómharbha' (18.4), is registered by evoking old aural pleasures – the sweetness of poetry, organ and harp song, the sagas and genealogies – now hushed (17.1–4).

The loneliness that Eóghan Ruadh mac an Bhaird documents in 'Anocht as uaigneach Éire', 'Ireland is lonely tonight', is to a remarkable degree acoustic, counted out in long incantations of absence. '*Gan* rádha rithlearg molta / *gan* sgaoileadh sgeóil chodalta' (*No* [lit. 'without'] reciting of praise-poems; *no* telling of tales for sleep) (Ó Clérigh, *Beatha* II, p. 140: 7.1–2; my emphasis): no sound of children's laughter, mass prayers, praise poems; no stories told, books read, genealogies recited. The silence is total. No word is heard from Ireland: 'labhra uaidhe ní héistior' (9.4). In this silence, the poet picks up with singular acuity the implications for Irish: 'cosg ar cheól glas ar Ghaoidheilg', a stop to music, manacles on Irish (5.2). Like Loghlainn Uí Dhálaigh and others, Mac an Bhaird attributes the woes of the Irish to God punishing them for past wickedness, just as He had once punished mankind for the presumption of 'toir Neamhruaidh', Nimrod's tower (20.2). But far from loosing polyphony, this second Babel threatens the perfect language fashioned by Fenius and his seventy-two sages from the rubble of the tower (see p. 174 above).

Mac an Bhaird's unflinching recognition of reality was forced on him by his closeness to the O'Donnells as native power collapsed (Ó Buachalla, *Aisling Ghéar*, p. 58). His *envoi* to Rory O'Donnell, embarking on negotiations in London in 1603, in 'Dána an turas tríalltar sonn', 'Bold the journey attempted here', captures the pain of the newly circumscribed elite in a single line: 'doiligh earr na huaisleachta', the end of nobility is hard to bear (Bergin, *Bardic Poetry*, p. 27: 1.4). Others, too, sensed the passing of the old order and recognised its implications for Irish. For the mid-seventeenth-century poet Cían Ó hEachaidhéin, in 'Cinn dúinn comhairle, a Chormaic', the eclipse of the Gaelic order and the ascent of English were almost synonymous: 'táinic críoch ar dtéarma isteach, / mo dhíoth sa beurla ar biseach' (Our term drew to a close, / alas, as English spreads); in the new, anglicised order, the learned classes were 'bailbh bhodhra', deaf and dumb (Ó Donnchadha, *Cloinne Aodha Buidhe*, p. 120: 9.3–4; 29.1). But even before the end of the sixteenth century, Aonghus Fionn Ó Dálaigh interpreted defeat in precisely those terms. His *Ar Éirinn* sees Ireland as a defenceless woman who, beset by foreign assailants, has become 'balbh nó bodhar', dumb or deaf (McKenna, *Dánta*, p. 73: 1.3).

When Tadhg Dall lamented the departure of the future fourth Earl of Thomond and others for schooling in England, he was more prescient than he could have known in his choice of synecdoche: 'Rugadh go Lunainn tar lear / glóir budh aoibhne rem aigneadh' (taken overseas to London / the sounds loveliest to my mind) (Knott, *Poems* I, p. 257: 4.1–2); the voices so translated would be, quite literally, anglicised. Another exile, the Old Englishman William Nugent, pined for all that he had left behind, including Irish, 'labhra dhiamhuir ar ndúthchus', our birthright mystic speech (Murphy, 'Poems of Exile', p. 13: 1.4). An anonymous poet writing in the early seventeenth century states his predicament starkly, 'Aonar dhamhsa eidir dhaoinibh', I am alone among the people; gone are the bardic schools and the scholar-poets, and with them 'fáthfhoras focal', mystic words (Bergin, *Bardic Poetry*, p. 160: 11.4). A silence which would inevitably redound on the demotic language was falling on polished utterance and it was not happening unnoticed by the poets.

ENGAGEMENT

Irish-language resistance

The Elizabethan writing of Ireland feigned an English-speaking world by taking over, ventriloquising or ignoring the native voice. The bardic poetry caught intimations of a coming silence. But the challenge which Irish offered to the monophone intentions of the policymakers and the monophone pretensions of the colonial texts was far from muted. Ireland proved to be more unaccountable than the English narrative allowed, its patterns more plural, elusive and irreducible – and part of that plurality was linguistic.

There was considerable native resistance to the incursion of English. Most simply, if ultimately most disablingly, blank ignorance of the invader's language held English at bay. In Ó Clérigh's biography of Hugh O'Donnell, the unfathomable world of English enters the text through a miasma of incomprehension. English is just another of the threatening martial noises that attend the foreign incursion, 'iongnaithe a nerradh agus a nerlabra agus la fogarthorman a ttrompadh agus a ttapúr agus a ccaismert catha' (the strangeness of their apparel and their speech and the racket of their trumpets and tabors and war-songs) (*Beatha* I, pp. 32–4). But there were less passive responses. By the late sixteenth century, language was becoming a badge of identity for Irish-speakers while English served as a metonym for the colonists. In 'Fuasgail Fódla a ua Eóghain' (1598), 'Rescue Ireland, Descendant of Eóghan', Muiris Mhic Gearailt urges Dónall MacCarthy to extirpate 'tréad throdach bheárlach bhrothach', the bellicose, English-speaking, ferocious herd (Williams, p. 69: 11.3). Likewise, 'Clíath mhínighthe ar maicne riogh', hails Philip O'Reilly (*d.* 1596) as a phalanx protecting the Gael against the varied depredations of the Gall: it identifies English as one of the invasive elements to be resisted. Philip is a 'cliath . . . re doirsibh gaillbhérla', a defence against the points of entry [literally 'doors'] of foreign speech (Carney, *O'Reillys*, p. 29: 10.1–2).

The centrality of Irish to the Gaels' self-definition encouraged Irish-speakers, as hostilities deepened, to become correspondingly contemptuous of English. Gaelic lords 'scoff that they have no wish to twist their minds by speaking English' (Stanihurst, *De rebus*, p. 145). When a chief of the O'Reillys discovered that his child had 'a stammer which made him almost dumb', Stanihurst tells us with evident irritation, he declared that the child should be sent away to learn English, affecting to believe that English required only 'a stuttering and incoherent articulation' (p. 145). Such attitudes were not lost on the Elizabethans. The anonymous author of the 'Discourse recommending the planting of colonies', recognised that 'for language, [the Gaels] so despise ours, as they think themselves the worse when they hear it' (*CSPI* 1598–9, p. 440). Newcomers repeatedly expressed indignation that Con *Baccach* had 'curs'd his Posterity if they should learn *English*' (Moryson, *History* I, 12; cf. Gainsford, *Tyrone*, p. 8). A rare glimpse into Hugh O'Neill's alertness to the politics of language comes during a parley with Geoffrey Fenton and Bishop Jones. At a crucial stage in the talks, 'he said he would have no more pleadings in English but that he would answer in Irish; and so he left them' (*CSPI* 1596–7, p. 485). The identification between the enemy and his tongue was so close that English could seal the fate of its speakers. Hugh O'Neill told the Old English go-between, Darby Newman, that Maguire 'hath bene soe hardlie dealte with' that he 'will not suffer a man to passe downe that weares a hatt on his head, or a cloke on his back, or that speakes a worde of english withoute takinge his head from his shoulders' (PRO SP 63/173/64.iv). After the relief of Enniskillen, O'Donnell pressed into Connacht, sparing no male between the ages of 15 and 60 who could not speak Irish (O'Sullivan, *Ireland under Elizabeth*, p. 82). The author of 'The Supplication' grimly approved of his opponents' harder line on linguistic exclusivity. The Irish were 'wiser' than the English: 'they see what force uniformitie of speeche hath to procure love and friendship, to continewe a societie and fellowshipe' and so 'proclaymed it in their campe deathe to speake Englishe' (Maley, p. 65). As the Nine Years War progressed, the linguistic polarisation deepened. Moryson complained that Palesmen

though they could speake English as well as wee, yet Commonly speake Irish among themselues, and were hardly induced by our familiar Conversation to speake English with vs, yea Common experience shewed, and my selfe and others often obserued, the Cittizens of Watterford and

Corcke hauing wyues that could speake English as well as wee, bitterly to
chyde them when they speake English with vs. (*Shakespeare's Europe*, p. 213)

The hegemony of English, contested in the field, could not be fully
secured even on the page. Irish leaves its trace as an absence that
must be accounted for and as a presence that must, however
elliptically, be acknowledged. The coincidence of muteness and
volubility gives these texts a surprisingly conflictual texture: exclusions are countered by intrusions, silence is interrupted by clamour
and a monophone impulse is challenged by the refusals and reversals
delivered by those who, though they will not be listened to, insist on
having their say. Gaps in the telling – puzzles, misreadings, *non
sequiturs*, silences – are inevitable. To speak only English in sixteenth-
century Ireland was to be shut out from a whole range of meanings,
to hit blanks. The newcomers were astray in a landscape where
words blocked access, where names yielded no meanings, where
language guarded its secrets and its silence was insolent and
threatening, not at all complicit with the effacement wished for it by
the English texts. Ralegh, 'in a strang country newly sett downe',
simultaneously loathing and coveting 'this loste lande', found that its
swirling intrigues confused his senses – and addled his imagery: he
felt 'like a fish cast on dry land, gasping for breath, with lame leggs
and lamer loonges' (Hennessy, *Ralegh*, pp. 174, 168, 177).

Two emblematic figures wander through this landscape, the
Frenchman James Cosharde and the Breton Guillame Tollare. After
landing at Smerwick with FitzMaurice, they wandered through the
countryside 'and were as well used as the contrie could doe' until
apprehended and 'examined' by Malby near Kilmallock. Cosharde
testified that after six or seven days walking he had arrived at a castle
by the sea, but he 'knoweth nether the name of the castle nor the
toune'. His comrade reported that 'the people of the contrie did
victuall them, but hee knoweth not their names' (Hogan and
O'Farrell, *Walsingham Letter-book*, pp. 181–2). It was in the French-
men's interest to play up their ignorance just as it served the English
writers' purpose to play down theirs. But both groups are abroad in
a landscape full of the blanks that come from not knowing the
vernacular.

The blanks are sometimes quite literal. O'Connor Sligo, caught
between irreconcilable allegiances to O'Donnell and the state, sent a
messenger, Mulrony Oge, to the administration with four blank
sheets symbolising, apparently, his inability to commit himself to

anything without O'Donnell's say-so. Confronted with his Irish-speaking emissary, the state, too, drew a blank: 'Mulrony durst not tell the cause of these blanks, for lack of a trusty interpreter both to the State and to O'Connor' (*CSPI* 1599–1600, p. 159). James Perrott is frequently caught short for a word – of a place, of a local chieftain – or of the native term for a rent collector 'which they called —' (*Chronicle*, p. 20). Indeed, his whole *Chronicle* ends on a blank. He is relating the rebellion of Cahir O'Dogherty:

As he went alonge he sent messages and wrate letters to stirre up the people whoe had any power in those partes to joyne with hym wherof one letter beinge written in Irish and translated into English for the strangenes of the stile and imperiousnes of command may well clayme a place in this passage of the storie — (p. 190)

At that very point, Perrott's text runs out. The translation eludes him. The strange imperiousness of the native may be unheard – but it is the colonial text that is mutilated.

Placenames provided a bedrock of linguistic resistance, imposing phonetic obstacles to the colonists' secure possession of the places so zealously catalogued. At some point, almost all the Elizabethan works reel off toponymic incantations as mantras of possession. But it is a stuttering recitation, tripped up by the obduracy of alien sounds. Even when the writers are most engaged in presenting Ireland as a geographical space, empty of people and inhabitants, a *chevaux de frise* of impenetrable names guards against appropriation. The Athloon Pursuivant d'Armes d'Irland recorded Sussex's journey through Ulster in 1556 as a toponomia. But his is a gapped and tattered songline: 'On Monday . . . the Lord Deputy removed from Bellah Clare to Morres Va— Carra Lisen Ree, by a river called —, by Dunmissa, in — country' (*CCM* 1, p. 259).

But the names withhold possession not just phonetically and semantically: encoded in their very existence are counter-claims to origin and ownership. Moryson picks his way through a landscape of insistently dual names: 'Dublin, called Divelin by the English, and Balacleigh (as seated upon hurdles) by the Irish' (Morley, *Ireland under Elizabeth*, p. 416). When revealed, the meanings of these obstructive sounds can be disconcerting. Campion learnt from his English–Irish hosts that Shane O'Neill had fortified an island in Tyrone 'which he named spitefully Foogh-ni-Gall, that is, the hate of Englishmenne' (*Two Bokes*, p. 139). In the end, the resistance would be ineffectual and the names would survive only as mangled sounds drained of sense. The pairing of old names with new implied a chronology of supersession: 'the king's Countie . . . being in tymes past called Offaly' (Hogan, *Description*, p. 81). Placenames would be haunted by the ghost of the original pronunciation but evacuated of reference or memory. Ralegh reduced the name of his plantation at Cúl na gCloc Fionn (ridge of white stones) to scrambled sounds – 'Cuolycloghsy Fynnay', 'Coultie Clo[f]inia' – thereby alienating meaning as well as title (Hennessy, *Ralegh*, pp. 233–4). Fish-rich rivers allure Derricke but 'their proper names I am / unable for to give' (*Image*, p. 27). Names were being lost. Camden mentions a little river running through FitzMaurice's territory which is 'now nameless' (*Britannia*, p. 1, 333). The loss was not trivial. James I used precisely that image when extolling the union – linguistic as well as religious and political – of England and Scotland:

For euen as little brookes lose their names by their running and fall into great Riuers, and the very name and memorie of the great Riuers swallowed vp in the Ocean: so by the coniunction of diuers little kingdomes in one, are all these priuate differences and questions swallowed vp. (*Workes*, p. 489)

Irish offered more than just the passive resistance of withholding meanings, however. There are rents in the colonial texts through which the ambient language sneaks back in, disrupting their monophone pretence. Sidney's account of a Christmas-tide raid on Shane O'Neill is itself prey to linguistic incursion. His journal records conversations from O'Neill's assembly in *faux* verbatim: ' "That is not possible" (quoth [O'Neill]) ". . . By O'Neyle's hande", quoth the messenger, "he is in this country, and not farre off, for I sawe the redd *bracklok* with the knotty clubb, and that is carried before none but himself" ' (Sidney, 'Memoir' 3, p. 42; my emphasis). Here, a residue of the unacknowledged original stows away inside a dialogue transposed from Irish into the narrator's tongue: by not making the journey fully out of Irish, *bratach*, 'standard', flags the occult translation.

CONTRAPUNTAL POLYPHONIES

These flashes of Irish irradiate the English texts with reminders that sixteenth-century Ireland was far more plural linguistically than the placid English surface of the colonial texts suggests. While the state sought to still dissent by marginalising Irish, there was a countervailing polyphony. The pattern of address and contestation which it allowed goes some way towards explaining why the silencing of Irish would fail to staunch the articulation of Irish dissent. The elite often knew more than one language. The Four Masters regularly eulogised dead chiefs as *ioldanach illaidin, agus i ngaoideilcc* ('skilled in Latin and Irish') and some, like Maurice, Lord Roche, for knowing Irish, Latin and English (*ARÉ* 2, pp. 1584, 1608, 1622; 3, pp. 1,875, 2,050, 2,177). The French nobleman who interpreted for Margaret Barnwall in St Malo had learned English and Irish with her family in Dublin; he explained that language-learning exchanges between Irish and French merchant families were not uncommon: 'Hiberni mittunt suos filios in Gallias, et Galli suos Hiberniam causa linguae discendae' (Moran, *Spicilegium*, p. 108). Florence MacCarthy, sniped St Leger, 'haith ben anye tyme this seven or eight yeares greatlie addicted to learne the Spanysh tonge'. When Florence attempted to win back Teig Hurley, his servant-turned-accusor, the insolent Teig retorted with 'an old proverb in the Spanish "Palabras y plumas el viento los lieven"'; another servant, Donogh-ne-buille, was 'a very good linguist' (MacCarthy, *Life*, pp. 30, 406, 409). Not only were more languages at play in sixteenth-century Ireland than just Irish and English – two Jesuits write in Portuguese to notify the Irish College in Lisbon of the defeat at Kinsale (Hogan, *Distinguished Irishmen*, p. 56) – but language-learning often bypassed English completely. A priest, Bernard O'Donnell, testified on examination that he had learned Latin from his father before travelling through Spain, Italy and Flanders to finish his clerical studies in Douai. The two Hughs employed him to reply to Philip II in their name. Yet, when he attended negotiations between Sir John Norris and the Irish, he was at a loss – because he knew no English (*CSPI* 1596–7, p. 351; 1599–1600, pp. 451–2).

Latin had considerable currency in sixteenth-century Ireland. It was the standard language of ecclesiastical communication and was sometimes used in official exchanges among members of the Gaelic elite. Turlough Luineach warned Brian O'Rourke in Latin against disobeying the queen; O'Rourke replied, 'with his owne hand in a faire irish character', in Irish (PRO SP 36/150/21). An intriguing glimpse of a Gaelic *ladino* is found in Moryson's story of a Bohemian baron's visit to O'Cahan. Arriving at O'Cahan's castle, the traveller is met by sixteen women 'all naked, excepting their loose mantles; whereof eight or ten were very faire, and two seemed very Nimphs'.

Seated by the fire among these revealingly cross-legged damsels, the
Bohemian does not know where to fix his 'chast eyes'. O'Cahan
enters, 'all naked excepting a loose mantle, and shooes'. These he
quickly sheds and entertains his guest 'after his best manner in the
Latin tongue'. 'So inshamed therewith' was the Bohemian, however,
that he dared not make eye-contact, much less converse (*Itinerary*
pt. 3, pp. 180–1).

The anglicisation of the Gaelic elite did not fall into place
overnight and, in the interim, negotiations with Irish-speaking lords
had to be conducted either through intermediaries or through a
mutual second language, usually Latin. Garrett Mattingly points out
that throughout western Europe, the use of Latin in negotiations was
declining well before 1600, as fewer ecclesiastics held state office and
Englishmen, abroad with their minority language, 'made shift with
whatever continental languages they happened to know' (*Renaissance
Diplomacy*, pp. 236–7). The Irish case indicates that, in its first colony,
English-language policy was setting a new course; but not all at once.
Latin held its own as a lingua franca among Irish-speaking leaders
and the English administration into the last quarter of the century.
Sidney enjoyed the comfort of a shared tongue at the end of his long
march through wild Mayo country: 'I founde *Mac William*[6] verie
sencible, though wantinge the *Englishe* Tongue, yet vnderstanding the
Lattin; a Lover of Quiet and Civylitie' (Collins, *Letters*, p. 104). Shane
Maguire, who badgered Sussex in blunt, half-mastered English,
seems to have been a precocious anomaly in 1560s Fermanagh,
where Latin was still the standard second language and English rare
enough to be almost as good as a cipher: he penned one letter to the
Lord Deputy 'bechetching you to wrytte me no more letters in
Latyn, becausse that I wold not that nother clerke nor non other
man of this contrey shuld knowe your mynd, wherfor doo you wryte
all your mynd in Englys' (Wright, *Queene Elizabeth*, pp. 110–11).

Latin retained its currency well beyond that. Grace O'Malley
conversed with the queen in Latin at Greenwich (MacCurtain,
'Women', p. 164). When Zubiaur sailed into Castlehaven in 1601, he
was given 'an account of the state of the kingdom' by Dermot
O'Driscoll, 'a shrewd man not unskilled in Latin' (O'Sullivan, *Ireland
under Elizabeth*, p. 143). The English clergyman Edmund Southern
became embroiled in a lively Latin joust with two friars in Navan in
1603 when he provocatively asked the younger, in Latin, if he was a
scholar. The feisty older man took up the challenge: 'Si ille non est,

Ego sum' (if he's not, I am), and demanded 'in great choler . . . what the like of him had to do in this country'. The friar then unleashed his tongue against the king: 'Es hereticus; pereat tecum, cum omnibusque illis qui receperunt auchtoritatem ab illo' (he's a heretic; he'll perish with you and all the rest who accept his authority), whereupon Southern accused him of treason and had him arrested. This served only to provoke the 'great concourse of people of all sorts' to join the fray in their vernacular, 'uttering their words with a confused noise in Irish'. For Southern, Irish may only have been so much noisy confusion, but when he saw two fellows kitted out in menacing loanwords – 'a tall fellow with trousers' and another with 'a skin' (*scian*, knife) – he, 'being but a lean and naked man', understood enough to beat a retreat (*CSPI* 1603–6, pp. 62–3).

When the minor northern lords surrendered to Mountjoy, their submissions were framed in Latin – but this time with a parallel English version (*CCM* 4, p. 287). By then a shift in the balance of power between the two languages was realigning the way language difference was managed. Anglophone and Gael no longer met in the relative neutrality – and parity – of a mutual second language; English was emerging as the medium of communication between coloniser and native. But a pattern of engagement and contestation was by then well established.

Talking across the language divide: interpreters

As small rents begin to show in the soundproofing woven by the English texts and as the polyphonic texture of exchanges becomes apparent, it becomes easier to spot other points where languages were meeting and being mediated. The colonial texts may have denied Irish but, in its actual linguistic fabric, Ireland was more sieve than shutter. Unexpected contacts and intriguing networks of communication point to the agency of well-placed mediators navigating between the two cultures. Docwra's complaint to Mountjoy that the 'loyal' Neal Garvey and his men 'give continual Advertisements, as well from us to the Rebels, as from them to us' gives a sense of the constant percolation of information (Moryson, *History* II, p. 249).

There is a tension in the English texts between their evocation of a boisterously noisy world of talk – querulous, taunting, boastful, treacherous – and their resolute inattention to the language which encoded much of this talk. Speech is reported energetically; language is glossed over. But the texts cannot airbrush all trace of linguistic mediation. Captain Humphrey Willis, who sailed with Docwra on the expedition to establish an English garrison on Lough Foyle, sent his cousin Simon, Cecil's secretary, a journal of the voyage out from Chester. Superficially, in complacently ignoring language, it seems to reproduce the obliviousness to indigenous tongues characteristic of the literature of encounter from Columbus' *Diarios* onwards. 'During our anchoring there, a pinnace was sent ashore two several times, and did talk with the enemy' (*CSPI* 1600, p. 201). Screened behind the metonymic 'pinnace' was the real but mystified agent who actually '*did* talk'. In all likelihood, the talking pinnace was Willis himself, whom Docwra reveals elsewhere to have interpreted for O'Dogherty: 'for him I sent first in the place of Captain Thornton because of his language'. But, even then, the translator's reprieve from oblivion was fleeting. Docwra's narrative proceeded to erase him through disingenuous ellipsis, recasting a bilingual trialogue as an English dialogue: 'I told him [O'Dogherty] . . .' (*CSPI* 1600, p. 195).

The invisibility of translators is their most manifest textual trait. But texts which at first seem sealed off from Irish are scored by a tracery of hair-line cracks, tiny fissures through which we glimpse languages in contact. Commissioners Wallop and Gardiner held talks with O'Neill and O'Donnell in January 1599. Their narrative creates the impression that all speeches are made in English, but stray pointers to intensive translation intrude. We see but cannot hear the first day's pantomime, staged on horseback when the Irish delegates refuse to get out of the saddle. Only the phrasing – 'We gathered from [O'Donnell's] speeches' – hints at meanings arrived at through indirect pathways of translation. These are revealed only when the Commissioners report that Hore, Wallop's secretary, a Wexfordman, 'hath by our sending had daily conference with them . . . which Hore we rather use for that he hath been interpreter betwixt us and O'Donnell'. Hore's role is made explicit when O'Neill and O'Donnell are asked to set down their terms, '[a]ccording to which they assented, requiring us to send Philip Hore to translate into English their demands, which we have performed accordingly' (*CCM* 3, pp. 142–5).

Sometimes the existence of interpreters can be inferred only from almost imperceptible wrinkles in the syntax which point to a linguistic baton-change, as here between 'utterance' (by Drury and

Fitton) and 'delivery' (by persons unknown): 'which words so by me uttered and delivered at my request to some of them hath undoubtedly bred no small terror in their minds' (*CCM* 2, p. 141). Fiach McHugh and Walter Reagh meet with Sir William Russell; of the parley itself we hear nothing except that 'the *effect* of theyr speech was to desier' pardon (Perrott, *Chronicle*, p. 92; my emphasis). Translators lurk behind circumlocutions like Sidney's reference to holding 'interparlaunce by commissioners' with Sorley Boy (*CCM* 2, p. 351). They are tucked away behind passive, impersonal constructions and uninformative past participles: Malby sent FitzWilliam 'Sorley Boy's petitions Englished'; FitzWilliam intercepted a letter from Hugh McMahon and 'cawsed it to be translated' (*CSPI* 1509–73, p. 525; Shirley, *Monaghan*, p. 84). Thomond and Carew's split-screen narration of Ormond's capture by Ony MacRory hints at their linguistic division of labour: 'I, the Erle of Tomond, willed Owney to put backe his men, and I, the Presydent, desyred his Lordship to be gone' (Gilbert, *Facsimiles* IV.1, p. liv). Even when the interpreter is solidly inside the frame, he is not necessarily listed in the credits: Russell's journal records that the proclamation of O'Neill and O'Donnell as traitors was 'delivered by one — both in English and Irish' (*CCM* 3, p. 232). The startling directness of the pursuivant's account of Sussex's journey into O'Carroll's country in June 1558, in blurting out that William Cantwell, 'my Lord's interpreter' was sent to 'Kelle Tobber' castle, resounds in the almost conspiritorial silence of the contemporary record with the starkness of an indiscretion (*CCM* 1, p. 274).

Richard Bingham's reports from Connacht are, through the twelve years of his governorship, largely impervious to the majority language. But the occluded layer of language activity – translators, interpreters, and the whole ambient world of Irish which his rendition habitually turned into English or silence – was disclosed when political necessity made a virtue of transparency. In 1590, Perrott was tried for treason. The charges included encouraging Con O'Clerie to write seditious verses against the queen (Henley, 'Treason'; Morgan, 'Fall of Perrot'). When Bingham was questioned about the rhymes, he was forced into a new explicitness about how language difference was handled. He did 'not generallie remember' the rhymes, except one which propounded that 'occonnor Duns . . . should be a swifte hungery greyhound, and should dryue all thenglishemen ouer the salte sea' (PRO SP 63/157/24). Suddenly, in a sequence of letters to

Burghley, Bingham's desire to distance himself from treasonable taint leads him to roll back the stony silence under which a team of translators had been invisibly beetling all along. Edward White, Clerk of the Council of Connacht, detained in connection with the offending verses, is finally unmasked as, *inter alia*, an indispensable translator when Bingham appeals for him to be restored to office 'in respect of his long experience *and the language*' (PRO SP 63/158/57; my emphasis). In upholding White's detention, FitzWilliam, too, nudges another language-worker out of the shadows: he counters that one Brereton, an M.A. 'and knowing the language of this country', has been appointed in his stead (*CSPI* 1588–92, p. 432). Before this storm in a couplet finally blows over, two other concealed translators are winkled out, 'White his boy Coursye, and Henry Renolds' who, Bingham records, 'had the interpreting of the rithmes' (PRO SP 63/161/1).[7]

The individual who crosses the lines – linguistically at least – often enters the text only *between* the lines. Unnoticed or erased, he usually exists only by implication, a medium who leaves no message to posterity. But, given his chance, the interpreter can fill in the gaps in his employers' texts. Lord Leonard Grey and Stephen Ap Parry – a Welshman settled in Laois (*CSPI* 1509–73, pp. 22, 49) – write parallel accounts of their journey through Munster and Connacht in 1538. By concentrating on processes, Ap Parry's version provides a syncopated accompaniment to Grey's no-nonsense focus on outcomes: for once, the 'how' supplements the 'what'. Grey records only the *fait accompli*: O'Carroll 'cam to me', Dermot O'Kennedy 'submitted himself unto Your Grace', as did 'McObrynes Arays', 'Dermound Omolrean', 'Ullyck Oburgh', 'Hugh Oflart', 'Molaghlyn Omadyn', 'Ochonor Roo' and others (*SPH8* III, pp. 58, 61); only the misshapenly anglicised names hint at the presence of another language. Grey mystifies the linguistic manœuvres that lay behind the completed Latin indentures, mentioning only that Brian O'Connor Faly and Ap Parry 'was they, whom I appoyntyd to tracte and comen' with the natives (p. 63). Ap Parry has no such reticence, specifying that the Irish

have a custome that they will have 'Sayers' betwen them, of all suche demaundes as the Lord Deputie shall demaund of them; wherin I and OChonour have byn 'Sayers', by my Lord Deputie, bytwen hym and all them afore rehersid; but we knew my Lordis plesure in every poynt, or we made any end with them. (p. 62, fn. 2)

Ap Parry's forthright exposition solves a puzzle and establishes a model, supplying the reader with the means of challenging the evasions of the end-obsessed colonial text by reinstating the procedures behind its production.

The anxiety of translation, implicit in surrendering meanings to the possibility of distortion and misrepresentation, encouraged Irish-speakers to highlight the process. 'Sheane McCongawney's Relation, written by himself in Irish, and translated afterwards into English' represents the deliberate attempt of a witness caught up in a conspiracy trial to safeguard himself against the perils of translation:

the cause why I have written this is, for the Council do not understand my language, and also for another reason, that I know not what the interpreter declares, and that I wot not but that he might leave some things unexpounded to the Lord Deputy or the Council which I should speak. (*CCM* 3, p. 76)

Interpreters who sought to ingratiate themselves with an administration predisposed to distrust bilinguals were quick to put their services on the record. Christopher Nugent, flagging his contribution in the Shane McConganny investigation, is at pains to tell Burghley that he had received a letter from the priest and 'the letter being in Irish I translated it' (*CSPI* 1588–92: 577). Later, when his nephew Richard was, rather embarrassingly, out with the rebels, he sent Mountjoy more than a dozen letters bagged by 'the intelligencer'. Those from Desmond and Ony MacRory, he explained officiously, he had 'translated verbatim' but had time only to prepare 'a brief of their differences' for the rest because of the messenger's haste (*CSPI* 1600, p. 125). Nugent, who regularly translated for the English, was aware, in a way that they were not, of the losses inherent in translation. He envisaged the Irish primer which he presented to Elizabeth as a means to overcome the 'defect' of translation. As the vernacular was 'the spetiall mean' whereby subjects 'learne obedience, and their Prynces, or Governors, understande their greves and harmes', a message 'delyvered by an interpretor, cann never carye that grace, or proper intellygence, which the tonge itselfe beinge understode expressith' (Gilbert, *Facsimiles* IV.1, p. xxxv).

Equally, arrangements taken for granted in Ireland had to be spelled out when exported. So, St Leger's report to Henry VIII on Morough O'Brien's surrender simply notes the presence of the chieftain's servant, Dr Nelan, an Ennis friar whose exact contribution is veiled behind the Delphic formula that he 'hathe moche travailled'. A later dispatch, however, detailing arrangements for Morough and Donough's investiture at Greenwich is more precise: they will be accompanied by James Sherlocke – a Waterford merchant – 'whiche James can well speake the language [*sic*] to interprete the same to your Highnes' (*SPH8* III, pp. 450, 454). When a spymaster in Flanders sent an Irish gentleman with intelligence from the Spanish camp to Essex, he specified that 'he should be examined with an Irish interpreter, being unable to utter his mind in any other language' (*Salis.* VIII, p. 401). Moreover, the state was happy to co-opt the translation process when it reinforced its own message. The preamble to the Latin indenture between 'Sir Donald O'Conchyr, *alias* O'Connor Sligo', and Elizabeth in January 1568 records that O'Connor came to Hampton Court and declared 'in his Irish tongue by an interpreter' that he was submitting to the illustrious princess, forgoing the uncivil practices of his ancestors (*CCM* I, p. 378).

To reinsert the interpreter into the narrative of sixteenth-century Ireland is to restore something of the discursive texture of the period and of the conflictual dialogue which was opening up between natives and newcomers. The interpreter is a necessarily hybrid figure, straddling, linguistically at any rate, two cultures. There were many such figures in Elizabethan Ireland. Their mixed heritage equipped the Old English to play the part of intermediaries. In 1520, Surrey met O'Carroll. The Lord Deputy never explains how he and the Gael managed their exchanges, but his throwaway reference to O'Carroll, the eighth earl of Ormond and Sir William Darcy 'communing to gathers in Irish' solves that puzzle (*CCM* I, p. 9). That Sir William, author of the 1515 document deploring the incursion of Irish into the colony, had himself not escaped contagion emphasises that, however unpalatable the qualification may have been to some of them, Palesmen were eminently fitted to act as interpreters. English–Irishmen weave through the colonial texts, oiling exchanges between the two sides so expertly that hardly a squeak is picked up in the official record. Manus O'Donnell communicated with the Dublin administration through the Old English merchant, John Fagan; Shane O'Neill's engagement with the English-speaking world was managed by the Flemings of Meath (Bradshaw, 'Manus "The Magnificent"', p. 98; Hogan, 'Shane O'Neill', p. 167).

Meanwhile, the increasing anglicisation of the Gaelic elite was bringing on a new crop of interpreters. Poets were often to the fore

in negotiations between the two cultures. When FitzMaurice de-
clined to confront Perrott, resplendent in scarlet 'Irish Trousses', in
single combat, he sent the poet, Conchobhar Ruadh Ó hIfearnáin,
with a 'cunning and subtle excuse' (Rawlinson, *Perrott*, p. 62; O'Rahilly, 'Irish Poets', p. 93; cf. Moran, *Catholic Archbishops*, p. 93).
Clergymen, particularly the handful of native Protestants, often
doubled as translators and interpreters. Christopher Bodkin, Archbishop of Tuam, assisted Dunne, the state interpreter, in a case heard
before the Council of Connacht (*CSPI* 1509–73, p. 428). Perplexed
by a prophecy linked in the popular imagination to Hugh O'Donnell, the Privy Council called on William Daniel for exegesis
(Meehan, *Rise and Fall*, p. 268).

References to translations provided by less exalted personages
show that a knowledge of English was spreading among the common
people. Mountjoy received Arthur O'Neill's demands 'by interpretation from the mouth of a barbarous messenger' (*CSPI* 1600, p. 229).
The queen, alarmed at the number of Irishmen serving in her army,
decreed that no band should comprise more than five natives 'and
they to serve for guides and interpreters' (*CSPI* 1592–6, p. 269). But
the ranks continued to swell with Irish recruits, many of whom
availed themselves of a chance to learn English. Between a third and
a half of Mountjoy's men were Irish (Moryson, *History* I, p. 276) and
the tension between mercenary allegiance and cultural loyalty
produced a remarkably open weave in communications between the
two sides. Those lacking the new lingua franca saw the need to
employ interpreters. The Archbishop of Cashel 'lent' Teig
O'Corkran to Maguire who had 'great use of his pen and his English
tongue' when dealing with Chichester (*CSPI* 1603–6, pp. 567–8).

The cast list of the colonial texts includes not only the principals,
both Irish and English, but also 'bit players' whose roles are never
quite defined and who shadow the main characters or move back
and forth between them with an ease and importance that is never
quite explained. One such figure is John Benyon who mediated, on
behalf of the administration, between Turlough Luineach and Hugh
O'Neill 'with the mildest words of persuasion' (*CSPI* 1586–8, p. 515).
Why Benyon was chosen as messenger and how he dealt with the
hibernophone Turlough – or in what language the 'mild words' were
uttered – is left a mystery. It is only when FitzWilliam is called to
account for the considerable sums he 'imprested' for his journey into
Connacht that circumstantial evidence receives the confirmation of

testimony: he justifies having kept Captain Benyon and Edward Byrne on his books because 'they be in credit with the Irishry and have the language' (*CSPI* 1588–92: 195).

Among the most intriguing of these enigmatic figures is the handful of Irish-born New Englishmen who served as interpreters. Captain William Piers who helped translate Turlough Luineach's 'badd speaches' for the Carrickfergus delegation was a second-generation New Englishman who thrived in the thick of translation (*CSPI* 1509–73, p. 211; *CCM* I, p. 491). Henry Duke, who stepped in to help Commissioners Gardiner and St Leger 'learn what [Hugh O'Donnell] said' (*CSPI* 1592–6, p. 224), grew up in the Meath marches, the son of a Kentish man. He sends FitzWilliam an 'Irishe letter', sent by O'Rourke to McMahon, 'translated, worde by worde' (PRO SP 63/137/10.xii). His intelligence reports use a hybrid lexicon that positions him midway between source and target languages: he notifies Perrott that the rebels in Brenny have made a 'keayshe'[8] over the river; he records the midnight arrival of 'an Irish Shenovine'[9] (*CSPI* 1586–8, p. 466; 1592–6, p. 235). His account of the 'dailie outrages' of O'Neill's followers seems to be written with the vigour of an Irish debate still ringing in his ears. He urges that the rebels' 'Irishe Sheanames shall no longer prevaile in clocking theire Rebellious attempts.' A marginal gloss, 'Irish Denialls', had to be supplied for FitzWilliam, to bring the residue of Irish clinging to the translation – *séanaim é*, 'I deny it' – fully into English (PRO SP 63/174/37.viii). The linguistic hybridity of this earlier generation of New Englishmen indicates that a significant shift in the pattern of newcomers' engagement with Irish took place in the latter half of Elizabeth's reign, as the cleavage between settlers and newcomers widened.

Doubly invisible in texts focused on male deeds are the women interpreters who were often well placed to move between the two languages. Sidney's accounts of his dealings with Turlough Luineach set the pattern: the role of the woman as linguistic go-between is first overlooked, then confirmed. For much of the 1570s, Sidney sent reports back to London of his meetings with Turlough. All skate around the issue of how he managed to communicate with this truculent Irish-speaker; many refer vaguely to Turlough's wife, the Earl of Argyle's daughter. When she visited Sidney in Armagh in November 1575, for example, he confined himself to observing that she was 'verye well spoken' (Collins, *Letters*, p. 77). When Turlough made excuses for not meeting the Lord Deputy the following year, Sidney blamed 'the fayre Speaches, and lewd Counsell of his Wyffe' (p. 164). A year later, Turlough entered into negotiations and their necessary corollary, a translation process.[10] Sidney's only reference then to the Countess is that she 'hath bene an Instrument, and cheife Counsellor, to frame hym to this Order of Obedience'; he suggests that Elizabeth 'bestowe a Garment vpon her, as a Token of your Favor' (p. 218). It is only in 1583, when Sidney sends Walsingham a memoir of his years in Ireland, that the Countess's role finally comes into focus. Not only was she 'a reverent speaker of the queen's Majesty' but 'she was a grave, wise, and well-spoken lady both in Scotch, English, and French' (*CCM* 2, pp. 349–50).[11] Another inter-preter steps out of the shadows, picking out a further thread in the web of talk that complicated the simplified polarities of war.[12]

CONTESTATION AND THE ORIGINS OF A CONFLICTUAL DIALOGUE

The sequelae of a language shift are complex and unpredictable. Elizabethan policy-makers were determined to refuse Irish a hearing and to promote English as part of an anglicising process designed to make Ireland 'quiet'. Far from being silenced, however, the Irish emerge as irrepressibly clamorous. Instead of recording a silent stand-off between the obduracy of Gaelic-speakers and the self-willed deafness of the English, the colonial texts hum with cross-currents of talk, leaks, spilled secrets and intrigue. Texts built on silence are rent by clamours; while they ignore indigenous speech, their pages hum with indigenous speakers and their subversive communications. (The change comes after Kinsale, when the record shows the colonial officials talking almost exclusively among them-selves.) The notion that silence is an invaluable accessory in the quest for domination, that the deaf ear is the agent and confirmation of power, needs to be questioned. Deafness, even deafness wilfully assumed, is scarcely an unmixed blessing. There is a tendency to presume that because English colonialism was characterised by linguistic inflexibility and self-imposed incomprehension this deaf-mute model constituted a colonial masterstroke, serving the colonist while disabling the native. But the disability cuts both ways: deafness can be a particularly self-denying way of excluding the other. If the texts show Englishmen attempting to dominate communications through exclusions and impositions, they also bear witness to the reversals met when the Irish began to play them at their own language games. English communicative abstinence found itself matched against Irish communicative inventiveness, with its dodges, evasions and deceits. Irish-speakers may have set limits on the incursion of English words but, as the extent of bilingual engagement evidenced above shows, they also sallied forth from their Gaelic base into direct, bilingual confrontation.

Defeat breeds compromises, with loyalty, with language. For the colonist, language is not negotiable. His language will dominate just as surely as his army and administration will. Where words fail, the colonial gaze takes over. The native can afford no such absolutes. 'An té nach bhfuil láidir ní foláir dó bheidh glic': ingenuity is needed where power is inadequate – and that calls on language, the coloniser's as well as one's own. Powerlessness can teach linguistic agility; survival argues for mastering the master's tongue. But mastery, even one succumbed to as a compromise with defeat, confers its own power. These paradoxes, where silence is pitched against clamour, domination (of Irish by English) against mastery (of English by the Irish), bring us to a central paradox: that the literal silencing of a language does not necessarily mean the metaphorical silencing of its speakers.

Nowhere is this shifting amalgam of compromise and duplicity, accommodation and contestation more apparent than at those moments when the two languages come into contact through the agency of interpreters. To cross between the languages of two antagonistic tribes was, in some ways, to slip across enemy lines. Those who made the journey across could return tainted by the encounter. Hybridity is an uncomfortable commodity in a polarised society and mistrust of the translator's duality was intensified by the growing strains between Old and New English. Linguistically, the interpreter was a half-caste whose *pureza de sangre* was ever in doubt. Rich ridiculed the practice of using Old English intermediaries in parleys:

those that were to appoint arbitrators in the behalf of the lion, made special choice of the fox and the sheep. The fox, being an ally to the wolf, and very near in affinity to him, would not press him further than the wolf himself liked.

These 'English with the Irish hearts', he sneered, were ever ready to speak for the rebels and to advance their case (*CSPI* 1599–1600, pp. 48, 50). Sir Henry Wotton came to Ireland in 1599 as Essex's secretary and was on hand when he negotiated with O'Neill. The experience left him bitterly mistrustful of Irish interpreters, as he told John Donne:

Whatsoever we have done, or mean to do, we know what will become of it, when it comes amongst our worst enemies, which are interpreters. I would there were more O'Neales and Macguiers and O'Donnells and Mac-Mahons, and fewer of them. (Smith, *Wotton*, p. 308)

A sense of disquiet often attends the idea of translation. The metaphors it attracts are instructive. As George Steiner points out, St Jerome speaks of 'capturing' meaning; Nietzsche talks of 'conquering' it; Steiner himself imagines 'hoarded dreams, patents of life . . . being taken across the frontier' (Steiner, *After Babel*, pp. 281, 260, 244). Mistrust is intensified in the colonial context where translation often slides into traduction. In his short story, '*Las dos orillas*', Fuentes uses Cortés' interpreter, Aguilar, to explore his own fascination with linguistic *mestizaje*. Fuentes' fictional Aguilar curses himself precisely for eliding translation and traduction: 'traduje, traicioné, inventé' (I translated, I traduced, I invented) (*El naranjo*, p. 18). Yet, if the inclination to mistrust interpreters is universal, there is an interesting difference between the New World and Ireland as to which side felt the mistrust most keenly. The evidence from America suggests that the duplicity of interpreters redounded most to the Indians' disadvantage. Cortés' sweep across Mexico towards Tenoctitlan and the destruction of the native world owed much to his success in harnessing the interpreters, Aguilar and Malinche, to his project; in Peru, the death of the last Inca was, Sarate believed, 'conspired by meane of his Interpreter' (Cortés, *Letters from Mexico*, pp. 17, 73; Sarate, *History*, fo. B.iii.r). Indians continued to have reason to suspect interpreters: exceptionally, interpreters were given the right to bear arms in order to defend themselves against aggrieved native monophones (Gonzalbo, *Historia*, p. 187; Heath, *Telling Tongues*, p. 12).

In Ireland, it is the English who most frequently voice qualms about the unreliability of interpreters. Bellingham chided an unidentified Irish lord for writing to him in Latin, telling him to find instead a 'trusty man who can vnderstande and wryt englyshe' because he doubted that 'lattyn letters' would 'be truly expovndyd' by 'fals and decytfull fryers' (PRO SP 61/1/139). Conversely, the London Commissioners investigating Perrott's treason were forced to examine Bishop Malachias O'Mollone in Latin because 'they dare not use the service of an Irish interpreter' (*CSPDom.* 1581–90, p. 688). The figure of Shealty in Robert Wilson's *The Three Lords and Three Ladies of London* suggests that by the 1590s the unreliable interpreter was emerging as a stock Irish type. Among the stage-Spaniards receiving a comeuppance in Wilson's xenophobic celebration of the Armada defeat is Spanish Pride who, not deigning to speak English, insists on using Latin (lines 1, 622–3). The 'Trowch man' necessitated by this insolence is Shealty, whose name Lord Pollicie glosses as 'An Irish word, signifieng liberty, rather remisnes, loosnes, if ye wil' (lines 1, 731–2).[13] Shakespeare's demonising of Cade – 'this devil' – in *Henry VI Part 2* included inventing a past for him as a transgressive shape-changer on the boundaries between Irish and English and, as York explains, duplicitly fluent in both:

> Full often, like a shag-haired crafty kern,
> Hath he conversèd with the enemy,
> And undiscovered come to me again
> And given me notice of their villainies.   (iii.i.367–70)

Articulate, fluent in civil tongues, in Ireland the confident Elizabethan loses control of meaning. He cannot follow the interpreter on his journey into a seeming babble of aspirates and gutturals. Hearing picks up only tones, inflections, raised voices, a burst of complicit laughter; the anxious gaze registers nudges, smiles, a wink.[14] Nor can he trust the message brought back from consort with the enemy. That such suspicions were well-founded is confirmed by those who could eavesdrop on both sides. Stanihurst's ignorance of Irish was less complete than he affected. Certainly, in the *Irish Chronicle*, he shows a sensitivity to the plasticity of meaning in its movement between languages quite foreign to his English-born contemporaries. He retells the story of Archbishop Alen's murder with a keen awareness of how ambiguities in language could be wilfully exploited. Hauled before Silken Thomas, Alen pleads for mercy; Thomas turns on his horse,

saying in Irish, '*Bir wem e boddeagh*' which is as muche in Englishe as 'Awaye with the Churle', or 'Take the Churle from mee', whyche doubtles he spake, as after he declared, meaning the Archbishop should bee deteyned as prisoner.

But the 'caitiffes' picked up the ambivalence of his phrasing and 'rather of malice than of ignorance, misconstruing his words . . . brayned and hackt [Alen] in gobbets' (*Chronicle*, p. 269). Stanihurst again spots the scope for manipulating the gap between bilingual agility and monoglot disability when he recounts how Skeffington[15] 'rewarded' Kildare's constable, Parese, for his unchivalrous betrayal of Maynooth castle with the pieces of silver which had bought his (dis)loyalty – and a sentence of beheading. Parese rues his misjudgement. Boyce, a Pale 'Gentleman of worship' and retainer of Kildare 'standing in the preasse, saide in Irishe, *Antragh*, which is asmuch in English as "too late"' (*Chronicle*, p. 279). Skeffington seeks a translation but Boyce, who has a different message for his English auditor, delivers a mischievously loose rendition:

M. Boyce willing to expounde his owne wordes, stept forth and answered, 'My Lord, I said nothing, but that Parese is seized of a towne neere the water syde named Baltra, and I woulde gladly know how he wil dispose it before hee bee executed.'

Skeffington, 'not mistrusting that M. Boice had glozed',[16] gets Parese to resolve the financial details 'and presently caused him to be cut shorter by the head' (pp. 279–80). Skeffington and Alen emerge from Stanihurst's text as emblematic figures, disadvantaged monophones astray in a world of plural meanings. This is precisely the positioning of the English newcomer and his text, suspicion an uncomfortable substitute for understanding. Beyond the language barrier, in the verso world of Irish, there were other pens at work recording engagements with the inverse foreign tongue. There, the voices that trail off into incomprehension and silence in English texts swell once more into meaning – and a confirmation of English suspicions.

Philip O'Sullivan Beare's account of the siege of Smerwick where, in his view, brutality confronted pusillanimity, finds only one honourable figure, 'an Irish gentleman of the Plunkett family', whom FitzMaurice had left as San Joseph's interpreter. Here, on the far side of the looking-glass, the interpreter's duplicity is endorsed as heroic subversion. Plunkett becomes the fulcrum of a narrative where bold language-acts confront merciless deeds. While San Joseph, 'a man of cringing disposition' keen to surrender, approaches Grey bareheaded, the interpreter keeps his head defiantly covered. Determined that the defenders should hold out against Grey,

Plunkett interpreted their speeches opposite ways, making the commandant say to the viceroy that he would lose his life rather than surrender, and making the viceroy say to the commandant that he was determined to give no quarter to the besieged. (*Ireland under Elizabeth*, p. 24)

For once, the reader is positioned alongside the devious interpreter, privy to mistranslations which those reliant on Plunkett can infer only from gestures. O'Sullivan and Donal O'Daly, who also tells this story, cast their glances in different directions when recording the opposed monophones' mutual realisation that meanings are out of kilter. O'Sullivan has San Joseph 'perceiving the false translations of the interpreter by the inconsistency of the viceroy's face' (p. 24) while for O'Daly 'the expression of Plunkett's features, and the fiery indignation of the Spaniard, caused Lord Grey to suspect that his words had not been rendered faithfully' (*Geraldines*, pp. 96–7). In O'Sullivan's version, the doomed Plunkett is arrested by San Joseph, in O'Daly's by Grey. The interpreter's power over language is ultimately circumscribed by his dependent-masters' power over him.

In the narratives of conquest, the keen-witted bilingual is regularly portrayed as a trickster, an alchemist of language who uses his skills to deceive, entrap or outsmart his opponent – or his master. Working alone in a privileged space where the monoglot cannot follow, the bilingual bends meaning to his will. One man caught doing so was 'Davies Omey', the young Scot that 'writeth' for Turlough Luineach. Escaping Turlough's surveillance as he moved from Irish into Latin and English, Omey altered O'Neill's intended message by adding accusations against Perrott, at the behest, apparently, of Sir Patrick Barnwall and Sir Henry Bagenal. Denouncing these 'bad practices', Perrott had Omey produce

the copy of the Irish letter which was the ground of that Latin letter which Turlough meant to have sent to Her Majesty at the first, with the translation thereof in English, under the hand of the said Davies.

Perrott was also able to send Burghley a letter, presumably in translation, from Turlough, which said, 'If there be any more in the Latin than is in the Irish it is falsely inserted by the translators.' Perrott could then conclude triumphantly: '[a]ll which being compared with the Latin letter that was devised and sent to Her Majesty will lay open the whole practice how I have been used therein' (*CSPI* 1586–8, p. 390).

In 1600, Ormond was captured by Ony MacRory in an episode that hinged on a linguistic misunderstanding. Ormond and Carew met MacRory and the Jesuit, Archer, for a parley. Finding that Carew spoke no Irish, Archer 'began to speak in English . . . piously and devoutly'. When Ormond interrupted with 'some silly argument', Archer 'chanced' to raise the staff supporting 'his aged limbs'. The hibernophone footsoldiers guarding him mistook this purely rhetorical flourish for a summons to arms – and seized Ormond (O'Sullivan, *Ireland under Elizabeth*, p. 123). Later, freed by his kidnapper, Ormond sent the queen a satisfied account of trumping the rebels linguistically at close of play. Just before releasing him, they produced a document for him to sign, intended to implicate him in their 'traiterous actions'. But the absence of their own secretary and of

> Archer the Jhesuith and such others of them as understood the English tonge enforced the traitors to committ the writing of that bill to one that wished better unto me, then unto them as by the stile thereof may appeare. (Graves, 'Ormonde', p. 428)

The bilingual-speaker and his unidentified translator-accomplice once more gull the monophones.

It is remarkable how often language difference features in episodes of deceit and chicanery. The power to manipulate language often conferred the power to manipulate *tout court*. Skullduggery often had a linguistic component, with double-dealing conspirators crossing back and forth between Irish and English. The uneasy suspicion that talk was used as a decoy, as war by other, fraudulent and seductive means, hung over exchanges across the language divide. It is there in Piers Walsh's report on the Great Water débâcle: looking back, he suspects that the rhymer and messenger sent by Fiach McHugh to Sir Henry Harington had come only 'to feed Sir Henry with fair words until their forces were ready to set upon him' (*CSPI* 1599–1600, p. 59). Another officer, Linley, is sure that the messenger's 15-minute dalliance 'was but a policy of the rebels that they might come near us'. Captains Mallory and Linley point the finger at Lieutenant Walsh himself who parleyed with the rebels without Harington's authority and was seen 'shaking his hat' towards them (p. 90); their suspicions cost Walsh his life. Such anxieties were never far from official attitudes to contacts across the language frontier – and to those who facilitated them.

The interpreter was a mistrusted figure. Docwra commended his interpreter, Captain Willis, 'in whom I find singular use and honesty', but Willis's Irish birth was enough to put a question mark over his loyalty for the anonymous author of a memorandum on the causes of the war: 'certain captains were raised to companies, as Willis, Fuller, and others, who, being this countrymen . . . it is a disputable question whether it were better to have them all against us, or with us' (*CSPI* 1600–1, pp. 13, 123). So suspicious were the English of Irish interpreters that when Juan Wall, an Irishman, turned up in London as interpreter for the Spanish ambassador, Zúñiga, the English refused to deal with him and had him arrested instead (Walsh, *O'Neill*, p. 41). The fear that linguistic duality bred doubtful allegiance, ever the root of English mistrust of the Old English, intensified during the Nine Years War. 'Practising', commoning, conversing, talking: subjects of dubious loyalty and rebels were bound in a confederacy of insatiable talk. Convinced that the informal translations provided by mistrusted Irish officials subverted English interests, Justice Saxey proposed that official translations should be provided 'by an Englishman':

for an interpreter sworn (as is used in Wales) who is subject to everyman's censure, if he interpret untruly, is more meet to inform the Court, than one of the Judges unsworn, whose untrue interpretation will be either favourably construed, or by silence allowed. (*CSPI* 1598–9, p. 394)

If ancestral ties were not enough to deflect suspicion from English-Irishmen crossing between the two languages, then Gaels who switched between English and a mother tongue that was believed to harbour all manner of abuses were even more deeply mistrusted. Florence MacCarthy, regarded by Carew as a 'Machiavellian ambodexter' and by Irishmen less ambivalently positioned than he as 'a damned counterfeit Englishman' (Judson, *Spenser*, p. 124), was the archetype of the unreliable bilingual. His 'tergiversations' and 'perpetual juggling' derived in part from a linguistic 'ambodexterity' which left him poised ambivalently between two worlds and, in the end, fatally at home in neither (Stafford, *Pacata Hibernia* I, pp. 138, 150). He trumpeted his usefulness when sending Carew an intercepted letter, 'in Irishe', from Donal MacCarthy to the Súgán Earl 'which I interpreted' (MacCarthy, *Life*, p. 292). But when Richard Boyle, in turn, intercepted letters from MacCarthy to Tomás Óg, he discovered that Carew's freelance interpreter and current house-guest was urging the rebel to hold out against his host. Among the many accusations of double-dealing building up against Florence was that he had sent 'a cunning letter written in Irish to the White Knight'; the vigorous translation is itself a play of ambivalences: 'Damnation, I cannot but commend me heartily to you, as bad as thou art.' Seeming so plastic in the hands of bilinguals like Florence, language became an unreliable currency: all would have been fine in

Munster 'if the protectees had meant in their hearts as they professed with their tongues' (Stafford, *Pacata Hibernia* I, pp. 135, 239, 120).

The very hybridity of the bilingual seemed to destabilise identity. For Patrick Crosby, who served the administration as a translator (*UJA* VI, p. 57), identity got displaced on to a no-man's-land between Irish and English: Ormond scornfully derided Crosby's claim to be 'only of English blood and surname' as fraudulent, insisting that he was really 'Mc y Crossane, one of the mere Irish' and of rhymer stock (*CSPI* 1601–3, p. 196). Crosby's subsequent career reminds us that new men like Boyle depended on accomplices like him to negotiate the linguistic as well as legal impediments that stood between them and a fortune. Crosby and his fellows – men like Francis Shane, the 'lynx-eyed native servitor' who translated an Irish document on landholdings for Burghley (Hill, *Flight*, p. 21) – 'had a foot in each camp, pursuing a course of profound ambiguity in the margin of rebellion, acting for all parties and especially themselves' (Ranger, 'Boyle', p. 273).

Most alarmingly, the identity of even native-born Englishmen proved fluid when tested by close contact; tales of Englishmen's degenerative drift are often built around fables of linguistic deceit. Intermarriage was always keenly mistrusted; ties of language had an irresistible force in luring Irish-speaking spouses to the rebels. Trollop used the case of Captain Tom Lee to reinforce his argument that all Englishmen married to Irishwomen – as well as all Irishmen – should be cashiered. Lee, hoping to entrap the rebel Walter Reagh, had sought to enlist one of Walter's associates. But when Lee engaged his wife, Elizabeth Eustace, 'as an interpreter between him and the fellow', she betrayed her husband's plot and his 'good purpose was prevented' (*CSPI* 1586–8, pp. 428–9).

At the heart of English-speakers' anxiety about translation and translators lay a fear of its transgressive quality. A vagrant shape-changer on the frontier between hostile factions, the mobile bilingual could turn language against its 'owners'. Silken Thomas, out-numbered by the English, had to rely on 'sodaine stratagemes' and 'knackes'. The success of one such 'knack' lay in ventriloquising the defenders' voices: Thomas 'deuised such of his horsemen that coulde speake English . . . to ryde to Trim, where a garrison lay, with hue and crie, saying that they were Captaine Salisburie his souldiours', to announce that 'the traytour' was burning a village outside the town. The English soldiers, 'suspecting no cosinage', sallied out, some to their deaths (Stanihurst, *Chronicle*, p. 281). David Barry got 'a boy that spake good English' to pretend to the garrison at Bantry Abbey that the loyalist Sir Owen MacCarthy required their assistance in recovering a prey taken by the 'traitors' – 'which treacherous message being believed of the soldiers', the English issued forth to be 'intrapped by an ambuscade laid for them' (*CSPI* 1574–85, p. lxxxvi).

Of course, the trick could be played on the other side. Francis Stafford, plotting with Manus O'Cahan, came up with a ruse to make 'a goode drafte on Ferdoroke Ochane'. They put out word that Manus was going about, collecting alms. One night, Manus rode out with twenty of Captain Warren's horsemen. When they came to the house where Ferdorough lay sleeping, they had the drum call out 'in Irish' that there was no need to fear: it was only Manus come abegging. One of the defenders, tumbling too late to the trick, said 'in Irish, Tardea smagh fourtough Shinn that is in English by god you haue gotten vs all wel' (PRO SP 63/134/36): Ferdorough's killers had used his language as a Trojan horse to pierce his defences. Patrick Plunkett, Lord Dunsany, brandished his fluency in Irish as an essential accessory to deception when petitioning Cecil for the command of Carrickfergus in 1600. He undertook to 'engage and corrupt his [O'Neill's] nearest followers and friends, yea his very wife', insisting that his edge over his competitor-conspirators was linguistic: 'I have all the helps and means that any other man hath, and I have the language very well for advantage' (*CSPI* 1600–1, p. 44).

The language of the enemy could be turned into a talisman, a charm to spirit its initiates away from harm. Pelham was troubled by the 'strange escape of Dr Sanders and John of Desmond'. He thought it uncanny that the pair, finding themselves surrounded by the Kilmallock garrison and 'being in the night above an hour in their company preserved in the dark by speaking English, and crying upon the English to execute the Irish' (*CCM* 2, p. 293). In his flight from Dublin Castle, Hugh O'Donnell relied on silence to slip unheard through the city's streets, 'gan fhoirchloisteacht do neoch' (unheard by any). But when he was joined by Turloch Buidhe O Hagan, O'Neill's seneschal, who 'spoke the language of the foreigner', 'no labhradh bérla na ttuath nechtrond', O'Donnell, shielded by the English-speaker, enjoyed the freedom of the 'English roads' (Ó Clérigh, *Beatha* i, pp. 20, 26).

The permeability of the language barrier is nowhere more evident

206 Language and conquest in early modern Ireland

than in the feverish trade in information. The Secretary of State, Geoffrey Fenton, was the energetic master of an extensive – if never entirely reliable – spy-ring. In a letter to Cecil in 1600, he contentedly parades his chief informants: 'my Irish priest in Dungannon', Piers Walsh,[17] 'whom Tyrone useth to employ to his confederates in Leinster' and 'an Irish soldier in Tyrone's camp'. He crows over the excellent returns on his £44.15s. investment in spies' fees, but urges Cecil to pay the next instalment, 'for you know the priest must be fed or else he will do nothing' (*CSPI* 1599–1600, pp. 387–9). Names are as unreliable as their owners: Richard Weston reports as 'William Gelle' on one occasion and as 'John Tomson' the next; when that is rumbled, he becomes 'Stephen Waterhouse' (*CSPI* 1596–7, pp. 251, 264, 282). The priest uses the code name 'Fr Jarkey'; Fenton contrives to place a 'gentlewoman' called Honora in the camp where Ormond is held captive and later informs Cecil that she will henceforth 'pass under the name of *Imperia Romana*' (*CSPI* 1600, pp. 169, 181). Following the logic of the sobriquet to vanishing-point, one informer trades as '*Sine Nomine*' (*CSPI* 1596–7, p. 449).

This world without names was also one without certainties. The spy was the incarnation of the duplicit translator, crossing back and forth not just between languages but between allegiances. Moving between camps entailed moving between languages: one Walter Tallent interpreted when Donal Groome came to inform on Niall Garbh – and was also on hand when Shane McManus Oge O'Donnell needed help to spill some beans (*CSPI* 1601–3, pp. 374–7). Weston-Gelle-Tomson-Waterhouse, the son of New English settlers and a minor Irish-language poet (Ó Fiaich, 'Weston'), represents the indeterminacy – nominal, linguistic, onto-logical – of the go-between to the full. Owen McHugh O'Neill came to Mountjoy in April 1600, 'in the night secretly by a privy way, disguised', to inform. To sell his tale, he crossed the language frontier: the participants included Mountjoy and 'one interpreter named Edward Tatle' (*CSPI* 1600, p. 310; Ó Fiach, 'The O'Neills', p. 43). But the direction of translation and transmission was far from one way: before the informer returned to Ulster, Hugh O'Neill already knew of his defection. McHugh had no doubts about who was responsible for the counter-espionage: Fenton's prized agent, Richard Weston who, McHugh averred, 'doth continually lie in Dundalk for intelligence' to bring back to . . . O'Neill (*CSPI* 1600, p. 311). Once again, the bilingual's proves to be a forked tongue.

Those who, in Stanihurst's phrase, could turn their tongues could, with equal facility, turn their coats.

Ironically, those who 'vented' 'the treasure of our tongue' on Ireland's 'strange shores' (Daniel, 'Musophilus', lines 958–9) came to mistrust words. But signs, in which the English invested their trust instead, were scarcely more reliable. As a token of one of his many reforms, Hugh O'Neill 'had cookes, hys meate well dressed and decently served'. The optimistic English soothsayers were willing to 'finde hope of his good meaninge' (Perrott, *Chronicle*, pp. 73–4). But whether opting for the raw or the cooked, O'Neill's purpose was unchanged. While the authorities were pleased to interpret his purchase of 'riche furniture for his howse, of beddinge, arras, carpettes' as a sign that he 'would reduce this contrie unto civilitie', he subverted their optimistic auguries: in a further gesture of home improvement, he imported lead to roof his castle in Dungannon, 'which afterwards was turned to a worse use of shotte and bullettes to annoy the State' (pp. 67–8).

So it is that texts which represent language monophonically resonate with discordant voices. Natives denied textual recognition for their own language enter the texts as irrepressible communicators, operating in an unidentified space between two languages. Irish communicative wiles vex the commentators obliged to report them. The natives are 'sharpe witted' (Campion, *Two Bokes*, p. 19), full of 'subtleties and sly shifts' (Spenser, *View*, p. 23); they are 'dissembling Temporisers' and masters of 'coulorable evasions' (Moryson, *History* II, p. 330; *Shakespeare's Europe*, p. 216). Their vigour in contestation becomes their defining trait: 'These rebellious People, are by Nature clamorous', their complaints 'strayned to the highest points of calamity, sometymes in hyperbolical tearmes' (Moryson, *History* I, p. 116; *Shakespeare's Europe*, p. 484). Bishop Aylmer, entrusted with custody of the volatile priest, Denys Roghan, complained, with an eloquent intransitive, that 'his Irish mouth lavished' (Strype, *Aylmer*, p. 107).

The extravagance and excess of Irish utterances is played off against seemly English reticence. Sidney portrays himself as a plain-talking soldier, asking his audience in the Irish Parliament to 'beare with me; I take matters while I thinke on them as the cum nexte to hande; I canne no skil of written tales' (Campion, *Two Bokes*, pp. 147–8). Mountjoy disliked 'a free Speaker' and was himself 'sparing in Speech; but when he was drawn to it, most judicious therein, if not eloquent' (Moryson, *History* I, p. 110); that, too, is the impression reaching London: the 'Lord Mountjoy in Ireland will never discourse at table; eates in silence' (Manningham, *Diary*, p. 104). Verbally continent to the point of silence, the Englishman is hoist, not with his own petard, but with his own word.

Irish anglophones wielded the colonial language and its legal and diplomatic discourses against its 'owners'. Finín O'Driscoll accosts an English sailor, Roger Lover, moored in Baltimore, and with cool irony deploys the metropolitan tongue to tell him of English naval reversals at Plymouth. Lover seeks more detail; O'Driscoll produces a letter which the illiterate sailor has to give to his ship's master to read (*Salis.* XI, p. 79). Cecil is disconcerted not just by Florence MacCarthy – 'how probably that witty knave can argue' (*CCM* 4, p. 326) – but by the anglophile Earl of Thomond. He bridles at O'Brien's ambages and the uncertainty of cross-cultural communication inside a common language. When asked his purpose, Thomond 'will still reply "Nay, Sir, even in what please you I am yours to dispose" . . . and so would still hide himself in such sort as, before God, it did much trouble me' (*CCM* 4, p. 47).

The Irish lords practised the cut and thrust of diplomatic language with gusto. Bishop Jones sent Burghley an account of a series of talks held at the height of the Nine Years War, when the Crown Commissioners, Ormond, Fenton and the bishop, faced O'Neill. On the second day of hard talking, O'Neill is 'ticklish', demanding that negotiations be conducted through messengers and, as we saw earlier, refusing to have any further 'pleadings in English' (*CSPI* 1596–7, p. 485). Fenton and Jones take 'exception' to this development and persuade him to return. Fenton delivers written terms which O'Neill takes away for consideration. As the Commissioners ride back towards Dundalk, O'Neill's 'secretary for the Irish tongue' overtakes them and reads out a letter that has just arrived from Hugh O'Donnell while Miler McGrath, Archbishop of Cashel, provides a running translation (p. 486). Jones surmises that the 'most dangerous, cunning, and crafty' O'Neill (p. 488) deliberately showed them O'Donnell's 'proud and lofty' rejection, to force them into accepting his own 'unreasonable conditions' (p. 490). Next day, O'Neill's response to the articles is so 'crooked and untoward', quibbling over details line by line, that the talks break up (p. 487). When Wallop and Gardiner take over as the new commissioners, they denounce the northern lords' 'vnquiet discourses' to the English

Council 'with some amazement at their oratory, and cunning insinuation, whereby they might haue excused diuers things' – had the lords not, they intimate, chosen the wrong audience (Gainsford, *Tyrone*, p. 20).

The Irish refused English connotations, challenging them with dissenting counter-definitions, causing pairs of contested terms to spring up. Because the Gaels defined their rising as a war, not a rebellion, '[t]hese outlawes are not by them termed Rebels, but men in Action' (Moryson, *Shakespeare's Europe*, p. 194). Lord Deputy Russell insists that he is embarking on 'a cessation of armes' with O'Neill; O'Neill terms it, 'thoe not rightly, a truce' (Perrott, *Chronicle*, p. 114). Shane O'Neill is proclaimed traitor by Sidney but the new name is refused with insolent humour. 'An Irish gestor standinge by and hearing Oneal denounced with addicion of a newe name, traytor: Except (quoth he) a traitor be a more honourable title then Oneal, he shall never take yt uppon him by my consente' (Campion, *Two Bokes*, p. 140).

The 'guylefull' Hugh O'Neill (Perrott, *Chronicle*, p. 8) played the colonists' language games against them in a manner which they found singularly galling. Exasperation is never far from English accounts of his negotiation style. 'Of a high, dissembling, subtile, and profound Wit', he repeatedly out-manœuvres them 'by feigned Countenance and false Words' (Moryson, *History* I, pp. 17, 48). Moryson imagines 'that *Carthage* [n]ever bred such a dissembling fædifragous Wretch as *Tyrone*' (p. 62). He holds the ring with his web of words and wheedling as much as with military might. 'He writtes often; accuseth and excuseth much . . . knowes with whom he deales'; he is master of the 'large answer' and of advocation (Perrott, *Chronicle*, pp. 72–3). His skilful manœuvres simultaneously dismay and disarm the English: he repeatedly talks senior officials into pardons and concessions, 'accordinge to his wonted and well experienced maner of dissimulation'; his subtle protestations 'thoe scarce beleived . . . yet were they accepted' (Perrott, *Chronicle*, pp. 160, 113). Even the animal metaphors foisted on him pay bitter tribute to his communicative ingenuity. He is a 'Viper', a 'crafty Fox', a 'wily Serpent' who could 'change like Proteus into all shapes, that might bring aduantage to his treasons' (Moryson, *History* II, p. 225; I, p. 38; E. S. C., *Government*, p. 22). At the height of his power, he grows insolent in his breaches of English decorum: 'he not only omitted his wonted observation of reverence in writting to that State, but slighted them, and used rather commination than any dutifull or decent wordes' (Perrott, *Chronicle*, p. 157).

Spenser's Malengin, the shaggy-haired, fastness-dwelling raider, is the very type of an Irish rebel – and personifies 'Guyle'. He is 'crafty' and lives off 'his owne wylie wit'. His most lethal armament is linguistic: he is 'smooth of tongue, and subtile in his tale' (*FQ* v.ix.5.1,6). Eloquence is his weapon of choice against the decoy-damzel: 'He gan with guilefull words her to perswade' (12.5). Even the animal forms which he assumes – fox, snake (17,19) – when seeking to evade Talus' violence are those used by the Elizabethans to characterise their maddeningly loquacious Irish adversaries. But Malengin's end, too, replays the ultimate impotence of verbal dexterity against might. The Talus-silenced 'Guyle' is 'left a carrion outcast; / For beasts and foules to feede vpon for their repast' (19.8–9).

For these are paradoxes that rebound on all. In opting for mastery of communications, the natives were, increasingly, having to master the only language which the English could hear. The ultimate price of communicative agility might be language – their language. The Elizabethan wars in Ireland marked a crucial shift in the balance of power in the island. The Gaelic lords were crushed. The Old English were marginalised. The English gained control. In parallel, a shift occurred in the balance of linguistic power. Expression remained unstaunched – but the language in which it was articulated, especially in public fora, was shifting. The Irish Caliban was learning to curse the *boddai Galt* as an 'English churl' and his 'profit on't' was deeply ambivalent. The Elizabethan conquest did little to alter the fact that Irish was still the language of the people: Stephen White noted in 1602 that 'scarcely one in a thousand of the Old Irish know even three words of any tongue except Irish' (Walsh, 'Irish Language', pp. 247–8; Lynch, *Cambrensis*, p. 191). As the medium of their artistic expression and that of the exiled writers on the continent, Irish was entering a century of extraordinary vitality (Ó Hifearnáin, 'Capuchon'). But the ascendancy of the New English meant that it was exiled from political and economic power. Irish is missing from the record of the Irish Confederacy, half a century after Kinsale. Even by the early seventeenth century it was becoming haunted by a sense of absence. Céitinn consciously wrote against oblivion, undertaking *Foras Feasa* so that Ireland and its noble companies would not 'do dhul i mbáthadh, gan luadh ná iomrádh do bheidh orra' (go under without mention or deliberation being made of them) (*Foras Feasa*, p. 76).

But the very vigour of Céitinn and his contemporaries' 'writing back' demonstrated that threnodies for the silenced tongue were premature. By the end of the war, we are seeing not so much the clash of two languages as the clash of two incommensurate communication styles. With the new order settling into place, the old language barrier is replaced by a new communications barrier as a conflictual dialogue opens up. A common language is being used to frame discrepant meanings. A language shift that had its origin in a refusal to hear, a passion to be heard and deep mutual misunderstanding was unlikely ever to guarantee shared meanings. Moryson's experience in Ireland led him to conclude that its complexity was such that no governor sent there could ever hope to understand it (*Shakespeare's Europe*, p. 189). Perrott heard 'a greate counsellor of this kingdome confesse he understoode lesse Ireland then any other' (*Chronicle*, p. 6). A failure to understand, originally rooted in language difference, was being translated, by the late sixteenth century, into a pattern of misunderstanding that would henceforth be only partly linguistic.

As early as the 1570s, Brian Ó Gnímh captured the desolation of the poet adrift – 'ar mearbhall' – on a rising tide of English which reduced his words to the lonely call of seabirds: 'mé an murdhuchan an mhuir Goill', I am the guillemot, the English the sea (Walsh, *Chiefs and Leaders*, p. 74: 13.3). The long ebb of the Irish language had begun. But the rising tide of English came freighted with a complex cargo from the wreckage of the Gaelic world.

Conclusion

Scríte in uisce, le clipe de sciathán rotha,
ar scothóg feamainne mar phár.
Nuala Ní Dhomhnall, 'An Mhurúch agus Focail Áirithe'

Two last texts, pitched at the poles of an incomprehension that is linguistic, artistic and epistemological and held in tense equipoise only by their shared subject, an Irish-speaker caught up in the havoc of a changing world, act out, in their own way, the paradox which, from the start, marks the experience of linguistic colonisation in Ireland. Some time in the 1580s, Tadhg Dall Ó hUiginn addressed 'D'fhior chogaid comhailtear síothcháin', 'By a man of war is peace kept', to Brian na Murrtha O'Rourke, the lord of Breifne who challenged English rule in the north-west throughout the 1580s and who has made minor appearances throughout this work. The poet urges O'Rourke to unleash a maelstrom of destruction, driving the 'fir Saxan',[1] 'Saxon men', from Ireland (Knott, *Poems* I, p. 108: 2.2). The poet conjures up images of apocalyptic violence: 'múir chloch 'na gcuiltibh fiaidhmhíol', the 'stone castles' of the Pale reduced to 'lairs for savage beasts'; a famine-stricken mother eating 'mír do chridhe a céidleanaibh' (a bite of the heart of her first-born) (19.1; 20.4). Ó hUiginn stands the Elizabethans' taxonomy of 'civil' and 'barbarian' on its head: the English are 'danair loma léirchreachaigh'[2] (rapacious, destructive barbarians) who pillage 'Gaoidhil na ngníomh gcathardha'[3] (the Gaels of civil deeds) (32.4; 3.2). The poet puts his faith in war, not words, warning O'Rourke 'ná meallaid le millsi briathar' (let [the English] not beguile with sweet words) (32.1); the Irish must be like 'an chineóil shionnchamhail' (35.2), 'the fox tribe', who foiled the treacherous lion's attempt to lure them to his cave. Instead of talk, the poet advocates a terrible extirpation leading to silence: 'ríoghnaibh roisgfliucha', wet-eyed queens, will raise 'éighmhe loma loisgniucha', sharp shrieking wails, over their dead (71.2, 4); afterwards, nothing will remain of the English 'acht rádh go rabhsad uair éigin' (21.3), but to say that once upon a time they were.

O'Rourke rose once more in 1589 and was defeated by Bingham's forces. He fled to Scotland; James VI handed him over to Elizabeth to be tried for treason in London (Morgan, 'Extradition'). In his *Annales* entry for 1591, Stow gives an extended account of the trial. He details the Crown's charges: that O'Rourke had conspired with the Spanish, sheltered Armada survivors – these included, we recall, Captain Cuellar – and, most provocatively,

> caused the picture of a woman to bee made, setting to her Maiesties name, and caused it to bee tyed to an horse tayle, and to bee drawne through the mire in derision of her Maiesty. And after caused his Galliglasses to hew the same in pieces with their axes, vttering diuers traiterous and rebellious wordes against her Maiestie. (p. 763)

His Scottish gaoler, Lord Scrope, had complained that O'Rourke, apart from 'some broken Latin', 'will not shewe to understand any other language then that of his owne countrey' (O'Grady, *Catalogue*, p. 422). So, in the London courtroom, blinking in the unwonted spotlight, is an interpreter, '*Iohn Ly* of Rathbride, a Gentleman out of Ireland . . . who did expound and declare in Irish . . . all speeches vttered by the Judges, and the sayd *O Royrke*' (Stow, *Annales*, pp. 62–3; cf. *CSPI* 1586–8, p. 244). Stow structures his telling around the cut and thrust of the courtroom exchanges. The chieftain demands, through Lye, that he be shown the depositions which FitzWilliam and Bingham made against him, that 'a good man of Law to bee assigned vnto him' and that the queen 'bee one of the Iury to passe vpon him'. These demands are construed as 'his refusall to bee tryed' – 'beeing obstinate therein, [he] was guiltie of his owne death' – so the Lord Chief Justice requires Lye to expound 'vnto him his iudgement': O'Rourke is to be taken on a hurdle to the place of execution, hanged 'vntill he were halfe dead, then to bee let downe, and his members and bowels to bee taken out, and burnt in the fire, his head to bee striken off, and his body to be quartered' (p. 763).

The drama of translation continues in Tyburn. With '*O Royrke* yet standing vpon the Cart', Lye exhorts him to repent 'the filthy and odious treasons that he committed against her Maiestie'. O'Rourke responds 'obstinately', still rehearsing legal arguments. Lye then interprets for both sides as the chieftain and the spectators to his execution argue to and fro. Miler McGrath, too, is on hand and is 'willed by the standers by, to counsell the sayd O Royrke' who argues the toss defiantly. O'Rourke is deemed, one last time, to be 'obstinate' – 'and so the Cart went from him' (p. 764).

The distance that separates Stow's pacy reportage from Tadhg Dall's *grísacht* – a poem of instigation whose icy poise is achieved through the balance between the ferocity of its imagery and the restrained, formulaic archaism of its expression – maps out the space explored in this book. Stow's account and the colonial documentation on which it draws replay the manœuvres that characterised the Elizabethans' engagement with the Irish language and its speakers. Read against the annalist's triumphalist narrative, Ó hUiginn's antiphon sounds as an anthem not only for its doomed patron but for the culture which sustained them both.

The interest of Stow's narrative is that different aspects of the Elizabethans' engagement with language – with Irish – are picked up in his telling. As a report of a trial which focused on a 'treason of the image' (*CSPI* 1588–92, p. 405), it dramatises the Elizabethans' impulse to privilege spectacle over words. It is revealing that the most scandalous case of criminal defamation from sixteenth-century Ireland centres not on words, but on an image. The English reports which stand behind Stow's account pronounce O'Rourke's words 'traiterous and rebellious' but never record them directly. Instead, they focus on a spectacle. One John Ball writes that 'I sawe the pictar of a woman carved in a block standinge vpon whelles of small tymber'; he gives no sense of encountering any language other than English in Breifne; yet the language difference which his account suppresses can be inferred from a give-away loanword: 'it was made for a callyaghe' (PRO SP 63/151/96). But equally, Stow's account of the trial itself bears out my contention that, when it became expedient, language difference was foregrounded. If in Ireland the idiom used in reporting O'Rourke's 'traitorous pageant' (*CSPI* 1588–92, p. 143) is relentlessly visual, that of his English trial is notably verbal. In the London courtroom – as in Ulster on the eve of plantation and in Guiana – translation is dramatised to give a show of due process to the proceedings.

Something else is being dramatised in Stow's account: it is a pageant of cultural nationalism. Brady sees 'common law thought' underpinning English cultural nationalism (*Chief Governors*, p. xi); I have argued that language is another vital element in that equation.

Here, in the triumphant pageant of English law, dramatised through translation, language moves centre-stage, in the courtroom and in the public theatre of execution. English is the language of power; Irish the rebel's tongue.[4]

Above all, O'Rourke's entry into English narrative illustrates what I contend is the paradoxical outcome of linguistic colonisation in Ireland: its mixture of contestation and silence. Catherine Belsey argues that '[t]he supreme opportunity to speak was the moment of execution' (*Subject of Tragedy*, p. 190). O'Rourke turned the dock and the tumbrel into a stage for defiant counter-argument in a drama that grimly bears out Dollimore and Sinfield's paradox that 'to silence dissent one must first give it a voice' ('History and Ideology', p. 215). Further, Stow's account is positioned at precisely the same disadvantage as those of Elizabethans writing from Ireland: here again is a monophone text mistakenly assuming that it controls meaning in a diglossic world. Stow confidently 'quotes' the 'good exhortations' which Lye and McGrath deliver in Irish. But once in the hands of the 'fox tribe' of wily bilinguals, meaning is no longer guaranteed. An Irish genealogical tract destabilises Stow's account by listening in to the other half of the unreliable bilingual's message: under cover of 'exhorting' O'Rourke, it suggests, McGrath, Protestant Archbishop and Fransciscan apostate, 'tug absolóid os íosal dhó' (gave him absolution in a whisper) (Carney, 'Tract', p. 245).

But there is silence too. O'Rourke eventually withdraws into his own silence: 'no more could be had of him, but fell to his prayers' (Stow, *Annales*, p. 764). His speech from the tumbrel is framed by violence and narrated as a flashback: first comes Stow's announcement – with its ironic mirroring of Ó hUiginn's violent iconography of the heart – that O'Rourke was hanged and

his members and bowels burned in the fire, his heart taken out and holden vp by the hang-man, naming it to be the Arch-traytors heart, and then did he cast the same into the fire, then was his head stricken off, and his body quartered. But before this was done: the sayd *O Royrke* yet standing vpon the Cart . . . (p. 764)

The silence which Tadhg Dall had hoped for fell the other way. It fell, very literally, upon his patron, whom the Four Masters eulogised 'ar dhuasaibh duanmholta' (for rewarding praise-poems) (*ARÉ* 3, p. 1,906). But it is an equivocal silence. However paradoxically, in Stow's narrative O'Rourke does still speak after death. And earlier, when O'Rourke heard the sentence passed on him, 'he answered nothing but sayd, if that were their will, let it be so' (p. 764): his response – like that of the culture he represents – is suspended in an oxymoron of speech and silence.

Glossary: the colonial wordlist

Baco: *baccach*, lame
Baghall: *bachal*, crozier
Ballibetagh: *Baile biattaig*, land measurement
Ban: *bán*, white
Banno: *beannaithe*, blessed
Bard: *bard*, category of poet
Beg: *bec*, small
Betagh: *bíattach*, base client
Bodrag: *búaidread*, disturbance
Boilie: *buile*, summer pasturing
Bonnought, bonies: *búanacht*, quarterage
Bonny: *bunad*, basic
Bonnyclabbe: *bainne clabhair*, curd-like milk product
Boy: *buidhe*, yellow
Brehon: *brethemhan*, judge

Callyaghe: *caillech*, old woman, hag
Caple: *capall*, horse
Carrow: *cearrbhach*, card-player
Codie: *cuid oidhche*, guesting
Coigny, quoynes: *coindmhedh*, billetting
Coin: *cáin*, tax
Corbe: *comarbae*, ecclesiastical heir
Coshery: *cóisearacht*, feasting
Cott: *cot*, small boat
Creete: *crech*, plunder
Creight: *caoruigheacht*, a herd of cattle and its cowherds
Cummerick: *commairce*, legal protection

Daloney: *dílmainech*, mercenary

217

Erinach: *airchinneach*, monastic superior

Gald: *gallda*, foreign
Galloglass: *gallóglach* (mercenary) soldier
Garran: *gearrán*, gelding
Garvy: *garb*, rough
Glib: *glib*, fringe
Glin: *gleann*, valley

Iriach: *éraic*, fine

Keayshe: *ces*, wattle hurdle
Kerne: *ceithearnach*, footsoldier
Kincogish: *cin comocuis*, (liability for) kinsman's crime

Mahon: *mathghamhan*, bear
Monashul: *mná siubhal*, travelling women
More: *mór*, big

Nettying: *nighe*, washing
Nevog: *naomhóg*, coracle

Oge: *óg*, young, junior

Rath: *rath*, earthen rampart
Roe: *rúad*, red

Sassona: *Sasanagh*, Saxon
Skelaghes: *scealaithe*, storytellers
Skene: *scian*, knife
Soren: *sorthan*, free quarterage
Sragh: *srath*, fine
Stocagh: *stócach*, soldier
Sugan: *sugán*, straw rope

Tamist: *tánaiste*, heir presumptive
Tarbert: *tarberd*, isthmus
Tath: *tath*, measurement of land
Termon: *tearmann*, ecclesiastical sanctuary
Tow sel: *tóstal*, meeting place

Uriaghes: *úr rí*, underlord
Usquebagh: *uisce beatha*, whiskey.

Notes

INTRODUCTION

1 Unless otherwise stated, translations in the text are mine.
2 Likewise, Brian Friel's *Making History*, like his *Translations*, is insistently monophone in its staging of linguistic difference. What would have been, for the bilingual Hugh O'Neill, changes in language between Irish and English, are represented in the play merely as shifts between RP – and Ulster-accented English.
3 Several of his speeches come verbatim from Spenser, cf. *Mutabilitie*, p. 12; *View* p. 104.
4 Equally anachronistically, Kilroy's *The Great O'Neill* depicts sixteenth-century Ireland as moribund, portraying Hugh O'Neill as a European-ising moderniser keen 'to throw off the chains of a dead past' (p. 42).
5 Extending the comparison between linguistic colonisation in Ireland and Latin America to the present, it can be argued that the energy of writers like Eduardo Galeano and Carlos Fuentes comes, in part, from their historically informed engagement with the originary moment of '*encuentro*'.
6 Linguists estimate that between 50 per cent and 90 per cent of the world's languages will be either extinct or on the way to extinction by the end of the century; even the lower estimate implies the loss, on average, of one human language every fortnight (Crystal, *Language Death*, pp. 18–19).

1 CONQUEST, COLONIAL IDEOLOGIES AND THE CONSEQUENCES FOR LANGUAGE

1 Several translators of Spanish works – Carew, Googe, Fenton – had close connections with Ireland (Underhill, *Spanish Literature*). Henry Bynneman, who, by publishing translations of Spanish accounts of the *conquista*, provided the 'strongest propaganda for colonization yet seen in England' (Parker, *Books*, p. 90), was a servant of Sir Christopher Hatton, an architect of the Munster plantation.

2 'Le colonisateur doit s'appeler Colon', as Todorov incisively puns (*Conquête*, p. 42).

3 Edward Gray's assumption that pre-Enlightenment Europeans sub-scribed unswervingly to the referential model leads him to understate the first English colonists' readiness to judge Indian languages to a degree that belies a simple faith in the underlying universality of all tongues; it holds him back from exploring why, for example, 'in much the way that the English viewed Welsh or Gaelic, many of them came to regard Algonquian tongues as inferior languages' (*New World Babel*, p. 48).

4 Dutch travellers to the Cape unfailingly imagined the click sounds of the Khoisan to be like 'the clucking speech' of turkeys (Raven-Hart, *Cape*, pp. 19, 52, 63).

5 Spanish, in contrast, was an eminently Christian tongue: the expression *hablar en cristiano*, 'to speak Christian', is still used colloquially as synon-ymous with 'hablar castellano.'

6 Topsell catalogued the pygmies under 'The Ape' in his *Historie of Fovre-footed Beastes*, 'bicause they haue no perfect vse of reason . . . and though they speak [,] yet is their language imperfect' (p. 3).

7 Matthew Arnold demonstrates the longevity of the reflex in imagining that Irish and its 'despised literature' could serve as a spiritual supple-ment to worldly-wise English (*Works*, p. 305).

8 Ironically, while Adrian IV's *Laudabiliter* (1155), which granted Ireland to Henry II, served as a precedent for *Inter caetera*, for Protestant Eliza-bethans it was more an embarrassing anachronism than a validation of their renewed conquest.

2 'A BAD DREAM WITH NO SOUND': THE REPRESENTATION OF IRISH IN THE TEXTS OF THE ELIZABETHAN CONQUEST

1 In 1603, George Owen noted that while the myriad Wexfordmen migrating to Pembrokeshire 'saye, they vnderstande noe Irishe, neyther doth anye well vnderstande his Englishe' (*Pembrokeshire*, p. 40).

2 The first Earl of Essex's 'Estimate of the Charges in the Province of Ulster' included 16d. a day for 'Edmonde Boy', the Earl's interpreter. (His guide earned a penny more but the real money – 2s. a day – lay in piping) (Shirley, *Monaghan*, p. 48). William Dunne/Doyne and Thomas Cahill are the only two official interpreters identified in Lascelles' *Liber munerum publicorum Hiberniae*.

3 The reader lulled into assuming that Sir Turlough 'must have' spoken English should recall the Four Masters' eulogy of Sir Roger Gilla Duv O'Shaughnessy: he was a valued ally of the English, 'though not skilled in Latin or English' (*ARÉ* 3, p. 1631).

4 At times, as when Bingham scornfully notes that the Burkes 'sent their messengers and letters crying out for peace (as they term it)' and declare that they will 'never be subject to any foreigners (as they termed it)' (*CSPI*

1588–92, pp. 545, 591), such phrases not only occlude the language from which they were translated – Bingham is commenting on a 'bagfull' of letters in Irish – but also ring round their meanings with disbelief.

5 The Irishmen in shadowy attendance on him – his 'verie good guide', Patrick Fagaw, the soldier who saved his life, or Captain Piers, identified above as the translator of Turlough Luineach's 'badd speaches' and who served with Ralegh in Munster – could have doubled as interpreters.

6 Derricke's Plate XI, on the other hand, depicts Rory Óg speaking Latin.

7 Malby and Piers's report that Somhairle Buidhe MacDonnell and his son, Alexander Óg 'signed' an accord, 'the hands of both being led on the pen', suggests the scope for exploiting linguistic disadvantage – especially since the MacDonnells were known to speak 'nae language but Erse' (*CSPI* 1509–73, p. 358; Walsh, 'Irish Language', pp. 244–5).

8 *gearrán*, gelding; *capall*, horse. Loanwords from Irish are glossed on pp. 217–8.

9 See Greene, 'War Cry', for etymology.

3 'WILDE SPEECH': ELIZABETHAN EVALUATIONS OF IRISH

1 'As the bee draws honey from the thyme and the spider poison, so one takes good or evil from a language according to one's character.'

2 These included Christopher Nugent and James Knowde (*CSPI* 1600, p. 125; *CSPDom.* 1598–1601, p. 569)

3 The irresistible lure of racy speech for even the most recalcitrant learner is captured in the smutty relish with which Moryson produces 'Cacatrouses' (*Irish Sections*, p. 111).

4 *recte*, isthmus.

5 *gallóglach*, lit. foreign warrior.

6 *coindmhedh*, billetting.

7 *cin comocuis*, a kinsman's offence.

8 *commairce*, legal protection.

9 Herbert had won Nicholas Keenan, Dean of Ardfert, for the Reformed Church by giving him certain books of controversy 'as Mr. [William] Whitaker's and Sadæll's' [ie. Antoine Chandieu] – whose works were published in Latin (*CSPI* 1588–92, p. 192); exchanges could equally have flowed in the other direction.

10 Some newcomers' only brush with language-learning, Davies acidly implied, lay in mastering the semiotics of corruption. Playing on the fact that cattle were used as bribes, he recommended that those investigating irregularities in the Church of Ireland be 'such as never heard a cow speak and understand not that language' (Bagwell, *Tudors* 3, p. 476).

11 Tellingly, Cuellar, who self-consciously models his tale on '*libro[s] de*

cabellerías' (books of romance) (pp. 346–6), had access to a rhetorical option, the picaresque, not available to his English contemporaries.

12 Bodley's editor, Bishop Reeves, demurred from translating this passage: 'Plura, quae Anglicè nolunt propriè exprimi, Latinè amplius reddita sunt'; nor did C. L. Falkiner include it in his translation (*Illustrations*, p. 339).

13 In reconstructing it, I have drawn on the works of Beacon, Campion, Churchyard, Davies, Derricke, Dymmok, Farmer, Gainsford, Gerrard, Harington, Hooker, Moryson, Payne, Perrott, Rich, Spenser and Stafford.

14 *Recte, gleann*, pl. *gleanna*, valley.

15 Thevet, followed by Duret, similarly recorded that '*diroit qu'ils pleurent ou gemissent, lors qu'ils prononçent leur parole*' (Thevet, *Cosmographie*, fo. 671r; Duret, *Thresor*, p. 875).

16 A levy; unusually, this represents a translation – of *gearradh* – rather than a transliteration.

17 The Earl of Desmond's war cry, *Pápa abú*, implies 'victory to the Pope'.

18 Language is caught up in the blurring of boundaries between Gaels and Englishmen in Drayton's *Sir John Oldcastle*: Harpool, decked out in Mack Chane's 'lowsie mantle, and a paire of broags . . . in habite Irish, but in speech, not so', is emblematic of 'intricate confusion' (*Works*, pp. 457, 463). Is it purely coincidental that he shares a surname with Robert Hartpool, the marcher captain who married 'out' to an O'Byrne?

19 For Shakespeare's comparable use of the Acrasia/Circe motif in Mortimer's seduction by Welsh/women in *Henry IV*, pt. 1, see Neil, 'Broken English'. Leslie Dunne, 'The Lady Sings in Welsh', has a related discussion of how that play marginalises both Welsh and women.

20 *Táiplis*, a game similar to backgammon.

21 *recte, mathghamhan*.

22 Dekker's Irish footman in *The Honest Whore* blithely confesses 'I know not a letter a de Booke y faat la' (*Works* i, p. 94).

23 *recte, conas tá tú*.

24 All-comers co-opted genealogy to back expansionist claims. When Diego Ortiz de Urizar came to Munster in 1574 to reconnoitre for Philip II, he was happy to use the alleged Spanish origin of the Irish to legitimise potential annexation (Tazón Salces, 'Politics, Literature, and Colonization', p. 32). There is, therefore, nothing casual in Spenser's interest in disparaging Spanish links, linguistic and otherwise, with Ireland (*View*, pp. 43–4).

25 *recte, marcach*.

4 'TRANSLATING THIS KINGDOM OF THE NEW': ENGLISH
LINGUISTIC NATIONALISM AND ANGLICISATION
POLICY IN IRELAND

1 In imagining that Ireland's 'uncouth language' darkened Lord Deputy
   Surrey's mind and in finding its present-day citizens 'Irishly talkative',
   however, Calder is more helpful in illustrating the persistence of
   linguistic stereotypes than in tracing their origin (*Revolutionary Empire*,
   pp. 42, xv).

2 He interrogated Bishop O'Hurley by putting him 'to the torture . . .
   which was to toast his feet against the fire with hot boots' (*CSPI*
   1574–85, p. 498).

3 Helgerson uses this quotation to set up his analysis of the late Elizabethans' 'discourses of nationhood', but he does not follow through on the
   parallel project of linguistic imperialism which it implied (*Forms of Nationhood*, p. 2). Not unreasonably, Grillo finds 'particularly striking' social
   historians' 'almost total lack of attention to any relationship between
   English language and national identity' (*Dominant Languages*, p. 44).

4 In his 'Fvnerall Poeme Vpon the Death of the late noble Earle of
   Deuonshire', Daniel rejoiced that, because of Mountjoy's victory, the
   'imperiall Crowne / Stands boundlesse in the west' instead of being
   'pent' at home (*Works* 1, p. 178: lines 181–2).

5 For Timias' allegorical kinship with Ralegh, cf. Koller, 'Spenser and
   Ralegh'.

6 Another participant in Bryskett's symposium, Nicholas Dawtrey, was
   equally sceptical about the power of civility to transform. Even 'the
   civilist of all these Irish rases', he told the queen, quickly revert and
   reversion is directly linked to Irish and the practices it memorialises.
   Accordingly, they can be kept in check only as long as 'the sworde
   hangeth over there heades' (PRO SP 63/174/62.i).

7 FitzWilliam, petitioning Burghley on the bishop's behalf, perversely
   used Lyon's want of Irish as an almost miraculous confirmation of his
   evangelising prowess: 'it is wonderfull . . . that . . . one man, not
   learned in theire owne Language, in so shorte a tyme coulde have
   brought them to the like perfection' (PRO SP 63/141/42).

8 *scian*, knife.

9 The Geraldine historian, Donal O'Daly, lamented that after the fall of
   the Desmonds 'you were subjected to every contumely if you spoke the
   vernacular' (*Geraldines*, p. 139).

10 *búaidred*, disturbance.

11 Talus is allegorically related to Sir Richard Bingham, 'the Flail of
   Connacht' (Highley, *Crisis*, p. 120).

12 To judge from Brian Senior's rare English borrowings in the *Annals*,
   English was little more than an uncomprehended, minor incursion: he
   speaks of '*cing Hanri*' but also of '*cing Maria*' (*ALC*, p. 398).

5 NEW WORLD, NEW INCOMPREHENSION: PATTERNS OF
CHANGE AND CONTINUITY IN THE ENGLISH ENCOUNTER
WITH NATIVE LANGUAGES FROM MUNSTER TO MANOA

1 When the Spanish commander yielded Smerwick, Ralegh 'who had the
   ward of that daie, entered into the castell, & made a great slaughter'
   (Hooker, 'Historie', p. 439). The West Munster variant of 'Beware the
   bogeyman!', *'Cughat an Rawley'* – 'Ralegh's coming!' – survived into the
   twentieth century (O'Rahilly, *Massacre*, p. 23).

2 Pelham urged English explorers not to remain 'pent at home, like
   sluggardes' but to roam '[l]ike as the fishes . . . [t]hrough all the Ocean';
   Bingham enjoined them to 'fish for lucke, while sluggardes lye at home'
   (Dedic.).

3 Barlow brought back 'two of the Savages being lustie men, whose
   names were Wanchese and Manteo', to be trained as interpreters
   (Hakluyt VIII, p. 310). The absence of interpreters on the first, 1584,
   voyages means that the 'very many words' which Barlow recounts with
   no hint of incomprehension can have been 'understood' only retro-
   spectively. Like the 'good' Irishman before him, Manteo, who served
   the English on subsequent voyages to Virginia, 'behaved himself . . . as
   a most faithfull Englishman', as White contentedly recorded (Hakluyt
   VIII, p. 396).

4 The episode echoes a moment in Münster's account of Columbus' third
   voyage, as relayed in Eden's translation. When Columbus, newly landed
   on a small Caribbean island, confronted the natives 'the admirall, (as
   well as he could by signes) allured them to communicacion'. But the
   Indians were suspicious and Columbus, realising 'that he could nought
   preuayle, by signes and tokens, he determined with Musical instrumentes
   to appease their wildnesse. As the minstrelles therefore blewe theyr
   shaulmes, the barbarous people drew neare, suspecting that noyse to bee
   a token of warre, whereupon they made ready theyr bowes and arrowes'
   (Arber, *Three English Books*, p. 35).

5 *Caoruigheacht* means 'a herd of cattle and its keepers' (Nicholls, *Gaelicised
   Ireland*, p. 185). Lane confuses the collective noun with the individual
   heads of cattle.

6 Only by reading *The discoverie* as a narrative isolated from extratextual
   realities of power can Mary B. Campbell find in it a 'responsible rhetoric'
   (*Witness*, p. 254).

7 Thomas Hacket dedicated his translation of Thevet's *The New found
   Worlde, or Antarctique* (1568) to Sir Henry Sidney in yet another instance of
   the connections between the colonisation of Ireland – where Hacket
   imagines Sidney 'brideling of the Barbarous' – and the Americas.

8 English borrowings from New World languages were far more lexically
   limited and phonetically distorted than were Spanish borrowings (Tuttle,
   'Borrowing', pp. 604–5).

9 Brinsley's *Consolation for our Grammar Schools* (1622), commissioned by the Virginia Company, would seek to teach English to 'the verie sauages . . . whether Irish or Indian' (fo. A.IV).

10 Ralegh's annotations to his copy of the *Faerie Queene* indicate that he identified himself with Calidore (Norbrook, *Poetry and Politics*, p. 145). And, indeed, in his move from Ireland to the New World Ralegh seems to switch from Timias-esque tough squire to exemplar of civil conversation.

11 Harriot's difficulty in conveying the distinction between the literal and the metaphorical bedevilled European attempts to translate Christian abstractions into Amerindian languages. It echoes the breakdown between Atawallpa, last Inca of Peru, and the Franciscan who attempted to convert him. Ringed by *conquistadores* in the square of Cajamarca, Atawallpa was approached by the friar, Valverde, who extended a Bible and the injunction, mediated through a hapless interpreter, Felipillo, that the Inca hear the word of God. Atawallpa held the book to his ear and, saying 'this book does not speak to me', cast it to the ground. His 'blasphemy' sealed his fate and that of his empire (MacCormack, 'Atahualpa', p. 150).

12 Chapman imagined Englishmen setting 'their glad feet on smooth *Guianas* breast' (*Plays and Poems*, p. 281: line 164)

6 THE CLAMOROUS SILENCE

1 Newcomers' interest in Irish was almost exclusively instrumental, as when Carew had an Irish language pseudo-prophecy concocted to bolster one of his land-claims (O'Curry, *Lectures*, p. 635; O'Sullivan, 'Tadhg O'Daly').

2 In a series of richly suggestive explorations of other instances of creative cross-fertilisation, Mac Craith traces how poets like Cearbhall Ó Dálaigh, Riocard do Búrc and Ó hEóghusa borrowed from Elizabethans like Harington to reshape Irish love poetry.

3 A work like Menchu's *Me llamo Rigoberta Menchu*, which painfully documents in hesitant Castilian the oppression of the *indigenas* in Guatemala, is both an act of repossession and a testimony to the difficulties and perils of doing so.

4 Caball, too, rejects O Riordan's analysis ('Gaelic Mind'). Rather, he argues, several late sixteenth-century poets imbued traditional motifs with a new political charge (*Poets and Politics*).

5 The sense of *allmhardha*, an epithet regularly applied to English, glides from 'strange', and 'foreign' to 'uncouth' and 'barbarous'.

6 Seán Mac Oliver Burke.

7 Similarly, when the Council's Commissioners charged Bingham with blocking Provost Marshal Fowle from 'draw[ing] the rebels to a treaty' (*CSPI* 1588–92, p. 173), his defence highlighted linguistic realities

usually screened from view: he had not sent Fowle to parley with the Burkes 'for that he vnderstoud not their language' (PRO SP63/148/39).

8 *ces*, a causeway of hurdles.

9 *seanbhean*, old woman.

10 Translation leaves its trace in Sidney's remark that O'Neill 'exhibited his Peticions in Writing'. Negotiations conducted through interrogatories and letters allowed for the language barrier to be managed – and downplayed.

11 Her mother, Calvagh O'Donnell's wife and Shane O'Neill's captive-paramour, was 'not unlernyd in the Latyn tong, speketh good French, and . . . som lytell Italyone' (O'Grady, *Catalogue*, p. 57).

12 I explore the role of interpreters and translators more fully in 'Uncovering the Invisible Interpreters of Sixteenth-Century Ireland', in *Irish Historical Studies*, forthcoming.

13 *Silteach*, 'prodigal', 'lavish', fits, while its near-homophone *sílteach*, 'given to imagining things', nicely extends the range of associations.

14 The anxiety is captured in Dekker's observation that, since Babel, malefactors can 'stand gabling with strange tongues, and conspire together (to his owne face) how to cut a third mans throat' (*Wonderful Year*, p. 187).

15 Chief Governor, 1530–2.

16 'Speciously adorned' (*OED*).

17 This is not the executed lieutenant.

CONCLUSION

1 By the late sixteenth century, Irish had begun to distinguish between *Sasanaigh* (New English) and *Gaill* (Old English), reflecting a shift in political alignment (Ó Buachalla, 'Poetry and Politics', p. 159).

2 *Danar* literally means 'Dane' thence 'viking' and, by extension, 'barbarian' (*DIL*).

3 The derivation of '*cathardha*' from '*cathair*', 'city', mirrors that of 'civil'.

4 The project of linguistic transformation that flowed from a nationalism so wedded to its vernacular is exemplified by the experience of O'Rourke's own son, who went from being George Bingham's hostage to Oxford; unlike his father, Brian Óg had no need of an interpreter in his fraught dealings with the English state (O'Grady, *Catalogue*, p. 465; Collier, *Egerton Papers*, p. 145).

Bibliography

Acosta, Juan de, *De procuranda indorum salute*, trans. Francisco Mateos, Madrid: Colección España Misionera, 1952.

Adorno, Rolena, 'Reconsidering Colonial Discourse for Sixteenth- and Seventeenth-Century Spanish America', *Latin American Research Review* 26 (1991): 135–45.

Affergan, Francis, *Exotisme et Altérité*, Paris: Presses Universitaires de France, 1987.

Aldrete, Bernardo de, *Del origin y principio de la lengua castellana ò romance que oi se usa en España*, 1606, 2 vols. (vol. II: *Ideas Lingüísticas de Aldrete*), ed. Lidio Nieto Jiménez, Madrid: Consejo Superior de Investigaciones Científicas, 1972–5.

Alexander, A. F., 'The O'Kane Papers', *Analecta Hibernica* 12 (1943): 69–127.

Alvar, Manuel, *La lengua como libertad*, Madrid: Cultura Hispánica, 1982.

Andrews, J. H., 'The Maps of the Escheated Counties of Ulster, 1609–10', *Proceedings of the Royal Irish Academy* 74C (1974): 133–70.

Andrews, Kenneth R., N. P. Canny and P. E. Hair, eds., *The Westward Enterprise: English Activities in Ireland, the Atlantic, and America 1480–1650*, Detroit: Wayne State University Press, 1978.

Arber, Edward, ed., *The First Three English Books on America*, Birmingham, n. p., 1885.

Armitage, David, 'Literature and Empire', *The Origins of Empire: British Overseas Enterprise to the Close of the Seventeenth Century*, in *The Oxford History of the British Empire*, vol. I, ed. Nicholas P. Canny, Oxford University Press, 1998, 99–123.

Arnold, Matthew, 'On the Study of Celtic Literature', *The Complete Prose Works*, ed. R. H. Super, Ann Arbor: University of Michigan Press, 1962, 291–395.

Asensio, Eugenio, 'La lengua compañera del imperio', *Revista de Filología Española* 43 (1960–2): 399–413.

Assmann, Jan, 'Translating Gods: Religion as a Factor of Cultural (Un)-Translatability', *The Translatability of Cultures*, ed. Sanford Budick and Wolfgang Iser, Stanford University Press, 1996, 25–36.

Bagenal, Philip, *Vicissitudes of an Anglo-Irish Family*, London: Ingleby, 1926.
Bagwell, Richard, *Ireland under the Tudors*, 3 vols, 1885–1890, London: Holland Press, 1963.
Bailey, Richard W., 'The Conquests of English', *The English Language Today*, ed. Sidney Greenbaum. Oxford: Pergamon, 1985, 9–19.
Images of English: A Cultural History of the Language, Cambridge University Press, 1991.
Bartley, J. O., *Teague, Shenkin and Sawney*, Cork University Press, 1954.
Bathe, William, *Ianua Linguarum: A Gate to the Languages*, trans. William Welde, London, 1615.
Baudot, George, 'Dieu et le Diable en langue nahuatl dans le Mexique du XVIème siècle avant et après la conquête', in Bénassy-Berling *et al.*, eds., 145–57.
Beacon, Richard, *Solon His Follie*, Oxford, 1594.
Belsey, Catherine, *The Subject of Tragedy*, London: Methuen, 1985.
Bénassy-Berling, Marie-Cécile, Jean-Pierre Clément and Alain Milhou, eds., *Langues et cultures en Amérique Espagnole coloniale*, Paris: Presses de la Sorbonne Nouvelle, 1993.
Bergin, Osborn, ed., *Irish Bardic Poetry*. Re-edited by David Greene and Fergus Kelly, Dublin Institute for Advanced Studies, 1970.
Bhabha, Homi, *The Location of Culture*, London: Routledge, 1994.
Bishop, Elizabeth, *Complete Poems*, London: Chatto and Windus, 1991.
Blank, Paula, *Broken English: Dialects and the Politics of Language in Renaissance Writings*, London: Routledge, 1996.
Bodley, Josias, 'Discriptio itineris Capitanei Josiae Bodley in Lecaliam apud Ultoniensis, Ann. 1602', *Ulster Journal of Archaeology* 2 (1854): 73–95.
Boland, Eavan, *Object Lessons*, London: Vintage, 1995.
Borde, Andrew, 'The First Boke of the Introduction of Knowledge', ed. F. N. Furnivall, *EETS* e. s. 10 (1870): 111–222.
Borst, Arno, *Medieval Worlds: Barbarians, Heretics and Artists in the Middle Ages*, trans. E. Hansen, Cambridge: Polity, 1991.
Bottigheimer, Karl S., 'Kingdom and Colony: Ireland in the Westward Enterprise, 1536–1660', in Andrews *et al.*, eds., 45–64.
Bradshaw, Brendan, 'The Elizabethans and the Irish', *Studies* 65 (1977): 38–50.
'Sword, Word and Strategy in the Reformation in Ireland', *The Historical Journal* 21 (1978): 475–502.
The Irish Constitutional Revolution of the Sixteenth Century, Cambridge University Press, 1979.
'Manus '"The Magnificent": O'Donnell as Renaissance Prince', in Cosgrove and McCartney, eds. (1979), 15–36.
'The Tudor Reformation and Revolution in Wales and Ireland: the Origins of the British Problem', *The British Problem, c. 1534–1707*, ed. Brendan Bradshaw and John Morrill, London: Macmillan, 1996, pp. 39–65.

Brady, Ciaran, 'Court, Castle and Country: the Framework of Government in Tudor Ireland', in Brady and Gillespie, eds., 22–49, *The Chief Governors*, Cambridge University Press, 1994.

Brady, Ciaran and Raymond Gillespie, eds., *Natives and Newcomers*, Dublin: Irish Academic Press, 1986.

Brady, William M., ed., *State Papers Concerning the Irish Church in the Times of Queen Elizabeth*, London: Longmans, Green, Reader and Dyer, 1868.

Breathnach, Pádraig A., 'The Chief's Poet', *Proceedings of the Royal Irish Academy* 83C (1983): 37–79.

Brerewood, Edward, *Enquiries Touching the Diversity of Languages and Religions through the Chief Parts of the World*, 1614, London, 1674.

Brinsley, John, *A Consolation for our Grammar Schooles*, 1622, ed. Thomas Clark Pollock, New York: Scholars' Facsimiles, 1943.

Bryskett, Ludowick, *A Discovrse of Civill Life*, London, 1606.

Bryson, Anna, *From Courtesy to Civility: Changing Codes of Conduct in Early Modern England*, Oxford: Clarendon Press, 1998.

Bullock-Davies, Constance, *Professional Interpreters and the Matter of Britain*, Cardiff: University of Wales Press, 1966.

Burke, Peter, *Popular Culture in Early Modern Europe*, London: Temple Smith, 1978.

Caball, Marc, 'The Gaelic Mind and the Collapse of the Gaelic World: An Appraisal', *Cambridge Medieval Celtic Studies* 25 (1993): 87–96.

Poets and Politics: Continuity and Reaction in Irish Poetry, 1588–1625, Cork University Press, 1998.

Calder, Angus, *Revolutionary Empire: The Rise of the English-Speaking Empires from the Fifteenth Century to the 1780s*, London: Cape, 1981.

Calder, George, ed., *Auraicept na n-Éces*, Edinburgh: Grant, 1917.

Calvet, Louis-Jean, *Linguistique et colonialisme: petit traité de glottophagie*, Paris: Payot, 1974.

Camden, William, *Annales: The True and Royall Historie of the Famous Empresse Elizabeth*, trans. Abraham Darcie, London, 1625.

Britannia, trans. Edmund Gibson, London, 1722.

Remains Concerning Britain, ed. R. D. Dunn, University of Toronto Press, 1984.

Campbell, Hugh T., *Getting to Know Waiwai: An Amazonian Ethnography*, London: Routledge, 1995.

Campbell, Mary B., *The Witness and the Other World*, Ithaca: Cornell University Press, 1988.

Campion, Edmund, *Two Bokes of the Histories of Ireland*, 1633. Ed. Alphonsus F. Vossen. Assen: Van Gorcum, 1963.

Canny, Nicholas P., 'The Ideology of English Colonisation: From Ireland to America', *William and Mary Quarterly* 30 (1973): 575–98.

The Formation of the Old English Elite in Ireland, Dublin: National University of Ireland, 1975.

The Elizabethan Conquest of Ireland: A Pattern Established, 1565–76, Hassocks, Sussex: The Harvester Press, 1976.

The Upstart Earl: A Study of the Social and Mental World of Richard Boyle, First Earl of Cork, Cambridge University Press, 1982.

'Edmund Spenser and the Development of an Anglo-Irish Identity', *Yearbook of English Studies* 13 (1983): 1–19.

Carew, George, trans. *The Historie of Araucana, Translated out of the Spanish into Englishe prose allmost to the ende of the 16: canto*, ed. Frank Pierce, Manchester University Press, 1964.

Carew, Richard, 'The Excellencie of the English Tongue', Camden, *Remains* (1984): 37–44.

Carney, James, ed., *Poems on the O'Reillys*, Dublin: Irish Manuscript Commission, 1950.

 ed., 'Tract on the O'Rourkes', *Celtica* 1 (1950): 238–79.

Carroll, Clare, 'Representations of Women in Some Early Modern English Tracts on the Colonization of Ireland', *Albion* 25 (1993): 379–94.

Castañeda Delgado, P., 'La Iglesia y la Corona ante la nueva realidad lingüística en Indias', *I Simposio de Filología Española*, Zaragoza: Libros Pórtico, 1990: 29–41.

Céitinn, Seathrún, *Foras Feasa ar Éirinn*, ed. David Comyn, vol. 1, London: Irish Texts Society, 1902.

Chambers, Anne, *Granuaile: The Life and Times of Grace O'Malley c. 1530–1603*, 1979. Dublin: Wolfhound Press, 1993.

Chapman, George, *Plays and Poems*, ed. Jonathan Hudston. Harmondsworth: Penguin, 1998.

Chiappelli, Fredi, Michael J. B. Allen and Robert L. Benson, eds., *First Images of America: The Impact of the New World on the Old*, 2 vols. Berkeley: University of California Press, 1976.

Chiarelli, Bruno, 'Commémoration d'un peuple et d'une culture disparus', *L'art Taïno*, ed. Jacques Kerchache. Paris: Paris-Musées, 1994, 222–5.

Churchyard, Thomas, *A Generall Rehearsal of Warres*, London, 1579.

Clément, Jean-Pierre, 'Les Créoles et le débat sur le quechua au XVIIIème siècle', Bénassy-Berling *et al.*, 119–32,

Clendinnen, Inga, '"Fierce and Unnatural Cruelty": Cortés and the Conquest of Mexico', Greenblatt (1993): 2–47.

Coe, Michael D., *Breaking the Maya Code*, Harmondsworth: Penguin, 1992.

Cohen, Murray, *Sensible Words: Linguistic Practice in England, 1640–1785*, Baltimore: Johns Hopkins University Press, 1977.

Collier, J. Payne, ed., *The Egerton Papers*, Camden Society first series, 12, London, 1840.

Collins, Arthur, ed., *Letters and Memorials of State*, vol. 1, London, 1746.

Collinson, Patrick, *The Birthpangs of Protestant England*, New York: St Martin's Press, 1988.

Corcoran, Timothy, ed., *State Policy in Irish Education A.D. 1536–1816*, Dublin: Fallons, 1916.

Cortés, Hernan, *Letters from Mexico*, trans. Anthony Pagden. New Haven: Yale University Press, 1986.

Cosgrove, Art, 'Hiberniores Ipsis Hibernis', in Cosgrove and McCartney, eds., 1–14.

Cosgrove, Art and Donal McCartney, eds., *Studies in Irish History Presented to R. Dudley Edwards*, University College, Dublin, 1979.

Cox, Virginia, *The Renaissance Dialogue*, Cambridge University Press, 1992.

Crofton, Henry Thomas, *Crofton Memoir*, York: privately printed, 1911.

Cronin, Michael, *Translating Ireland*, Cork University Press, 1996.

Crosby, Alfred W., *Ecological Imperialism*, 1986, Cambridge University Press, 1993.

Crystal, David, *Language Death*, Cambridge University Press, 2000.

Cuellar, Francisco de, 'Carta de uno que fué en la Armada de Ingalaterra y cuenta la jornada', *La Armada Invencible*. Ed. Cesáreo Fernandez Duro, vol. II, Madrid: Sucesores de Rivadeneyra, 1885, 337–70.

Cunningham, Bernadette, 'Native Culture and Political Change in Ireland, 1580–1640', in Brady and Gillespie eds. (1986): 148–70.

'A View of Religious Affiliation and Practice in Thomond, 1591', *Archivium Hibernicum* 48 (1994): 13–24.

Curtis, Edmund, 'The Spoken Languages of Medieval Ireland', *Studies* 8 (1919): 234–54.

Daniel, Samuel, *The Poeticall Essayes*, London, 1599.

The Complete Works in Prose and Verse, ed. Alexander Grosart, vol. I, London: privately printed, 1885.

Poems and A Defence of Ryme, ed. A. C. Spague. London: Routledge and Kegan Paul, 1950.

Daniel, William, trans. *Tiomna Nvadh*, Dublin, 1602.

Leabhar na nVrnaightheadh gComhchoidchiond, Dublin, 1608.

Davies, John, *A Discovery of the True Causes why Ireland was never Entirely Subdued*, 1612, Shannon: Irish University Press, 1969.

Dawson, Jane, 'Calvinism and the Gaidhealtachd in Scotland', ed. Andrew Pettigrew *et al.*, *Calvinism in Europe, 1540–1620*, Cambridge University Press, 1994.

Dawtry, Nicholas, 'A booke of questions and answers concerning the warrs or rebellions of the kingdome of Irelande', ed. Hiram Morgan, *Analecta Hibernica* 36 (1995): 79–132.

De Blácam, Aodh, *Gaelic Literature Surveyed*, 1929. Dublin: Talbot Press, 1973.

De Breffny, Brian, 'An Elizabethan Political Painting', *Irish Arts Review* 1 (1984): 39–41.

De Brún, Padraig, 'Litir Ó Thor Londain', *Éigse* 22 (1987): 49–53.

De Fréine, Seán, *The Great Silence*. Dublin: Foilseacháin Náisiúnta, 1965.

Dekker, Thomas, *The Dramatic Works*, ed. Fredson Bowers, vols. I & II, Cambridge University Press, 1953–5.

The Wonderful Year and Selected Writings, ed. E. D. Pendry, London: Edward Arnold, 1967.

Delisle, Jean and Judith Woodsworth, eds., *Translators through History*, Amsterdam: John Benjamins, 1995.

Derricke, John, *The Image of Irelande*, 1581, ed. J. Small; notes, Sir Walter Scott, Edinburgh: Black, 1883.

Dewar, Mary, *Sir Thomas Smith: A Tudor Intellectual in Office*, London: Athlone Press, 1964.

Dollimore, Jonathan and Alan Sinfield, 'History and Ideology: the Instance of *Henry V*', *Alternative Shakespeares*, ed. John Drakakis, London: Routledge, 1985.

Donawerth, Jane, *Shakespeare and the Sixteenth-Century Study of Language*, Urbana: University of Illinois Press, 1984.

Draper, John W., 'Linguistics in *The Present State of Ireland*', *Modern Philology* 17 (1919–20): 471–86.

Drayton, Michael, *The Works of Michael Drayton*, ed. John William Hebel *et al.*, vol. I, Oxford: Blackwell, 1961.

Du Bellay, Joachim, *La Deffence et Illustration de la Langue Francoyse*, 1549, ed. Henri Chamard, Paris: Marcel Didier, 1970.

Dubois, Claude-Gilbert, *Mythe et langage au seizième siècle*, Paris: Éditions Ducrois, 1970.

Dunne, Leslie C., 'The Lady Sings in Welsh: Women's Song as Marginal Discourse on the Shakespearean Stage', *Place and Displacement in the Renaissance*, ed. Alvin Vos, New York: Medieval and Renaissance Texts and Studies, 1995.

Dunne, T. J., 'The Gaelic Response to Conquest and Colonisation: The Evidence of the Poetry', *Studia Hibernica* 20 (1980): 7–30.

Duret, Claude, *Thresor de l'histoire des langues de cest vnivers*, Cologne, 1613.

Durkacz, Victor E., *The Decline of the Celtic Languages*, Edinburgh: John Donald, 1983.

Duviols, Jean-Paul, 'Langue et évangélisation dans les missions jésuites de Paraguay', in Bénassy-Berling *et al.*, eds., 275–88.

Dymmok, John, 'A Treatice of Ireland', *Tracts Relating to Ireland*, ed. Richard Butler, vol. II, Dublin: Irish Archaeological Society (1843): 1–90.

E. C. S., *The Government of Ireland under Sir John Perrott, 1584–88*, London, 1626.

Edwards, Philip, *Threshold of a Nation*, Cambridge University Press, 1979.

    ed., *Last Voyages: Cavendish, Hudson, Ralegh*, Oxford: Clarendon Press, 1988.

Ellis, Steven, *Tudor Ireland: Crown, Community and the Conflict of Cultures, 1470–1603*, London: Longman, 1985.

Elyot, Thomas, *The Boke named the Gouenour*, 1531, ed. H. H. S. Croft, vol. I, London: His Majesty's Stationary Office, 1880.

Falkiner, Caesar Litton, ed., *Illustrations of Irish History and Topography*, London: Longmans, 1904.

Farmer, William, 'Chronicles of Ireland', ed. Caesar Litton Falkiner, *The English History Review* 22 (1907): 104–30, 527–52.

[?Farwell, James], *The Irish Hudibras, or Fingallian Prince*, London, 1689.

Fellheimer, Jeannette, 'Hellowes' and Fenton's Translations of Guevara's *Epistolas Familiares*', *Studies in Philology* 44 (1947): 140–56.

Fenton, Geoffrey, trans., *Certaine Tragicall Discourses, written oute of French and Latin*, London, 1567.

A Discourse of the Ciuile Warres and Late Troubles in Fraunce, drawn into English, London, 1570.

Actes of Conference in Religion, London, 1571.

Golden Epistles, gathered as well out of the remaynder of Gueuaraes workes, as other authors, London, 1575.

The Historie of Guicciardin, conteining the warres of Italie, reduced into English, London, 1599.

Florio, Giovanni, *His First Fruites*, London, 1579.

Ford, Alan, *The Protestant Reformation in Ireland, 1590–1641*, Frankfurt: Verlag Peter Lang, 1985.

'The Protestant Reformation in Ireland', in Brady and Gillespie, eds. (1986), 50–74.

Foster, Roy F., *Modern Ireland: 1600–1972*, Harmondsworth: Penguin, 1989.

Foucault, Michel, *The Order of Things*, London: Tavistock, 1970.

Friel, Brian, *Making History*, London: Faber and Faber, 1989.

Fuentes, Carlos, *Valiente mundo nuevo*, Madrid: Mondadori, 1990.

El naranjo, Madrid: Alfaguara, 1993.

Fuller, Mary C., *Voyages in Print: English Travel to America, 1576–1624*, Cambridge University Press, 1995.

Gainsford, Thomas, *The Glory of England*, London, 1618.

The true exemplary and remarkable history of the Earle of Tyrone, London, 1619.

Gerrard, William, 'Lord Chancellor Gerrard's Notes of his Report on Ireland', *Analecta Hibernica* 2 (1931): 93–291.

Gilbert, Humphrey, *Queene Elizabethes Achademy*, ed. F. J. Furnivall, *EETS* e.s. 8 (1869): 1–12.

Gilbert, John Thomas, ed., *Facsimiles of the National Manuscripts of Ireland*, vols. IV, 1 & 2, London: Her Majesty's Stationary Office, 1882.

Gillies, William, ed., 'A Poem on the Fall of the Gaoidhil', *Éigse* 13 (1969–70): 203–10.

Gillingham, John, 'Images of Ireland, 1170–1600', *History Today* 37 (1987): 16–22.

Giraldus Cambrensis, *The History and Topography of Ireland*, trans. John J. O'Meara, Harmondsworth: Penguin, 1982.

Gonzalbo Aizpuru, Pilar, *Historia de la educación en la época colonial: el mundo indígena*, México: Colegio de México, 1990.

Goodman, Godfrey, *The Fall of Man or the Corruption of Nature*, London: 1616.

Googe, Barnabe, trans., *The prouerbes of the noble and woorthy souldier Sir Iames Lopez de Mendoza . . . with the paraphrase of P. Diaz of Toledo*, London, 1579.

Gosson, Stephen, *The Schoole of Abuse*, London, 1579.

Graves, James, 'The Taking of the Earl of Ormonde, A.D. 1600', *Journal of the Historical and Archaeological Society of Ireland* 3 (1860–1): 388–432.

Gray, Edward G., *New World Babel*, Princeton University Press, 1999.

Greenblatt, Stephen J., *Sir Walter Ralegh: The Renaissance Man and His Roles*, New Haven: Yale University Press, 1973.
'Learning to Curse: Aspects of Linguistic Colonisation in the Sixteenth Century', in Chiapelli 2 (1976): 561–80.
Marvelous Possessions: The Wonder of the New World, Oxford: Clarendon Press, 1991.
ed. *New World Encounters*, Berkeley: University of California Press, 1993.
Greene, David, 'The Irish War Cry', *Ériu* 22 (1971): 167–73.
Greenfeld, Liah, *Nationalism*, Cambridge, MA: Harvard University Press, 1992.
Grey Egerton, P., ed., *A Commentary on the Services and Charges of William Lord Grey of Wilton*, London: Camden Society first series, 40 (1847).
Grillo, R. D., *Dominant Languages: Language and Hierarchy in Britain and France*, Cambridge University Press, 1989.
Gruzinski, Serge, *La colonisation de l'imaginaire*, Paris: Gallimard, 1988.
Guazzo, Stephen, *The Ciuile Conuersation of M. Stephen Guazzo*, trans. G. Pettie, London, 1586.
Hadfield, Andrew, 'Briton and Scythian: Tudor Representations of Irish Origins', *Irish Historical Studies* 28 (1993): 390–408.
Literature, Politics and National Identity: Reformation to Renaissance, Cambridge University Press, 1994.
Hadfield, Andrew and John M. McVeagh, *Strangers to that Land: British Perceptions of Ireland from the Reformation to the Famine*, Gerrards Cross: Colin Smythe, 1994.
Hakluyt, Richard, *The Principal Navigations Voyages Traffiques & Discoveries of the English Nation*, vols. VIII & X, Glasgow: MacLehose, 1903–5.
Hall, Edith, *Inventing the Barbarian*, Oxford: Clarendon Press, 1991.
Hamilton, A. C., *The Spenser Encyclopedia*, Toronto University Press, 1990.
Hanzeli, Victor E., *Missionary Linguistics in New France*, The Hague: Mouton, 1969.
Harcourt, Robert, 'A Relation of a Voyage to Guiana', *The Harleian Miscellany*, vol. VI, London: White and Murray, 1810, 487–519.
Harington, John, *Nugae Antiquae*, ed. Thomas Park, vol. I, London: Vernor and Hood, 1804.
A Short View of the State of Ireland, 1605, ed. William Dunn Macray, Anecdota Bodleiana 1, Oxford, 1879.
The Letters and Epigrams of Sir John Harington, ed. Norman Egbert McClure, Philadelphia: University of Pennsylvania Press, 1930.
Harris, F. W., 'The Commission of 1609: Legal Aspects', *Studia Hibernica* 20 (1980): 31–55.
Harrison, Alan, 'The Shower of Hell', *Éigse* 18 (1981): 304.
Hart, John, *An Orthographie*, London, 1569.
Harvey, Elizabeth D., *Ventriloquized Voices*, London: Routledge, 1992.
Healy, George R., 'The French Jesuits and the Idea of the Noble Savage', *William and Mary Quarterly* third series 15 (1958): 143–67.

Heaney, Seamus, 'An Open Letter', *Ireland's Field Day*, ed. Seamas Deane *et al.*, Indiana: University of Notre Dame Press, 1986, 19–30.

Heath, Shirley Brice, *Telling Tongues: Language Policy in Mexico, Colony to Nation*, New York: Teachers College Press, 1972.

Hechter, Michael, *Internal Colonialism: The Celtic Fringe in British National Development*, London: Routledge and Kegan Paul, 1975.

Helgerson, Richard, *Forms of Nationhood: The Elizabethan Writing of England*, University of Chicago Press, 1992.

Henley, Pauline, *Spenser in Ireland*, Cork University Press, 1928.

'The Treason of Sir John Perrot', *Studies* 21 (1932): 404–22.

Hennessy, John P., *Sir Walter Ralegh in Ireland*, London: Kegan Paul, Trench, 1883.

Herbert, William, *Croftus sive de Hibernia liber*, ed. Arthur Keaveney and John A. Madden, Dublin: Irish Manuscripts Commission, 1992.

Hernández de León-Portillo, Ascensión, 'Lengua y cultura náhuatl en el Colegio de Santa Cruz de Tlatelolco', Bénassy-Berling *et al.* 135–43.

Highley, Christopher, *Shakespeare, Spenser, and the Crisis in Ireland*, Cambridge University Press, 1997.

Hill, George, *The Flight of the Earls*, Belfast: Northern Whig, 1878.

Hindley, Reg, *The Death of the Irish Language*, London: Science Paperbacks, 1990.

Hodgen, Margaret T., *Early Anthropology in the Sixteenth and Seventeenth Centuries*, University of Philadelphia Press, 1964.

Hogan, Edmund, ed., *The Description of Ireland . . . in anno 1598*, Dublin: Gill, 1878.

Distinguished Irishmen of the Sixteenth Century, London: Burns & Oates, 1894.

Hogan, James, 'The Tricha Cét and Related Land Measures', *Proceedings of the Royal Irish Academy* 38c (1929): 148–235.

'Shane O'Neill Comes to the Court of Elizabeth', ed. Séamus Pender, *Féilscribhinn Torna*, Cork University Press, 1947, 154–70.

Hogan, James and N. McNeill O'Farrell, eds., *The Walsingham Letter-book*, Dublin: Irish Manuscript Commission, 1959.

Hogan, Jeremiah Joseph, *The English Language in Ireland*, 1927, Maryland: McGrath, 1970.

Holinshed, Ralph, *Chronicles of England, Scotland and Ireland*, 1586, 6 vols., London: Johnson *et al.*, 1807–8.

Hooker, John, 'The Irish Historie composed and written by Giraldus Cambrensis, and Translated into English . . . together with the Supplie of the said Historie . . . vnto . . . 1587', in Holinshed, vol. 6, 99–461.

Hughes, Thomas *et al.*, *The Misfortunes of Arthur*, ed. J. Payne Collier, London: S. Prowett, 1828.

Hulton, Paul and David Beers Quinn, ed., *The American Drawings of John White*, 2 vols, Chapel Hill: University of North Carolina Press, 1964.

Husson, Jean-Philippe, 'Contresens, malentendus, quiproquos: ce qu'il

advint du quechua lorsqu'on en fit une langue d'évangélisation',
Bénassy-Berling *et al.*, 257–74.

Irwin, Patrick J., 'Ireland's Contribution to the English Language', *Studies*
22 (1933): 637–52.

Jackson, Donald, 'The Irish Language and Tudor Government', *Éire-Ireland*
8 (1973): 21–8.

James I, *The Workes of the Most High and Mighty Prince James*, London, 1616.

Jenkins, Raymond, 'Spenser and Ireland', *English Literary History* 19 (1952):
131–42.

Jennings, Francis, *The Invasion of America: Indians, Colonialism, and the Cant of
Conquest*, Chapel Hill: University of North Carolina Press, 1975.

Jones, Ann Rosalind and Peter Stallybrass, 'Dismantling Irena: The
Sexualising of Ireland in Early Modern England', *Nationalisms and
Sexualities*, ed. Andrew Parker *et al.*, London: Routledge, 1992, 157–71.

Jones, R. Brinley, *The Old British Tongue*, Cardiff: Avalon, 1970.

Jones, Richard Foster, *The Triumph of the English Language*, Stanford University Press, 1953.

Jones, W. R., 'The Image of the Barbarian in Medieval Europe', *Comparative
Studies in Society and History* 13 (1971): 376–407.

'England against the Celtic Fringe: A Study of Cultural Stereotypes',
Journal of World History 13 (1971): 155–71.

Jorden, Edward, *A Briefe Discourse of a Disease Called the Suffocation of the Mother*,
London, 1603.

Joyce, James, *A Portrait of the Artist as a Young Man*, 1916, London: Granada,
1977.

Judson, Alexander C., *The Life of Edmund Spenser*, Baltimore: Johns Hopkins
University Press, 1945.

Kearney, Richard, *Transitions: Narratives in Modern Irish Culture*, Dublin:
Wolfhound Press, 1988.

Kempe, William, *The Education of Children in Learning*, London, 1588.

Kiberd, Declan, *Idir Dhá Chultúr*, Baile Átha Cliath: Coiscéim, 1993.

Kiernan, Victor, 'Language and Conquerors', *Language, Self and Society: A
Social History of Language*, ed. Peter Burke and Roy Porter, Cambridge:
Polity Press, 1991, 191–210.

Kilroy, Thomas, *The Great O'Neill*, Oldcastle: Gallery Press, 1995.

Kinsella, Thomas, 'The Divided Mind', *Irish Poets in English*, ed. Seán Lucy,
Cork: Mercier, 1973, 208–18.

The Dual Tradition, Manchester: Carcanet, 1995.

Knott, Eleanor, ed. and trans., *The Bardic Poems of Tadhg Dall Ó Huiginn*, 2
vols., London: Irish Texts Society, 1922.

Koller, Katherine, 'Spenser and Ralegh', *English Literary History* 1 (1934): 37–60.

Kobayashi, José María, *La educación como conquista: empresa franciscana en
México*, México: El Colegio de México, 1974.

Kozinska-Frybes, Joanna, 'Le plurilinguisme dans le théâtre religieux de la
Nouvelle-Espagne', Bénassy-Berling *et al.*, 171–88.

Kupperman, Karen O., *Settling with the Indians: The Meeting of English and Indian Cultures in America, 1580–1640*, London: J. M. Dent, 1980.

Las Casas, Bartolomé de, *The Spanish Colonie*, trans. M. M. S., London, 1583.

Brevísima relación de la destructión de las Indias, 1552, ed. Manuel Ballesteros Gaibrois, Madrid: Fundación Universitaria Española, 1977.

Lascelles, Rowley, ed., *Liber munerum publicorum Hiberniae*, London, 1824.

Laurence, Patricia, 'Women's Silence as a Ritual of Truth: A Study of Literary Expressions in Austen, Bronte, and Woolf', ed. Elaine Hedges and Shelley Fisher Fishkin, *Listening to Silences: New Essays in Feminist Criticims*, Oxford University Press, 1994.

Le Clézio, J. M. G., *Le Rêve mexicain*, Paris: Gallimard, 1988.

Lee, Joseph J., *Ireland 1912–1985*, Cambridge University Press, 1989.

Leerssen, Joep T., *Mere Irish and Fíor-Ghael*, Amsterdam: John Benjamins, 1986.

Lennon, Colm, *Richard Stanihurst the Dubliner 1547–1618*, Dublin: Irish Academic Press, 1981.

Lestringant, Frank, *Le Huguenot et le Sauvage*, Paris: Aux Amateurs de Livres, 1990.

Lhuyd, Humfrey, *The Breuiary of Britayne*, trans. Thomas Twyne, London, 1573.

Lievsay, John Leon, *Stefano Guazzo and the English Renaissance, 1575–1675*, Chapel Hill: University of North Carolina Press, 1961.

Lloyd, David, 'Translator as Refractor: Towards a Re-reading of James Clarence Mangan as Translator', *Dispositio* 7 (1982): 141–62.

Lodge, John, ed., *Desiderata curiosa Hibernica*, vol. 1, Dublin: Hay, 1772.

Longfield, Ada K., *FitzWilliam Accounts, 1560–1565*, Dublin: Irish Manuscript Commission, 1960.

Lynch, John, *Cambrensis Eversus*, vol. 1, ed. and trans. Matthew Kelly, Dublin: The Celtic Society, 1848.

Lyon, John Henry H., *A Study of the Newe Metamorphosis, written by J. M., gent., 1600*, New York: Columbia University Press, 1919.

McAdoo, Henry R., 'The Irish Translations of the Book of Common Prayer', *Éigse* 2 (1940): 250–7.

Mac Airt, Seán, ed., *Leabhar Branach*, Dublin Institute of Advanced Studies, 1944.

McCabe, Richard, *The Pillars of Eternity*, Dublin: Irish Academic Press, 1989.

MacCarthy, Daniel, *The Life and Letters of Florence Mac Carthy Reagh*, London: Longmans, Green, Reader and Dyer, 1867.

McCarthy Morrogh, Michael, 'The English Presence in Early Seventeenth Century Ireland', in Brady and Gillespie (1986), 171–90.

The Munster Plantation: English Migration to Southern Ireland, 1583–1641, Oxford: Clarendon Press, 1986.

MacCormack, Sabine, 'Atahualpa and the Book', *Dispositio* 36–8 (1989): 141–68.

Mac Craith, Mícheál, *Lorg na hIasachta ar na Dánta Grá*, Baile Átha Cliath: An Clóchomhar, 1989.
'Gaelic Ireland and the Renaissance', ed. Glanmor Williams and Robert O. Jones, *The Celts and the Renaissance*, Cardiff: University of Wales Press, 1990.
'*Beatha Aodha Ruadh Uí Dhomhnail*: beathaisnéis de chuid an Renaissance', *Irisleabhar Mhá Nuad* (1994): 45–94.
Mac Cuarta, Brian, 'Mathew de Renzy's Letters on Irish Affairs, 1613–1620', *Analecta Hibernica* 34 (1987): 107–82.
'Conchubhar Mac Bruaideadha and Sir Matthew de Renzy (1577–1631)', *Éigse* 27 (1993): 122–6.
MacCurtain, Margaret, 'Women, Education and Learning in Early Modern Ireland', *Women in Early Modern Ireland*, ed. Margaret MacCurtain and Mary O'Dowd, Edinburgh University Press, 1991, 160–78.
McEachern, Clare, *The Poetics of English Nationhood, 1590–1612*, Cambridge University Press, 1996.
McGuinness, Frank, *Mutabilitie*, London: Faber and Faber, 1997.
McKenna, Lambert, ed., *Dánta do chum Aonghus Fionn Ó Dálaigh*, Dublin: Maunsel, 1919.
ed., *The Book of O'Hara*, Dublin Institute of Advanced Studies, 1951.
Mahon, Derek, *Selected Poems*, London: Viking, 1991.
Maley, Willy, ed., 'The Supplication of the Blood of the English Most Lamentably Murdered in Ireland, cryeng out of the yearth for revenge (1598)', *Analecta Hibernica* 36 (1995): 1–77.
Salvaging Spenser: Colonialism, Culture and Identity, London: Macmillian, 1997.
Mannheim, Bruce, *The Language of the Inka since the European Invasion*, Austin: University of Texas Press, 1991.
Manningham, John, *Diary*, ed. W. Tite, Camden Society first series, 99, London, 1868.
Mant, Richard, *History of the Church of Ireland*, vol. 1, London: Parker, 1840.
Marron, L., 'Documents from the State Papers Concerning Miler McGrath', *Archivium Hibernicum* 22 (1958): 75–189.
Martinell Gifre, E., *Aspectos lingüisticos del descubrimiento y de la conquista*, Madrid: Consejo superior de investigaciones, 1988.
Mattingly, Garrett, *Renaissance Diplomacy*, London: Jonathan Cape, 1955.
Maxwell, Constantia, ed., *Irish History from Contemporary Sources (1509–1610)*, London: Allen & Unwin, 1923.
Mazzio, Carla, 'Staging the Vernacular: Language and Nation in Thomas Kyd's *The Spanish Tragedy*', *Studies in English Literature* 38 no. 2 (1998): 207–32.
Meehan, Charles Patrick, *The Fate and Fortunes of Hugh O'Neill and Rory O'Donnell*, Dublin: Duffy, 1868.
The Rise and Fall of the Irish Franciscan Monasteries, fifth edn., Dublin: Duffy, 1877.

Menchu, Rigoberta, *Me Llamo Rigoberta Menchu*, ed. Elizabeth Burgos, México: Siglo Veintiuno, 1993.

Mhág Craith, Cuthbert, ed., *Dán na mBráthar Mionúr*, vol. 1, Dublin Institute of Advanced Studies, 1967.

Mignolo, Walter D., 'Literacy and Colonisation: The New World Experience', *Hispanic Issues* 4 (1989): 51–96.

'Teorías renacentistas de la escritura y la colonización de las lenguas nativas', *I Simposio de Filología Iberoamericana*, Zaragoza: Libros Pórtico, 1990, 171–99.

The Darker Side of the Renaissance: Literacy, Territoriality and Colonization, Ann Arbor: University of Michigan Press, 1995.

Milhou, Alain, *Langues et identités dans la Peninsule Iberique*, Rouen: Université de Rouen, 1989.

'Les politiques de la langue à l'époque moderne', in Bénassy-Berling *et al.*, eds., 15–40.

Miller, Shannon, *Invested with Meaning: The Ralegh Circle in the New World*, University of Philadelphia Press, 1998.

Montague, John, *The Rough Field*, third edn., Dublin: Dolmen Press, 1979.

Montaigne, Michel de, *The Essayes or Morall, Politike and Millitarie Discourses of Lo: Michaell de Montaigne*, trans. John Florio, London, 1603.

Montrose, Louis, 'Professing the Renaissance: The Poetics and Politics of Culture', *The New Historicism*, ed. H. Aram Veeser, London: Routledge, 1989, 15–36.

'The Work of Gender in the Discourse of Discovery', in Greenblatt (1993) 177–217.

Moody, T. W., F. X. Martin and F. J. Byrne, eds., *A New History of Ireland: Early Modern Ireland 1534–1691*, vol. III, Oxford: Clarendon Press, 1975.

Moran, Patrick Francis, *History of the Catholic Archbishops of Dublin*, Dublin: Duffy, 1864.

ed., *Spicilegium Ossoriense*, first series, Dublin: Kelly, 1874.

Morgan, Hiram, 'The Colonial Venture of Sir Thomas Smith in Ulster, 1571–1575', *Historical Journal* 28 (1985): 261–78.

'Extradition and Treason-Trial of a Gaelic Lord: the Case of Brian O'Rourke', *The Irish Jurist* 22 (1987): 285–301.

Tyrone's Rebellion: The Outbreak of the Nine Years War in Tudor Ireland, Woodbridge: Boydell Press, 1993.

'Tom Lee: the Posing Peacemaker', ed. Brendan Bradshaw, Andrew Hadfield and Willie Maley, *Representing Ireland: Literature and the Origins of Conflict, 1534–1660*, Cambridge University Press, 1993, 132–65.

'The Fall of Sir John Perrot', *The Reign of Elizabeth I: Court and Culture in the Last Decade*, ed. John A. Guy, Cambridge University Press, 1995, 109–25.

'Giraldus Cambrensis and the Tudor Conquest of Ireland', *Political Ideology in Ireland, 1541–1641*, Dublin: Four Courts, 1999.

Morley, Henry, ed., *Ireland under Elizabeth and James the First*, London: Routledge, 1890.

Moryson, Fynes, *An History of Ireland, from the Year 1599–1603*, 2 vols, Dublin, 1735.

An Itinerary, 1617, 3 parts in 1 volume, Amsterdam: Da Capo Press, 1971.

Shakespeare's Europe, Unpublished Chapters of Fynes Moryson's Itinerary, with an Introduction, and Account of Fynes Moryson's Career, ed. Charles Hughes, London: Sherratt & Hughes, 1903.

The Irish Sections of Fynes Moryson's Unpublished Itinerary, ed. Graham Kew, Dublin: Irish Manuscripts Commission, 1998.

Mulcaster, Richard, *Elementarie*, 1582, ed. Ernest Trafford Champagnac, Oxford: Clarendon Press, 1925.

Muldoon, James, 'The Indian as Irishman', Essex Institute Historical Collections 111 (1975): 267–89.

Murphy, Andrew, 'Shakespeare's Irish History', *Literature and History* third series, 5 (1996): 39–60.

Murphy, Gerald, 'Poems of Exile by Uiliam Nuinsean Mac Barúin Dealbhna', *Éigse* 6 (1948–52): 8–15.

Murphy, Michael A., 'The Royal Visitation of Cork, Cloyne, and the College of Youghal', *Archivium Hibernicum* 2 (1913): 173–215.

Mustapha, Monique, 'Langue, mission et politique chez José de Acosta (1540–1599)', in Bénassy-Berling *et al.*, 233–56.

Neil, Michael, 'Broken English and Broken Irish: Nation, Language, and the Optic of Power in Shakespeare's Histories', *Shakespeare Quarterly* 45 (1994): 1–32.

Newman, Karen, *Fashioning Femininity and English Renaissance Drama*, University of Chicago Press, 1991.

Nicholls, Kenneth, *Gaelic and Gaelicised Ireland in the Middle Ages*, Dublin: Gill and Macmillan, 1972.

Ní Dhomhnaill, Nuala, *Cead Aighnis*, Daingean: An Sagart, 1998.

Ní Dhonnchadha, Máirín, '*Caillech* and Other Terms for Veiled Women in Medieval Irish Texts', *Éigse* 28 (1994–5): 70–96.

Niranjana, Tejaswini, *Siting Translation: History, Post-Structuralism, and the Colonial Context*, Berkeley: University of California Press, 1992.

Norbrook, David, *Poetry and Politics in the English Renaissance*, London: Routledge and Kegan Paul, 1984.

O'Brien, Flann, *At Swim-Two-Birds*, 1939, Harmondsworth: Penguin, 1967.

Ó Buachalla, Breandán, 'Na Stíobhartaigh agus an t-Aos Léinn: Cing Séamas', *Proceedings of the Royal Irish Academy* 83c (1983): 81–134.

'Poetry and Politics in Early Modern Ireland', *Eighteenth-Century Ireland* 7 (1992): 149–75.

Aisling Ghéar: Na Stíobhartaigh agus an tAos Léinn 1603–1788, Baile Átha Cliath: An Clóchomhar, 1996.

Ó Cearnaigh, Seán, *Aibidil Gaoidheilge 7 Caiticiosma*, ed. Brian Ó Cuív, Dublin Institute of Advanced Studies, 1994.

Ó Cianáin, Tadhg, *The Flight of the Earls*, ed. Paul Walsh, Dublin: Gill, 1916.

Ó Clérigh, Lughaidh, *Beatha Aodha Ruaidh Uí Dhomhnaill*, ed. Paul Walsh, Dublin: Irish Texts Society, vol. 42 (1948); vol. 45 (1957).

Ó Cuív, Brian, 'The Irish Language in the Early Modern Period', in Moody *et al.* eds., (1975), 509–45.

O'Curry, Eugene, *Lectures on the Manuscript Material of Ancient Irish History*, Dublin: Duffy, 1861.

O'Daly, Donal, *The Geraldines*, 1650, trans. Charles Patrick Meehan, third edn. Dublin: Duffy, 1878.

O'Daly, J., trans., 'Panegyric on Thomas Butler, the Tenth Earl of Ormonde', *Transactions of the Kilkenny Archaeological Society* 1 (1849–51): 470–85.

Ó Donnchadha, Tadhg, ed., *Leabhar Cloinne Aodha Buidhe*, Dublin: Irish Manuscripts Commission, 1931.

O'Donovan, John, ed., 'Letter of Florence MacCarthy to the Earl of Thomond, on the Ancient History of Ireland', *Journal of the Kilkenny and South East of Ireland Historical Society* n.s. 1 (1856–57): 203–29.

'Military Proclamation, in the Irish Language, Issued by Hugh O'Neill, in 1601', *Ulster Journal of Archaeology* 6 (1858): 57–65.

'Errors of Edmund Spenser: Irish Surnames', *Ulster Journal of Archaeology* 6 (1858): 135–44.

Ó Fiach, Tomás, 'Richard Weston agus 'beir mo bheannacht go Dundalk', *Seanchas Ard Mhacha* 5 (1970): 269–88.

'The O'Neills of the Fews', *Seanchas Ardmhacha* 7 (1973–4): 1–64, 263–315.

O'Flaherty, Roderick, *A Chorographical Description of West or h-Iar Connaught*, ed. John Hardiman, Dublin: Irish Archaeological Society, 1846.

Ó Glaisne, Ristéard, *Gaeilge i gColáiste na Trínóide*, Baile Átha Cliath: Preas Choláiste na Trínóide, 1992.

O'Grady, Standish H., ed., *Catalogue of Irish Manuscripts in the British Museum*, vol. 1, London: The British Museum, 1926.

Ó Hifearnáin, Tadhg, 'Capuchon, Lame et Lange: l'irlandais et l'Europe continentale au dix-septième siècle', *L'Irlande et ses langues: actes du colloque 1992 de la société française d'études irlandaises*, ed. Jean Brihault, Rennes: Presses Universitaires de Rennes, 1992.

Ó hInnse, Séamus, ed., *Miscellaneous Irish Annals*, Dublin Institute for Advanced Studies, 1947.

Ó Laidhin, Tomás, ed., *Sidney State Papers, 1565–70*, Dublin: Irish Manuscript Commission, 1962.

Ó Maolchonaire, Flaithrí, *Desiderius*, ed. Thomas F. O'Rahilly, Dublin: The Stationary Office, 1941.

Ó Mathúna, Seán P., *An tAthair William Bathe C. Í. 1564–1614: Ceannródaí sa Teangeolaíocht*, Baile Átha Cliath: Oifig an tSoláthair, 1980.

O'Rahilly, Alfred, *The Massacre at Smerwick*, Cork University Press, 1938.

O'Rahilly, T. F., 'Irish Poets, Historians, and Judges in English Documents, 1538–1615', *Proceedings of the Royal Irish Academy* 36c (1921–4): 86–120.

O'Riordan, Michelle, *The Gaelic Mind and the Collapse of the Gaelic World*, Cork University Press, 1990.

Orpen, Goddard Henry, trans., *The Song of Dermot and the Earl*, Oxford: Clarendon Press, 1892.

O'Sullivan, Anne, 'Tadhg O'Daly and Sir George Carew', *Éigse* 14 (1971–2): 27–38.

O'Sullivan, Anne and Pádraig Ó Riáin, eds., *Poems of the Marcher Lords*, London: Irish Texts Society, 1987.

O'Sullivan, M. D., 'Barnabe Googe, Provost-Marshall of Connaught 1582–1585', *Journal of the Galway Archaeological and Historical Society* 18 (1938): 1–39.

O'Sullivan Beare, Philip, *Ireland under Elizabeth, Being a Portion of 'The History of Catholic Ireland'*, trans. Matthew J. Byrne, Dublin: Sealy, Bryers and Walker, 1903.

Ó Tuama, Seán, 'Gaelic Culture in Crisis: The Literary Response 1600–1850', *Irish Studies: A General Introduction*, ed. Tom Bartlett *et al.*, Dublin: Gill and Macmillian, 1988, 28–43.

Owen, George, *The Description of Pembrokeshire*, 1603, vol. 1, ed. Henry Owen, London: the Honourable Society of Cymmrodorion, 1892.

Pagden, Anthony, *The Fall of Natural Man*, Cambridge University Press, 1982.

  Lords of All the World: Ideologies of Empire in Spain, Britain and France c. 1500–1800, New Haven: Yale University Press, 1995.

Parker, John, *Books to Build an Empire*, Amsterdam: N. Israel, 1965.

Parker, Patricia, 'Fantasies of "Race" and "Gender": Africa, *Othello*, and Bringing to Light', in *Women, 'Race', and Writing in the Early Modern Period*, ed. Margot Hendricks and Patricia Parker, London: Routledge, 1994, 84–100.

Pastor, Beatrice, 'Silence and Writing: the History of the Conquest', *Hispanic Issues* 4 (1989): 121–63.

Pawlisch, Hans S., *Sir John Davies and the Conquest of Ireland: A Study in Legal Imperialism*, Cambridge University Press, 1985.

Payne, Robert, *A Briefe Description of Ireland*, London, 1589.

Paz, Octavio, *El laberinto de la soledad*, 1950, México: Colección Popular, 1990.

Peckham, George, *A Trve Reporte, of the late discoueries, and possession . . . of the Newfound Landes*, London, 1583.

Pennington, Loren E., 'The Amerindian in English Promotional Literature 1575–1625', in Andrews *et al.*, 175–94.

Pereña, Luciano, *Genocidio en America*, Madrid: Mapfre, 1992.

Pérez, Joseph, 'Una nueva conciencia', ed. Jean Canavaggio, *Historia de la literatura española*, vol. II, Barcelona: Editorial Ariel, 1994, 1–35.

Perrott, James, *The Chronicle of Ireland, 1584–1608*, ed. Herbert Wood, Dublin: Irish Manuscript Commission, 1933.

Pinkerton, William, 'Barnabe Googe', *Notes and Queries* third series 3 (1863): 141–3, 181–4, 241–3, 301–02, 361–2.

Pratt, Mary Louise, *Imperial Eyes: Travel Writing and Transculturation*, London: Routledge, 1992.

Quinn, David Beers, ed., *The Voyages and Colonialising Enterprises of Sir Humphrey Gilbert*, vol. I, London: The Hakluyt Society, 1940.

ed., ' "A Discourse of Ireland" (circa 1599): A Sidelight on English Colonial Policy', *Proceedings of the Royal Irish Academy* 47C (1941–2): 151–66.

'Sir Thomas Smith (1513–77) and the Beginnings of English Colonial Theory', *Proceedings of the American Philosophical Society* 89 (1945): 543–60.

ed., *The Roanoke Voyages*, 2 vols, London: The Hakluyt Society, 1952.

The Elizabethans and the Irish, Ithaca: Cornell University Press, 1966.

'The Munster Plantation: Problems and Opportunities', *Journal of the Cork Historical and Archaeological Society* 71 (1966): 19–41.

'Renaissance Influences in English Colonisation', *Transactions of the Royal Historical Society* fifth series, 26 (1976): 73–93.

introd., *John Derricke's Image of Ireland*, Belfast: Blackstaff Press, 1985.

Thomas Harriot and the Problem of America, Oxford: Oriel College, 1992.

Quinn, David Beers and Kenneth W. Nicholls, 'Ireland in 1534', in Moody *et al.*, 1–38.

Rafael, Vincent L., *Contracting Colonialism: Translation and Christian Conversion in Tagalog Society under Early Spanish Rule*, Ithaca: Cornell University Press, 1988.

Ralegh, Walter, *The History of the World*, London, 1614.

Ranger, Terence, 'Richard Boyle and the Making of an Irish Fortune, 1588–1614', *Irish Historical Studies* 10 (1957): 257–97.

Raven-Hart, R., ed. and trans., *Cape Good Hope 1652–1702: The First Fifty Years of Dutch Colonisation as seen by Callers*, vol. I, Cape Town: A. Balkema, 1971.

Rawlinson, Richard, ed., *The History of Sir John Perrott*, London, 1728.

Rich, Barnabe, *Allarme to England*, London, 1578.

A True and Kind Excuse, London, 1609.

A New Description of Ireland, London, 1610.

A Catholicke Conference, London, 1612.

Anothomy of Ireland, 1615, ed. Edward M. Hinton, *Proceedings of the Modern Languages Association* 55 (1940): 73–101.

The Irish Hubbub, London, 1617.

Roberts, Peter R., 'The Welsh Language, English Law and Tudor Legislation', *Transactions of the Honourable Society of Cymmrodorion* (1989): 19–75.

Ronan, Myles V., *The Reformation in Ireland under Elizabeth, 1558–1580*, London: Longmans, 1930.

Rowse, A. L., *Sir Richard Grenvill of the 'Revenge'*, 1933, London: Cape, 1977.

Ryan, M. T., 'Assimilating New Worlds in the Sixteenth and Seventeenth Centuries', *Comparative Studies in Society and History* 23 (1981): 519–38.

Said, Edward, *Culture and Imperialism*, London: Chatto and Windus, 1993.

Salesbury, William, *A Dictionary in Welsh and English*, 1547, Menston: Scholar Press, 1969.

Salmon, Vivian, *Thomas Harriot and the English Origins of Algonkian Linguistics*, The Durham Thomas Harriot Seminar No. 8, 1993.

Sarate, Augustine, *The Strange and Delectable History of the Discouerie and Conquest of the Prouinces of Peru, in the South Sea*, trans. T. Nicholas, London, 1581.

Sharpham, Edward, *The Fleire*, London, 1610.

Sheehan, Bernard W., *Savagism and Civility: Indians and Englishmen in Colonial Virginia*, Cambridge University Press, 1980.

Sheidley, William E., *Barnabe Googe*, Boston: Twayne, 1981.

Shirley, Evelyn Philip, ed., *Original Letters and Papers in Illustration of the History of the Church in Ireland*, London: Rivington, 1851.

The History of the County of Monaghan, London: Pickering, 1879.

Shirley, John W., 'American Colonization through Raleigh's Eyes', *Raleigh and Quinn: The Explorer and his Boswell*, ed. H. G. Jones, Chapel Hill: North Carolina Society, 1987, 103–21.

Shuger, Debora K., *Habits of Thought in the English Renaissance*, Berkeley: University of California Press, 1990.

Sidney, Henry, 'Sir Henry Sidney's Memoir of his Government of Ireland', ed. H. F. Hore, *Ulster Journal of Archaeology* first series, 3 (1855): 33–52, 85–109, 336–57; 5 (1857): 299–323; 8 (1860): 179–95.

Simms, Katharine, 'Bards and Barons: The Anglo-Irish Aristocracy and the Native Culture', *Medieval Frontier Societies*, ed. Robert Bartlett and Angus Mackay, Oxford: Clarendon Press, 1989, 177–97.

Smith, G. Gregory, ed., *Elizabethan Critical Essays*, 1904, vol. 1, Oxford University Press, 1950.

Smith, L. Pearsall, *The Life and Letters of Sir Henry Wotton*, vol. 1, Oxford: Clarendon Press, 1907.

Smith, Roland M., 'The Irish Background to Spenser's *View*', *Journal of English and German Philology* 42 (1943): 499–515.

'More Irish Words in Spenser', *Modern Language Notes* 59 (1944): 472–7.

'Spenser, Holinshed, and the *Leabar Gabhála*', *Journal of English and Germanic Philology* 43 (1944): 390–401.

Smith, Sir Thomas, *Literary and Linguistic Works*, ed. Bror Danielsson, Stockholm: Almqvist & Wiksell, 1963.

Spenser, Edmund, *The Prose Works*, ed. Rudolf Gottfried, Variorum Edition, Baltimore: Johns Hopkins University Press, 1949.

A View of the Present State of Ireland, 1633, ed. W. L. Renwick, Oxford: Clarendon Press, 1970.

The Faerie Queene, 1596, ed. Thomas P. Roche, London: Penguin, 1978.

The Yale Edition of the Shorter Poems of Edmund Spenser, ed. William A. Oram *et al.*, New Haven: Yale University Press, 1989.

Speroni, Speron, *I Dialogi*, Vinegia, 1542.

[Stafford, Thomas,], *Pacata Hibernia: Ireland appeased and reduced, or a historie of the late warres of Ireland*, 1633, 2 vols, ed. Standish H. O'Grady, London: Downey & Co., 1896.

Stanihurst, Richard, *The First Fovre Bookes of Virgil his Aeneis Translated*, Leiden, 1582.

Holinshed's Irish Chronicle, 1577, ed. Liam Miller and Eileen E. Power, Dublin: Dolmen Press, 1979.

'On Ireland's Past: *De rebus in Hibernia gestis*', trans. Lennon, 131–60.

Steele, Colin, *English Interpreters of the Iberian New World from Purchas to Stevens*, Oxford: Dolphin, 1975.

Steiner, George, *After Babel: Aspects of Language and Translation*, second edn. Oxford University Press, 1992.

Stokes, Whitley, ed., 'The Gaelic Maundeville', *Zeitschrift für celtishe Philologie* 2 (1899): 1–63, 226–312.

Stow, John, *Annales, or a Generall Chronicle of England*, London, 1631.

Strype, John, *Historical Collections of the Life and Acts of . . . John Aylmer*, 1701, Oxford: Clarendon Press, 1821.

Tardieu, Jean-Pierre, 'Les Jésuites et la *lengua de Angola* au Pérou', in Bénassy-Berling *et al.*, 191–204.

Tazón Salces, J. E., 'Politics, Literature, and Colonization: A View of Ireland in the Sixteenth Century', *The Clash of Ireland: Literary Contrasts and Connections*, ed. C. C. Barfoot and Theo D'Haen, Amsterdam: Rodopi, 1980.

Techo, Nicolás del, *Historia de la Provincia del Paraguay de la Compañía de Jesús*, 1673, trans. Manuel Serrano y Sanz, 6 vols. Madrid: Uribe, 1897.

Thevet, André, *The New found Worlde, or Antarctike*, trans. Thomas Hacket, London, 1568.

La Cosmographie vniverselle, vol. II, Paris, 1575.

Todorov, Tzvetan, *La conquête de l'Amérique*, Paris: Seuil, 1982.

Tonkin, Humphrey, *Spenser's Courteous Pastoral*, Oxford: Clarendon Press, 1972.

Topsell, Edward, *The Historie of Fovre-footed Beastes*, London, 1607.

Tuttle, Edward F., 'Borrowing versus Semantic Shift: New World Nomenclature in European Languages', in Chiappelli 2, 595–611.

Tymoczko, Maria, *Translation in a Postcolonial Context*, Manchester: St Jerome, 1999.

Underhill, John Garrett, *Spanish Literature in the England of the Tudors*, New York: Columbia University Press, 1899.

Venuti, Lawrence, *The Translator's Invisibility: A History of Translation*, London: Routledge, 1995.

Verstegan, Richard, *A Restitution of Decayed Intelligence in Antiquities*, 1605, London, 1673.

Wallace, W. A., *John White, Thomas Harriot and Walter Ralegh in Ireland*, The Durham Thomas Harriot Seminar, no. 2, 1985.

Walsh, Micheline Kerney, *Hugh O'Neill: Prince of Ulster*, Dublin: Four Courts Press, 1996.

Walsh, Paul, 'The Irish Language and the Reformation', *The Irish Theological Quarterly* 15 (1920): 239–50.

Irish Men of Learning, ed. Colm Ó Lochlainn, Dublin: Three Candles, 1947.

Irish Chiefs and Leaders, ed. Colm Ó Lochlainn, Dublin: Three Candles, 1960.

Wardhaugh, Ronald, *Languages in Competition: Dominance, Diversity and Decline*, Oxford: Blackwell, 1987.

Ware, John, *The History and Antiquities of Ireland*, vol. II, Dublin, 1764.

Waswo, Richard, *Language and Meaning in the Renaissance*, Princeton University Press, 1987.

Welch, Robert, *Changing States: Transformations in Modern Irish Writing*, London: Routledge, 1993.

Wheatley, David, 'Samuel Beckett: An dátheangachas agus an deoraíocht', *An Fhealsúnacht agus an tSíceolaíocht*, ed. Ciarán Ó Coigligh and Diarmuid Ó Gráinne, Baile Átha Cliath: Coiscéim, 1992.

White, Hayden, *Tropics of Discourse: Essays in Cultural Criticism*, Baltimore: Johns Hopkins University Press, 1978.

Williams, Nicholas, ed., *Dánta Mhuiris Mhic Dháibhí Mhic Gearailt*, Baile Átha Cliath: An Clóchomhar, 1979.

I bPrionta i Leabhar, Baile Átha Cliath: An Clóchomhar, 1986.

Wilson, Robert, *Three Ladies of London and Three Lords and Three Ladies of London*, ed. H. S. D. Mithal, New York: Garland, 1988.

Wilson, Thomas, *The Arte of Rhetorique*, London, 1562.

Withers, Charles W. J., *Gaelic in Scotland, 1698–1981*, Edinburgh: John Donald, 1984.

Wright, Thomas, ed., *Queen Elizabeth and Her Times: A Series of Original Letters*, vol. I, London: Henry Colburn, 1838.

Index

Acosta, José de, 28–31, 88
Adrian IV, 220 fn. 2
Affergan, Francis, 6, 23, 60
Aguila, Don Juan de, 67–8
Aguilar, Gerónimo de, 198
Aldrete, Bernardo de, 28, 31, 33, 34
Alen, John, Archbishop of Dublin, 199–200
Alen, John, Master of the Rolls/Chancellor,
    42, 136, 142
Alexander VI, 36
Anchieta, José de, 134
Anglo-Norman conquest, 9–10, 16, 20, 41
Anglo-Saxon, 102, 105, 113
Ap Owen Gwyneth, 161
Ap Parry, Stephen, 43, 191–2
Aquinas, Thomas, 24
Arabic, 22, 34
Aramaic, 22
Archer, Fr James, 201–2
Arnold, Matthew, 220 fn. 7
Atawallpa, 198, 225 fn. 11
Aylmer, John, Bishop of London, 207

Babel, 24, 32, 103–4, 106, 180, 226 fn. 14
Bacon, Francis, 64
Ball, John, 214
Bagenal, Dudley, 124
Bagenal, Henry, 76–7, 201
Bagenal, Mabel, 77
Bagenal, Nicholas, 61
Bagenal, Samuel, 50
barbarism, 15–6, 18, 23, 30, 31, 34, 44, 65, 72,
    75, 100, 101, 116, 224 fn. 7
  barbarous tongues, 19, 23–4, 24, 28–9,
    31–2, 92, 102, 112
Barlow, Arthur, 152–3, 156, 164, 166, 168,
    224 fn. 3
Barnwall, Margaret, 43, 186
Barnwall, Sir Patrick, 201
Barry, David, 205
Barry, James, Viscount Barrymore, 44

Bathe, William, 134
Beacon, Richard, 47, 49, 137
Beaghan, John, 60
Beckett, Samuel, 2
Belleforest, François de, 111
Bellingham, Sir Edward, governor, 12, 198
Belsey, Catherine, 215
Benyon, John, 194–5
Berreo, Antonio de, 157–8, 159
Bingham, George, 78, 226 fn. 4
Bingham, John, 144
Bingham, Sir Richard, 44, 49, 59, 63, 78, 124,
    137, 144, 149, 156, 190–1, 213, 220 fn. 4,
    223 fn. 11, 224 fn. 2
Bishop, Elizabeth, 148
Blank, Paula, 64
Blount, Charles, Lord Mountjoy, governor,
    47, 50, 51, 64, 68, 75–6, 81, 100, 101,
    112, 139, 188, 192, 194, 206, 207–8,
    223 fn. 4
Bodkin, Christopher, 194
Bodley, Josias, 72–3, 77, 85–6
Boland, Eavan, 2
Borde, Andrew, 78
Boyle, Richard, 1st Earl of Cork, 21, 77, 203,
    204
Brady, Hugh, Bishop of Meath, 128, 130
Brecke, Simon, 104
Brereton, an M.A., 191
Brerewood, Edward, 90
Brinsley, John, 225 fn. 9
Brouncker, Sir Henry, 43
Brown, George, Archbishop of Dublin, 43
Browne, Sir Thomas, 77
Bryskett, Ludowick, 111, 115, 121, 122
Búrc, Riocard do, 225 fn. 2
Burgh, Thomas, governor, 63–4, 124
Burke, David, 143
Burke, Richard, 2nd Earl of Clanrickard, 44,
    144
Burke, Richard Óg, 176

247